ITALY

Welcome to Italy

Dorothy Daly

Collins
Glasgow and London

Cover photographs
Italian State Tourist Office, Van Phillips

Photographs
Italian State Tourist Office
p 21, 37, 67, 82, 87, 115

J. Allan Cash Ltd
p 101

Peter Baker Photography
p 76

Van Phillips
p 46, 58, 73

Regional maps
Matthews & Taylor Associates

Town plans
M. and R. Piggott

Illustrations
Barry Rowe

First published 1980
Copyright © Dorothy Daly 1980
Published by William Collins Sons and Company Limited
Printed in Great Britain
ISBN 0 00 410907 4

HOW TO USE THIS BOOK

he contents page of this book shows how the country is divided up into tourist
ons. The book is in two sections; general information and gazetteer. The latter is
nged in the tourist regions with an introduction and a regional map (detail below
). There are also plans of the main towns (detail below right). All the towns and
lages in the gazetteer are shown on the regional maps. Places to visit and leisure
cilities available in each region and town are indicated by symbols. Main roads,
railways, ferries and airports are shown on the maps and plans.

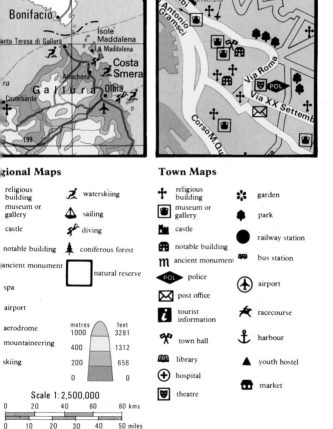

gional Maps

religious building	✈ waterskiing
museum or gallery	⛵ sailing
castle	diving
notable building	▲ coniferous forest
ancient monument	natural reserve
spa	
airport	
aerodrome	metres / feet
mountaineering	1000 / 3281
	400 / 1312
skiing	200 / 656
	0 / 0

Scale 1:2,500,000

0 20 40 60 80 kms

0 10 20 30 40 50 miles

Town Maps

✝	religious building	✽	garden
⊡	museum or gallery	●	park
🏰	castle	●	railway station
▦	notable building	🚌	bus station
m	ancient monument	✈	airport
POL	police	🏇	racecourse
✉	post office	⚓	harbour
𝒊	tourist information	▲	youth hostel
⚒	town hall	🏠	market
📖	library		
⊕	hospital		
▣	theatre		

CONTENTS

	page
A very brief History	6
Art and Architecture	6
Currency and Exchange Rates	10
How to Get There	10
Motoring	12
Accommodation	12
Camping	13
Youth Hostels	14
Food and Drink	14
Sport and Entertainment	15
General Information	16
Useful Addresses	19
Metric Conversions	19

The Lakes	20
Piemonte and Valle d'Aosta	24
Lombardia	28
Veneto	34
Liguria	51
Emília-Romagna	60
Toscana	69
Marche	80
Umbria	84
Lázio	89
Abruzzi and Molise	96
Campania	99
Púglia and Basilicata	106
Calábria	112
Sicília	116
Sardegna	123

| Key Words | 125 |
| Index | 126 |

Regions

1 The Lakes
2 Piemonte and Valle d'Aosta
3 Lombardia
4 Veneto
5 Liguria
6 Emília-Romagna
7 Toscana
8 Marche
9 Umbria
10 Lázio
11 Abruzzi and Molise
12 Campania
13 Púglia and Basilicata
14 Calábria
15 Sicília
16 Sardegna

Town plans

1 Torino 27
2 Milano 32-3
3 Padova 43
4 Trieste 45
5 Venezia 48-9
6 Verona 50
7 Génova 55
8 Bologna 62
9 Firenze 74
10 Pisa 77
11 Siena 78
12 Roma 92-3
13 Nápoli 104
14 Palermo 121

Note on place-names
In this book a stress accent has been used, where appropriate, on place-names as an aid pronunciation; *eg* Alássio.

A VERY BRIEF HISTORY

Italy as we know it today came to birth on 21 April 754 BC with the founding of the city of Roma (Rome).

At first not much larger than a village, Roma grew within a thousand years into a mighty empire circling the entire Mediterranean, including Spain, France and much of Germany, and stretching up to embrace parts of Britain. The thousand years from its foundation saw the rise and, alas, the fall, of one of the world's greatest civilizations.

In 395 AD Theodore divided the empire into two, the eastern and western empires. During the next 400 years Italy was repeatedly invaded. In return for protection, France was given power of empire over Italy, and in 810 AD Carlo Magno (Charlemagne) was crowned in Roma Emperor of the Holy Roman Empire, and there began the foreign domination of Italy.

Coeval with the invasions was the development of a great chain of monasteries in the country districts. San Benedetto, born in Nórcia in 480, founded the Benedettini (Benedictine Order); others followed. At this time an exodus from town to country is noticed: the monasteries offered protection for those who worked within their territory.

In the 9th and 10th centuries, however, came a return to the cities, to walled cities, high on the hills, far safer against attack than the country monasteries. These cities were more or less uniform in design, each with a large central square, a massive church for devotions, a belltower to summon the faithful, a fountain, a huge combined town hall and hall of justice.

Gradually the free *comunes* (city states) evolved, each city having its own form of government, often its own private army and, in the case of marine cities, a private navy as well. All owed allegiance to the central government, but, during the long periods of absentee emperors, each city realized the need for self-reliance and self-protection. Thus grew the spirit of individuality still to be observed in many Italian cities.

Most of these independent cities suffered greatly in the struggles against the German emperors Frederick Barbarossa and Frederick II, but they were the bases of the fabulous principalities such as the Medici of Firenze (Florence), Este of Ferrara and Montefeltro of Urbino, which during the Renaissance gave north Italy much of the art and architecture admire today.

From the 15th to the mid-19th centu Italy was fought over and dominated other European powers. The years af Waterloo saw the Austrians again in It but also the rise of a new national spi there were unsuccessful revolts betwe 1821 and 1848, then in 1859 Cavour, w the support of Napoleon III, defeated Austrians in Lombardia. In the next ye Garibaldi took Sicília (Sicily), then co quered Rome after a siege of 25 days. 1861 Victor Emmanuel became King Italy; Veneto was ceded by Austria 1866, and in 1871 Roma once ag became the capital of all Italy.

Only in 1946 was the Italian republic today proclaimed.

ART AND ARCHITECTURE

The earliest examples of art and archit ture in Italy stem from Greece a Etruria. Long before the founding Roma in 754 BC, the central portion of peninsula was inhabited by the Etr cans, who left splendid examples of w paintings and funerary monuments such centres as Tarquínia, Volterra, C tona and Chiusi, while others may seen in the museums of Firenze a Perúgia. The Greeks are remembe primarily by temples in Paestum, south Nápoli (Naples), and in Selinunte a Segesta, Siracusa (Syracuse) and Ta mina, the last four all being in Sicíli

As Roman power increased, architects began to express themselves great civic buildings and in commemo tive arches and columns. In the Fe Romano in Roma one sees the Basil Julia, built by Julius Caesar (46 BC), la rebuilt by Augustus. The Coloss erected in 69 AD under Vespasian, is

ample of Greek architecture adapted to ·man ideas of space. Other examples of ·man art are to be seen in the triumphal ch of Titus and Trajan's Column, ·ere one notices the cold classicism of ·eek portraiture giving place to vivid ·enesses of events and people. The ·ntheon (18–125 AD) is another fine ·nnant of Roman architecture. Around ·0 AD were erected the huge Terme di ·racalla (baths), which demonstrate the ·man love of spaciousness; a little later ·ne the Terme di Diocleziano. The ·silica di Massenzio in the Foro ·mano dates from 306–312 AD.

Painting was confined to wall decora- ·ns such as one sees in Pompei and ·colano, the cities near Nápoli ·stroyed in the eruption of Vesúvio in 79 ·. One of the finest examples of early ·tuary is the figure of Marcus Aurelius ·ich now dominates the Piazza del ·mpidoglio in Roma and which was ·npleted in 176 AD. The art of mosaic ·s highly developed. Starting as a floor ·coration, mosaics came to be used as ·ll embellishments, as in the Roman ·la at Piazza Armerina in Sicília. After · Edict of Milan (313 AD), which gave ·s freedom of worship to the Christians, ·saics began to appear as decorations in ·ristian churches. Statuary, too, ·veloped under Christianity.

·n the 5th century, Roma ceased for a ·ne to be the capital city, and the centre · activity moved to Ravenna, where a ·mber of magnificent churches were ·ilt during the next two centuries, lined ·ch some of the finest mosaics in the ·rld. Ravenna was in close touch with ·zantium, the capital of the eastern ·man empire, and there is a strong ·ental influence to be traced.

·rom the early Longobard period little ·nains but examples of the goldsmith's ·, In the Museo del Bargello in Firenze · charming 6th-century plaque in cop- ·, showing the Triumph of King ·ilupho; the treasury of the cathedral of ·nza houses the famous Iron Crown of

Monza, with which the Carolingian kings were crowned, so called because lining the gold crown is a band of iron, said to be a nail from the True Cross. Few churches were built during the following centuries, but in about 1000 AD there developed in Lombardia (Lombardy) what later came to be known as the Romanesque style. The church of Sant'Ambrogio in Milano (Milan) is a specially fine example; another is San Michele in Pavia; another the cathedral of Modena, begun in 1099 by the architect Lanfranco. Here, too, are some splendid early bas-reliefs.

Romanesque developed differently in various parts of Italy, while retaining more or less the same basic ideas of blind arches which make the cathedrals of this period so attractive. One splendid development is in Pisa in the Battistero (Baptistery), the Duomo (Cathedral) and the Campanile (Leaning Tower). The cathedral and the church of San Frediano in Lucca have similar ornate treatment. Firenze had its own interpretation, nota- bly in the geometric external decoration of the baptistery and the church of San Miniato al Monte, executed in vari- coloured marbles. Examples in Roma are the campanile (bell-tower) of Santi Giovanni e Paolo and the cloisters of San Giovanni in Laterano. The Basilica di San Marco in Venezia (Venice) is a blend of Romanesque and Byzantine, owing much to the design of the former church of SS Apostoli in Byzantium.

Painting and sculpture were now beginning to lose their Byzantine rigidity, and the mosaics of San Clemente and Santa Maria in Trastevere, both in Roma, offer an interesting parallel development. Two great painters emerge. Duccio di Buoninsegna (1278–1317) was almost the last of the Tuscan painters to reflect the influence of Byzantium, coupled in his case with the meticulous beauty associated with French miniature pain- ters. The Museo dell'Opera del Duomo in Siena houses his magnificent *Maestà*, once a double-sided altarpiece in the cathedral.

Cimabue (1240–1302), a Florentine, worked for a time in Roma, but he is principally remembered for his work in the enormous basilica at Assisi, begun two years after the death of St Francis in 1226. In Firenze, the Galleria degli Uffizi has a *Maestà* by this artist, and in the museum of the church of Santa Croce hangs a wonderfully impressive crucifix – badly damaged in the tragic floods of November 1966. But it is to Assisi one goes to see Cimabue at his finest, and to observe the influence cast by him on later generations of painters. Here were gathered together the leading artists of the period, not merely from Italy, but from other parts of Europe.

With the end of the Middle Ages, Gothic art and architecture began to supersede the Romanesque. Cimabue's pupil, Giotto, ranks as a Gothic painter, and the basilica of St Francis is also basically Gothic. The transition is most clearly marked in the sculpture of Nicola and Giovanni Pisano. In 1260 Nicola executed the pulpit in the baptistery in Pisa, where classical influence is still obvious. From 1266–8 he and his pupils sculpted the pulpit in the cathedral of Siena; later (1276–8), father and son worked on the Fontana Maggiore in the Piazza IV Novembre in Perúgia; in 1298 Giovanni began work on a pulpit in the church of Sant'Andrea in Pistóia, and between 1302 and 1310 he worked alone on the pulpit in the cathedral in Pisa. Here, the Gothic influence in both the architecture and the sculpture of the monuments is clearly visible.

Other great examples of Gothic architecture are the Basilica di Sant'Antonio in Padova (Padua) – a mixture of Gothic and Romanesque – Santa Maria Gloriosa dei Frari, Venezia, and the cathedrals of Siena, Génova (Genoa), Milano. One of Nicola Pisano's pupils, Arnolfo di Cambio, was not only a sculptor but also a notable architect. He was responsible for the cathedral of Firenze – begun 1296, the Brunelleschi cupola added in the 15th century – and conceived the cathedral of Orvieto, completed by Lorenzo Maitano, who sculpted the reliefs of the outer two of the panels dividing the entrance does.

The first great Gothic painter to emerge is Giotto (1267–1337), a pupil of Cimabue, architect of the Campanile (bell-tower) in Firenze, and painter of a series of frescoes in the upper church of St Francis in Assisi, and of the more mature series in the Cappella degli Scrovegni in Padova. Painting ceases to be the representation of a single moment in time and becomes a living narrative of events. In Assisi, look particularly at the miracle of the peasant drinking from the spring that gushes from the earth in answer to the prayer of St Francis; in Padova note the Kiss of Judas. Other frescoes by this great artist are to be seen in the Bardi and Peruzzi chapels in the church of Santa Croce in Firenze. In the Uffizi, compare his *Maestà* with those of Duccio and Cimabue.

During the 15th century, the great age of the Renaissance, sculptors, architects and artists succeeded in fusing classical

ideas with modern. The problem of pe[r]spective had been solved by Brunelles[chi] (1377–1446). In Firenze one should n[ote] particularly his cupola of the cathed[ral,] loggia of the Ospedale degli Innoce[nti] and exquisite Cappella dei Pazzi in [the] grounds of Santa Croce. Other conte[m]porary architects were Alberti (1404–7[ ], designer of the façade of Santa Ma[ria] Novella in Firenze, and Agostino Duccio, architect of the lovely little or[at]ory of San Bernardino in Perúgia.

Leading sculptors included Loren[zo] Ghiberti (1378–1455), sculptor of t[he] north and east doors of the baptistery [in] Firenze, also damaged by the Novemb[er] 1966 floods. In Siena, Jacopo della Que[r]cia (1374–1458) sculpted the Fonte Ga[ia] in the Campo, and a charming funera[l] monument to Ilaria del Carretto in t[he] cathedral of Lucca. In 1386 was bo[rn] Donatello who during the 80 years of h[is] life contributed much to Italian scul[p]ture; the *David* and the *St George* in t[he] Museo del Bargello in Firenze, a[nd] enchanting panel of child singers in th[e] Museo dell'Opera del Duomo and a fea[t] of sculpture in the Basilica [of] Sant'Antonio, Padova. The huge eque[s]trian statue outside, representing Ga[t]tamelata, one of the great soldiers of fo[r]tune, is possibly the finest statue of i[ts] kind, comparable only with Verrochio'[s] *Colleoni* in the courtyard of the church [of] Santi Giovanni e Paolo in Venezi[a.] Another sculptor to be influenced b[y] Donatello was Antonio del Pollaiol[o] whose statue of *Hercules and Antœus* ca[n] be seen in the Bargello, his monument [of] Pope Sixtus IV in the Vaticano.

Painters of this period are too nume[r]ous for more than a mention. The work [of] Masolino (1383–1435) and of Masacc[io] (b. 1401) is best seen in the frescoes in th[e] church of Santa Maria del Carmine i[n] Firenze – note particularly the drama [of] the *Flight from Eden*. Outstandin[g] among Florentine artists is the Domini[c]an friar, Beato Angelico (1400–55). [A] lovely series of his frescoes can be seen i[n] the Convento di San Marco in Firenze the *Deposition* in the museum gives a fin[e] impression of the spirituality of this mag[ic]al painter's work. A fine *Annunciation* i[s] in the little hill town of Cortona in Tos[cana (Tuscany).]

Paolo Uccello (1397–1475) is well known for his battle scenes, of which th[e] Uffizi has a fine example. Anothe[r] interpreter of the new ideas of perspective was Piero della Francesca (1416–92) – visitors to Arezzo should not fail to go t[o] the church of San Francesco to see hi[s] series of frescoes on the Legend of th[e] True Cross. In the Uffizi are his fine por[traits]

its of Federigo da Montefeltro and Bat-
ta Sforza. Luca Signorelli (1450–
25) is remembered for his series of fres-
es in the cathedral of Orvieto, massive
ures, no longer veiled with draperies –
nters were now beginning to be con-
ous of anatomy and were not afraid to
tray it. And at the height of the
naissance there comes Botticelli
45–1510), painter of dainty, aristocra-
figures in which one notices a sense of
ury coupled with a curious melan-
oly and wistfulness; the Uffizi has a
endid collection of his work, includ-
; *Spring* and *The Birth of Venus*. The
scoes on the walls of the Sistine
apel in Roma show a more serious
ect.

ne of the great 15th-century teachers
painting was Domenico Ghirlandaio
45–94), in whose studio the famous
chelangelo was for a time a student.
irlandaio painted two fine Last Sup-
s in Firenze, one in the refectory of the
rch of Ognissanti, another in San
rco. Perugino (1446–1523) – teacher
Raphael – worked in Umbria. Exam-
s of his work are to be seen in the
acoteca of Perúgia – splendid, calm
donnas, with a background of
brian countryside, often including
o Trasimeno – and in the Collegio
Cambio in Perúgia are some of his
st frescoes. Another Umbrian painter
Pinturicchio (1454–1513), who
ted the series of frescoes in the Lib-
Piccolomini in the cathedral of
na. Visitors to the town of Spello, bet-
n Perúgia and Spoleto, can see other
tings of his in the church of Santa
ria Maggiore. In Venezia the Bellinis
Carpaccio were enriching
rches. Jacopo Bellini (1400–70) and
two sons, Gentile and Giovanni, had
gift of creating images of alabaster-
luminosity. One of their finest works
e Predica di San Marco in the Palazzo
Brera, Milano; San Zaccaria, Venezia,
a *Madonna and Saints* and the Uffizi
Sacred Allegory.

mong architects of this period must
remembered Sansovino (1486–1570),
igner of the Loggetta and the Sanso-
o (or San Marco) Library in Venezia;
Palladio (1508–80), the pure classi-
beauty of whose designs is to be seen
great profusion in the city of Vicenza,
in the churches of San Giorgio Mag-
re and Il Redentore in Venezia. The
of geniuses – men who could express
mselves in virtually every medium –
n the Renaissance almost to the pres-
day is endless. Leonardo da Vinci
52–1519), architect, engineer, town
nner and great painter: in the Uffizi is

a lovely *Annunciation* (the scene set in the
open air), and in Milano the refectory of
the church of Santa Maria delle Grazie
houses his famous *Last Supper*.

Michelangelo (1475–1564), sculptor,
painter, architect, designed the Piazza del
Campidoglio in Roma, and was architect
of the cupola of San Pietro in Vaticano
and of the church of Santa Maria degli
Angeli in the midst of the Terme di Diocleziano. In Firenze he designed the
façade of the Basilica di San Lorenzo, and
the New Sacristy, where are housed the
tombs of the Medici family, which he also
sculpted. In Roma one can see his *Pietà*
in San Pietro in Vaticano, his *Moses* in
the church of San Pietro in Vincoli, and
in Firenze the much-copied *David* in the
Accademia. The ceiling of the Sistine
Chapel is the supreme example of his
work as a painter, a work achieved after
four years of almost superhuman fatigue.

Raphael (1483–1520) follows the rich
colourings of Perugino, but adds something of his own which is infinitely greater than anything his master produced.
The *Marriage of the Virgin* (Palazzo di
Brera, Milano), the *Madonna with the
Goldfinch* (Uffizi), the *Madonna della
Sedia* and the *Madonna of the Grand
Duke* (Pitti, Firenze) are among his finest
works. When in Roma do not fail to see
the great frescoes in the Raphael Stanze
in the Vaticano.

In the Veneto, too, there were splendid
painters at this time. Giorgione
(1477–1510), by whom there is a lovely
Tempest in the Accademia in Venezia,
and Titian (1477–1576), whose *Sacred
and Profane Love* and the smaller *Education in Love* are in the Galleria Borghese,
Roma. The Brera, Milano, Uffizi and Pitti, Firenze, also have Titians, and in the
Palazzo di Capodimonte, Nápoli, is his
portrait of Pope Paolo III. One of his
finest works is the altarpiece of Santa
Maria Gloriosa dei Frari in Venezia. Tintoretto (1518–98) and Veronese
(1528–88) are also well represented in
Venezia. The Accademia has several by
Tintorétto, including the large canvas of
San Marco freeing a slave, and the Scuola
di San Rocco has a splendid series which
includes the *Crucifixion* and *Christ before
Pilate*. Veronese's approach is more florid
than that of Tintoretto; more flamboyant
figures people his crowded canvases,
often giving one, even in his Biblical
scenes, a glimpse of the Venezia of his
day. The Accademia boasts a large and
impressive canvas of *Supper in the House
of Levi*, and another of the *Marriage of St
Catherine*, while his native city of Verona
has a splendid *Martyrdom of St Geórge* in
the church of San Giorgio Maggiore.

The 17th century ushered in the baroque period and is particularly associated in Roman architecture with Bernini (1598–1680), and with Borromini (1599–1667). The former, having designed the elaborate *baldacchino*, or canopy, in San Pietro in Vaticano, was later called upon to enrich its façade and to plan the grandiose oval piazza with the double colonnade. He, too, designed the fountain in Piazza Navona and the Fontana del Tritone in Piazza Barberini. Borromini's designs were even more flamboyantly baroque; visit the church of San Carlo alle Quattro Fontane and the church of Sant'Agnese in the Piazza Navona. The Fontana di Trevi, work of the sculptor Salvi, is another baroque landmark, and in Venezia fine examples are Longhena's church of Santa Maria della Salute, and Ca' Rezzonico. But to see the baroque in its full flowering one should visit the southern city of Lecce in Púglia where Zimbalo produced marvellous buildings in the local yellowish stone. Another great southern exponent was Vanvitelli, architect of the Royal Palace at Caserta, 12km from Nápoli.

In the 18th century the Venetian Tiepolo (1697–1770), much of whose painting is to be found in the Palazzo Labia and Ca' Rezzonico (Venezia), and in the Villa Pisani at Stra on the banks of the Brenta between Venezia and Padova, is outstanding. The Villa Valmarana near Vicenza has a fine series of rustic frescoes. Two extremely popular painters of this century were Antonio Canale, known as Canaletto (1697–1778), and Francesco Guardi (1712–93), both of whom have left unforgettable views of the Venezia of their day. Ca' Rezzonico on the Canal Grande has some fine Guardis.

By the late 18th century, baroque had given way to the neo-classicism of such artists and architects as Valadier (1762–1835), who planned the Piazza del Popolo in Roma, and Canova (1757–1822); the latter's recumbent statue of Paolina Borghese, sister of Napoleon, is in the Galleria Borghese, Roma. Out of neo-classicism in painting developed a movement closely resembling that of the French Impressionists. One of its leading exponents was Fattori (1825–1908), many of whose works are in the Galleria d'Arte Moderna, Palazzo Pitti, Firenze.

Of the moderns, one recalls Modigliani's (1884–1920) elongated figures with eyes that seem curiously out of focus; Giorgio di Chiciro (born 1888), painter of splendid horses; the Bergamesque sculptor Giacomo Manzù, sculptor of the new bronze doors of San Pietro in Vaticano, of a fine statue of C[ar]dinal Lercaro in San Petronio in Bolog[na] and of many other works which put h[im] among the truly great sculptors of Ita[ly] Annigoni is known for his portraits of [the] British royal family and other celebriti[es] but in the library of the Convento di S[an] Marco, Firenze, is an early *Deposit[ion]* which is well worth seeing. The work [of] the sculptor Marino Marini is equa[lly] famous. Finally, the Pirelli building [in] Milano is one of the most graceful exa[m]ples of post-war architecture, affirmi[ng] that the Italian genius is as vigorous a[s it] has ever been.

CURRENC[Y]

The unit of Italian currency is the *l[ira]* Since exchange rates fluctuate so cons[id]erably at the time of writing, no compa[ra]tive values are quoted here.

Banks are open from 08.30 until 13.[.] They remain closed on Saturdays, S[un]days and public holidays (see page [ ]) There are exchange offices (*cambio*) at [ ] large railway stations. Hotels, too, w[ill] change foreign currency and travelle[rs] checks, though at a less favourable rate [of] exchange than banks or recogni[sed] exchange offices.

HOW TO GET THER[E]

Boat and train Most routes from Lon[don] (Victoria) involve changing in Paris at [the] Gare du Lyon. Fast express trains se[rve] Génova, Milano, Pisa, Roma, Tori[no,] Venezia and Ventimiglia direct, and th[ere] are good train and coach connections [to] other towns and resorts. Seats, sleep[ers] and couchettes should be reserved [in] advance. Reductions are available [to] individuals making extended rail to[urs,] families, children, *etc*. For further inf[or]mation, see Useful Addresses (page [ ]) **Transatlantic routes** The main ports [of] entry are Génova and Nápoli. There [are] also services to Palermo and Messina [in] Sicília. Fares vary according to class a[nd] to the type of vessel. Tips, drinks, *etc* [can] add considerably to the basic cost. **Air travel** Alitalia and British Airw[ays] operate services to some or all of the f[ol]lowing airports: Génova, Milano, Náp[oli,] Pisa, Rímini, Roma, Venezia, on di[rect] scheduled flights. Various reductions [are] available for night and tourist flights, [ ] and there are several companies ope[n]ing charter flights. Further details [ ]

...ailable from travel agents and/or the ...lines involved (see Useful Addresses). From America there are direct air ser...es to Roma. Other services usually ...volve a change in Paris.

...ropabus This bus service is operated ...the railways of western Europe and ...vides swift, comfortable travel in air-...nditioned buses between many towns ...the continent. One can break one's ...urney at many places en route, but in ...e peak holiday season it is advisable to ...n one's stops and book well in ...vance.

...talian towns served by Europabus ...lude Torino, Génova, Milano, Ven-...a, Firenze, Ravenna, Perúgia, Roma, ...poli, Bríndisi. A great variety of tours ...also available, including 5- and 7-day ...rs of Sicília.

...ull details from Europabus, British ...ilways Travel Centre, London, SW1, ...Europabus (Overseas) Inc., 630 Fifth ...enue, New York 10020, USA.

...ternal Communications

...ains There are four different types of ...ns in Italy:

...pido; an inter-city express on which a ...plement is charged.

...rettissimo; a fast train, but which stops ...a few more stations than does the ...pido; usually 1st and 2nd class book-...is available.

...etto; fairly fast, but stopping at more ...ions than the *Direttissimo*.

...elerato; the slowest type of all, stop-...g at every station.

In addition to these, there are 'luxury' trains such as the *Settebello* (Milano, Bologna, Firenze, Roma), and the *Trans-Europ Express* on which all seats are reserved and there is a supplement charged over and above first-class fare.

Although great efforts are being made to improve services and travelling condi-tions, it is advisable to travel 1st class and to reserve your seat on most occasions. Second class is always overcrowded, and it is rarely possible to get a seat. Restau-rant cars are attached to long-distance trains; some serve a fairly good 'tray' lunch at a reasonable price.

As regards porters, you are advised to use only registered porters, who will wear a badge of identification, and whose charges − moderate − are fixed.

Coaches and buses Local buses connect with every town and village in Italy. There is an excellent network of long-distance buses between all main cities and resorts. Fares in the 36-seater luxury buses run by CIAT (*Compagnia Italiana Autoservize Turistici*) are comparable to 1st class rail fares. Other services are comparable to 2nd class rail fares. In many cases travel by bus is preferable to travel by rail. (See Europabus, opposite).

Planes Alitalia, Itavia, Alisarda and SAM operate between some 20 towns including Ancona, Bari, Bologna, Bríndisi, Firenze, Génova, Milano, Nápoli, Palermo, Pescara, Pisa, Réggio di Calábria, Rímini, Torino, Venezia and Verona.

Information is available from all tourist offices and from the offices of CIT (*Compagnia Italiana Turismo*) who have offices in 60 major towns and offer a service second to none in Europe.

MOTORING

Documents The only documents required are: the vehicle's registration book, third party (public liability) insurance cover, available in the form of a Green Card from your insurers; a valid driving licence. For British drivers this means your own driving licence accompanied by a translation available free of charge from motoring organizations. American motorists must obtain an International Driving Permit from the AAA.

Ferries Any of the northern cross-Channel routes are suitable, but these are heavily booked up and you are advised to make enquiries well in advance. There are regular sea services from Réggio di Calábria to Messina (Sicília) and from Nápoli to Palermo and Íschia.

Car-sleeper services operate from Ostend, Boulogne, Amsterdam and Paris to Milano, from Milano to Bríndisi, Roma, Villa San Giovanni and Réggio di Calábria. Although expensive, these services save time, energy, and hotel bills, and may be paid for in advance.

Rules of the road Drive on the right, overtake on the left. Before overtaking, you must indicate your intention and sound your horn (at night flash your lights). Unless otherwise indicated, traffic coming from the right always has priority.

Speed limits In November 1977 new speed limits came into force, and heavy fines will be due for any infraction of these rules. Posters with these limits clearly indicated in four languages (English, French, Italian and German) are placed in eye-catching positions at all frontier points, railway stations and airports. It is advisable to acquaint yourself with the Italian Highway Code as regulations are strictly enforced and the police may impose on-the-spot-fines. In such cases, it is wise to pay up and forget it.

Fuel and oil All the familiar brands are readily available. Foreign motorists must obtain a *Carta Carburante* from their motoring organizations or at the frontier. This will provide full information regarding the supplies of fuel and oil available, and the length of stay permitted. Fuel coupons may be purchased at the principal banks together with this card, or in

Italy at all the offices of the Automo[bile] Club on presentation of this *Carta C[ar]burante*. Remember to cash any unu[sed] vouchers at the border on leaving, as t[hey] cannot be refunded at home.

Road conditions The *Autostrade* for[m a] magnificent system of motorways wh[ich] is continually expanding. Altho[ugh] reasonable tolls have to be paid either [on] entering or leaving them, they save ti[me,] fatigue and fuel, and pass through so[me] magnificent scenery. Most of them [are] equipped with telephone boxes ev[ery] 2km for use in case of a breakdown.

Other roads are less satisfactory[:] crowded, dusty, bad surfaces – and [are] often cluttered with large trucks tow[ing] larger trailers. Many of them are 3-la[ne] but a sensible system of lane-mark[ing] *which must be observed* obviates the w[orst] dangers of this type of road.

Breakdowns In all areas you dial 116 [to] get in touch with the ACI, which [is] affiliated to the AA, RAC and AAA, [for] free assistance. Motorists must car[ry a] triangular warning sign, which may [be] bought in Britain or hired temporaril[y at] the frontier, to place 50 metres behin[d a] halted vehicle at night or in any ot[her] position where parking is not permitt[ed.]

Car rental You must have an Inter[na]tional Driving Permit and be over [21] years of age in order to rent a car. C[ars] may be booked in advance at most la[rge] railway stations (details from Itali[an] Railways), and the major airlines a[lso] offer car rental facilities.

Motels in Italy are excellent. Hach[ette] distribute an official Motel Guide [to] Europe, which is obtainable at most g[ood] bookshops. Information is also availa[ble] from the ACI provincial offices.

ACCOMMODATIO[N]

Hotels are officially classified in [5] categories: deluxe, 1st, 2nd, 3rd, and [4th] class. Charges vary within each c[lass] according to the region, situation, sea[son] and type of room chosen, but the price[s of] each establishment are fixed by the g[ov]ernment. Do not expect more than [you] pay for.

If you are considering a package t[our,] don't automatically plunge for [the] cheapest offered, or fall for the 'm[ystery] room' agent's silkiest sales talk. Go [to a] well-established agency and be guide[d by] their advice, then, if you are disappoin[ted,] *complain loudly* on your return ho[me –] even the best of agents is not infalli[ble,] but you will find he welcomes const[ruc]tive criticism and, when possible, [acts] upon it.

Hotel charges are not quoted here, but
member that to these prices must be
lded a 17 percent service charge, plus a
ossible further 12 percent owing to the
troduction of the IVA tax, similar to
AT, or to state taxes in the USA. Wine
id coffee are extras, and hotels may also
large for central heating in winter and
r conditioning in summer.

ensions (similar to a comfortable board-
g house) are also officially classified in
t, 2nd and 3rd categories.

Graded lists of hotels and pensions
ay be obtained from the Italian State
ourist Offices (see Useful Addresses).

ocande (inns), with very few exceptions,
e comparable with hotels of the 4th
tegory. On the whole, hotels are prefer-
le as having more facilities.

lberghi Diurni offer toilet facilities
nging from the simple *gabinetto* (lavat-
y) without wash-basin, to the luxury of
completely equipped bathroom. In
ntres such as Firenze, Milano, Roma,
ere are excellent *diurni* at the railway
ations, which feature rest rooms, writ-
g rooms, and *salons*, where one can get
aircut, shampoo, manicure, etc. Prices
e shown at the cash register and one
ys in advance.

CAMPING

here is an excellent camping guide,
ampeggi e villagi turistici in Italia, pub-
shed by the Touring Club of Italy,
nfortunately only in the Italian lan-
uage. If, however, you are not able to
ad the language, the Ente Turismo,
zienda Autonoma di Turismo, or the
fices of the CIT are extremely useful.
sually, at least one member of the staff is
ultilingual.

Your local tourist agent will also prove
elpful, or try the offices of CIT at 256
igh Street, Croydon CR9 1LL; 10
harles II Street, London SW1Y 4AB;
0 Fifth Avenue, New York, 10036; 333
orth Michigan Avenue, Chicago,
inois; 5670 Wilshire Boulevard, Los
ngeles, California 90036; the Italian
ate Tourist Office, 201 Regent Street,
ondon W1; the Italian Government
ourist Office, 630 Fifth Avenue, Suite
65, New York, 10020; 500 North
ichigan Avenue, Chicago 1, Illinois
611; 360 Post Street, Suite 801, San
ancisco, California 94108.

Camps offer a variety of accommoda-
on. Some have tents only, and the sign
noting these is **A** ; others have a
mbination of tents and bungalows,
cognizable by this sign **A C**. There
e also some delightful tourist villages,

the sign for which is **C C**. Snow camps
can be indicated by a white snow-crystal
within a dark surround.

Charges are not specified here, as they
change so quickly, but the 'tents only'
camp is cheaper than the bungalow type,
which in its turn is less costly than the
tourist village.

It must be remembered that there is a
tax (IVA, similar to VAT or state taxes in
the USA) to be added to all charges.

Most camps have a provision store and
bar and a service station. Many have
eating-places, varying from a restaurant
with service, to a self-service variety or a
snack bar. In most there is a shop where,
in addition to staple provisions, one can
buy cooking gas in cylinders; but, just in
case the cylinder available is not the right
type for your particular stove, pack a
spare.

In some camps there is an assembly
room, where one may chat with friends,
dance or listen to impromptu concerts.
Many seaside camps have their own private beach, quite a few have swimming
pools and, if you are staying on a really
luxurious camp site, there may even be a
doctor on the site.

If you are taking your dog on holiday,
remember that in some camps pets are
strictly NOT ALLOWED.

In camping literature – brochures, *etc*
– a sign indicates the nearest inhabited
place.

The bungalows on camp sites and in
tourist villages vary in type. They may be
of wood or concrete, and in the really
sunny south many have charming conical
straw roofs.

For really luxurious tourist village
holidays (but by no means of the cheapest
type) you are advised to try the Club
Mediterrane, but here it is advisable to
book well ahead, either at the headquar-
ters of the Club at Largo Corsia dei Ser-
vi, Milano, or in Viale Europa, Roma, or
through the CIT offices, the Italian State
Tourist Office, London, the Italian Government Tourist offices in USA or your
local travel agent.

Many sites provide especially for
families with children, and in some there
are organized games.

As a general rule, camping sites in the
north tend to be better and more efficient
than those farther south, a fact that
reflects the greater prosperity of the
northern half of the country.

Near or along the motorways, where
demand is greater, the camps tend to be
larger and consequently are usually better
equipped and better run. Also, the newer
the camp, the more efficient it tends to be.

One must not expect too much of a

camping holiday, or of the facilities portrayed so glowingly in brochures. So long as one remembers that all camping is bound to be to a certain extent 'roughing it', and doing a holiday 'on the cheap', then the experience will prove rewarding and probably better than one had dared to hope.

YOUTH HOSTELS

There are over 70 youth hostels in Italy, details of which can be obtained from the Associazione Italiana Alberghi per la Gioventù, 24 Via Guidobaldo del Monte, Roma, or from national organizations. The Centro Italiano Viaggi Istruzioni, Via Caetani 32, Roma, will provide information regarding students' hostels.

FOOD AND DRINK

Fish In the coastal centres one can enjoy a variety of fish dishes: scampi, octopus, squid and various shellfish and polypi. There are several unusual white fish which are worth sampling: *San Pietro* (John Dory) are similar to sole, and a Venetian speciality is *coda di rospo*, the tail of the 'frog fish', which has an excellent flavour and texture. A *fritto misto* of fish in any of these regions is an experience not to be forgotten; scampi, tiny mullet, baby octopus, squid, *etc*, are fried in very hot oil, and served piping hot with a slice of lemon and a green salad. In Génova *zimino*, a fish stew, is a delicacy; and *brodetto*, a fish soup, may be enjoyed on the Adriatic. Grilled tuna fish is of high quality in the south and in Sardegna (Sardinia). In the north there is pink-fleshed trout and in Veneto *baccalà* (salt cod) is a splendid winter dish, cooked in milk and oil and flavoured with onion. It may be served with *polenta*, which is a slice of a type of pasta made of maize flour.

Pasta is the generic name for any type of macaroni and comes in all varieties, from the long string-like to the *ravioli* or *tortellini* which are small circles or squares stuffed with spinach, *Ricotta* cheese or chopped meat before being served. Plain boiled macaroni or spaghetti are excellent served with a generous helping of butter and sprinkled with Parmesan cheese; a richer variety is *alla Bolognese*, served with a ragout composed of beef, chicken livers, herbs and tomato purée. In the south one's *pasta asciutta* (the name given to pasta not served in soup) frequently comes with a rich tomato sauce.

Lasagne − green or white − are ? large strips of pasta which are excelle when served *al forno*, a kind of savou first-course pudding cooked in the ov with a combination of Bolognese rago and béchamel sauce, coupled with gen ous amounts of grated parmesan. *Cann loni* is another outstanding variatio There are many varieties of filled pa which are delicious served as *pa asciutta* or dropped into a rich, clear ch ken soup. *Gnocchi*, which are tiny dun lings of semolina or potato, are simila treated.

Rice Dishes At one time rice dishes w associated with the north, *pasta* with ? south; nowadays the latter is obtainab all over Italy, but the former is still me or less confined to the north. A plain *ris to*, rice cooked in water or white wine an excellent dish, served simply with lump of fresh butter and generous he ings of grated Parmesan cheese (partic larly to be recommended for those rec ering from a bout of 'tummy' trouble). F there are more exotic varieties, such *risotto Milanese* which has beef marro incorporated in it, and a speciality of ? Veneto is *risi e bisi*, in which tender gre peas are incorporated with the rice. Oth combinations are *risotto* with *scampi* *vongole* (clams).

Soups Apart from the fish soups alrea mentioned, there are three outstandi soups to be found in Italy: *minestrone* thick rich soup of haricot beans, cele spinach, onions, peas, chopped ham, c rots, cabbage, tomatoes, herbs, and so o cooked together in meat stock and serv with grated parmesan cheese − ? unlike a well-made Scotch broth, a similarly almost a meal in itself; *zup Pavese* (Pavese soup) is a clear soup w a raw egg dropped into it just long enou to coagulate the white before servir *stracciatella*, a speciality of Roma, h also a basis of clear chicken soup, in which is whipped, just before servir beaten eggs combined with gra Parmesan cheese.

Meat The raw Parma ham (*prosciu crudo*) sliced paper-thin and served w fresh figs or a slice of melon makes delightful hors d'oeuvre, while in Lo bardia *bresaola* (dried salt beef) is goo

Veal is excellent in Italy, and when doubt as to what to order, one cannot wrong asking for a *costoletta Milane* which is a veal cutlet, beaten thin, coat with egg and breadcrumbs and fried butter; although a speciality of Mila this can be obtained all over Italy. richer variety is *costoletta alla Bologn* with grated Parmesan cheese and M sala added during the cooking. Again ologna one finds *scaloppe farcite*, which e thin slices of veal sandwiched with *osciutto crudo* and Gruyère cheese and ushrooms, fried and served with a rich uce. *Osso buco*, another Milanese dish, a veal shin bone, with the marrow left cooked in wine and stock with matoes and usually served with a plain hite *risotto*.

A great Roman speciality is *abbacchio forno*, roast baby lamb cooked whole; *pretto* (baby kid), similarly treated, is ually excellent. A delicious summer sh is *vitello tonnato*, thinly sliced roast al, served coated with a creamy sauce in hich is incorporated pounded tuna fish. The great winter dish of northern Italy *bollito*, chosen from the trolley which is ought one by the waiter, and on which e displayed beef, calves' head or feet, icken or turkey, *cotechino* (a rich salted rk sausage), all of them boiled. With is is usually served a piquant green uce (*salsa verde*). In Nápoli and the uth meat dishes are richer and usually rved with a thick sauce; *bistecca alla zzaiola* is a good rump steak, coated th a sauce composed of tomatoes, gar-, green and red peppers, and herbs, oked together in oil. Where poultry is ncerned, in addition to chicken and pon, it is rewarding to try roast *faraone* uinea fowl), quails, and *uccelletti* (tiny ng-birds roasted whole on a spit).

zza In Nápoli particularly, but nowa-ys all over Italy, are to be found *pizze* — en tarts of bread dough baked with any a number of toppings, the basis of hich is usually tomatoes, olives, cheese, t varied at times with anchovies and her additions.

egetables can be exotic. Artichokes are eap and excellent and are served some-mes with olive oil or, when very young d tender, sliced paper thin in a salad, or ed whole. Asparagus is a speciality of e Veneto and of Liguria and is of the rge, white variety. *Finocchio* (fennel — her like a bulbous celery in appear-ce, and tasting faintly of aniseed) is licious in salads or cooked and served th butter and grated Parmesan. Mush-oms are excellent.

uit Apart from the conventional anges, lemons, apples *etc*, autumn ings persimmons (*kaki*), and pomegra-tes, both of which are worth sampling. spring and summer, particularly ound Roma, there is an abundance of y, wild strawberries.

heeses are legion. The north gives one *aleggio* (at its best not unlike Camem-rt); *Bel Paese*, *Fontina*, *Provolone*, are worth trying, as are the *Mozzarella*, ade of buffalo milk, and *Ricotta* and

Pecorino (made of sheep's milk); grated *Parmesan* is widely used as a garnish to hot dishes as it does not coagulate.

Cost of Meals A *ristorante* is often expensive, a *trattoria* less so, and it is wise to choose one that has a priced menu exhibited on the door-post or in the window. To the price quoted will be added a service charge of 10 percent to 15 percent. You should also allow for a cover charge plus IVA tax, similar to VAT or the American state taxes. Wine and coffee are extra. Some restaurants have special tourist menus at fixed prices, but these tend to be a little uninspired — try experimenting with the native food, but only in a restaurant that has the prices indicated on the menu.

If money is running short, a *tosto* (a toasted sandwich consisting of a slice of ham and a slice of cheese between slices of bread) is a good standby with a glass of local wine, and can be obtained in any bar, and a plate of pasta is cheap and not to be despised.

Drinks Usually the local wine, white or red, is pleasant and not expensive. Some of the cruder varieties may need softening down with water. Such wine can be ordered by the carafe, half (mezzo) or quarter (quarto) carafe.

Whisky, brandy, gin and various liqueurs can be obtained at almost any bar, as can a variety of vermouth appetizers (not least among them Fernet-Branca, that infallible pick-me-up for an upset stomach). If one sits down at an outside table in a smart district, the price soars.

SPORT AND ENTERTAINMENT

Spectator sports The great national sports of Italy are football, basketball, tennis, racing (horses, cars, bicycles), boating, skiing and bobsledding. Golf is played, but not to a great extent. (Further details from the Federazione Italiana Golf, Viale Tiziano 70, Roma). Every town of any size has a football ground, basketball court and racecourse. Games and sporting events are widely advertised and the local Azienda Autonoma di Soggiorno (tourist office) or one's hotel can give full details and supply tickets.

International tennis championships are held in the Foro Romano, Roma, in May; others in Viaréggio at the end of August; in Catánia in Sicília in mid-March and in Réggio di Calábria in April. In April and May in Roma there is an

International Horse Show in the Piazza Siena; Catánia has a similar show in October. The main racecourses are in Roma, Faenza, Bologna, Merano and Nápoli. There is car and motorcycle racing at Monza in September; Cortina d'Ampezzo holds an international *Concours d'Élégance* at the end of July, and there is also racing at Caserta near Nápoli in June and at Siracusa in Sicília in April. A Motor Show is held in Torino in November; an Air Show is held in Génova in the same month.

The international motorboat race *Del Lario* takes place at Como in October; in September there is a sailing regatta at Portofino. International water polo takes place in Roma in May, while during July Ancona holds an international fair of fishing and water sports. Ice hockey championships are held at Cortina d'Ampezzo in August, in Torino – coupled with skating events – in February. From late December to early February the bobsled championships take place in Cortina.

On the less active side, there are bridge championships in Alássio in May and chess championships in Réggio nell' Emília in December. In July, there is a fashion show at the Palazzo Pitti, Firenze. Venezia holds an International Film Festival in August and September; Cortina has a festival of sports films in March, and there is a Film Review in Roma in September. Every other year, on even years, the Venezia Biennale art exhibition is held from June to October. Both Trieste and Roma have son et lumière (*suoni et luce*) spectacles during the summer evenings, the former at Castello Miramare, the latter in the Foro Romano. These are in a different language each evening, and you should find out when the English version is being held.

Winter sports in Italy

As soon as winter has settled in, almost everyone who can stand up on a pair of skis to enjoy the thrills and spills of this exhilarating sport. From early childhood Italians begin skiing, and at most winter resorts there are well-managed ski-schools and practice slopes.

Even in the hot summer days, ski fans will divide their annual holidays between a few days at the seaside and a few at some high resort, such as the Stelvio, where it is possible and pleasant to ski whatever the season.

Most of the resorts have skating rinks and many have sleigh-rides to tempt visitors; in Cortina d'Ampezzo it is great fun to get into a horse-drawn sleigh and go off, bells jingling, for a ride around the mountain.

There are numerous mountain refug where the night, or several nights, can spent. Among the many popular reso are Cortina d'Ampezzo, San Martina Castrozza, Moena Val di Fasso, Ortiséi the Dolomites, and farther west su lovely spots as Aosta in the valley of t same name.

Even those who do not ski or skate fi life in such centres agreeable; the sun hot, skies are blue, and it is easy to acqu a healthy tan and an even healthier app tite for the plentiful and excellent mou tain food, not to forget the mounta *grappa* or hot, spiced wine to warm o up after a spell in the fresh, crisp air.

Music festivals

The following are the more importa musical and theatrical events.

Firenze Maggio Musicale, May Music Festival, 10 May to end June. Summ theatre season, July. **Milano** Opera se son at Teatro alla Scala, December–Ma Piccola Scala lyric theatre, March–Ma **Nápoli** Lyric theatre, Campi Flegr July–August. Teatro San Carlo ope season December–May. **Óstia Antic** Performances in Roman Theat June–August. **Perúgia** Music Festiv September. **Ravenna** Organ Festiv church of San Vitale July–August. **Rom** Concert season of Accademia Sar Cecilia in the Basilica di Massenz July–August. Lyric theatre and ope Terme di Caracalla, July–August. Ope season December–June. **Siena** Mus week, September. **Spoleto** Festival of Two Worlds, June and July. **Venez** Concerts in Palazzo Ducale, July. Su mer season of lyric theatre at Teatro Fenice, July–August. **Verona** Opera a drama in Roman Theatre and Are July–August. **Vicenza** Drama at Tea Olimpico, September. Further details all the above events and many others m be obtained from the Italian State Government Tourist Office or from local tourist offices.

GENERAL INFORMATION

Passports and visas All visitors to Ita must hold a valid passport. Visas are r required. Passports may be obtained Britain at a passport office. Two passp photographs and one's birth certific are necessary when making applicati for a passport. The normal passport valid for ten years. A British Visito passport, valid for one year only, may

ined at any Department of Employ-
at and Productivity office. A birth cer-
ate or National Health insurance card
ecessary for identification.

merican citizens should apply in per-
to the Passport Division, Department
tate, in Washington DC, New York,
ton, Miami, Chicago, New Orleans,
Angeles, San Francisco, or Seattle. If
not possible to attend any of these
es, personal application should be
e before the clerk of any US District
rt System. Take along three un-
ached photographs, 6cm (2½in)
re, a witness who has known you for
ast two years unless you can produce
e identification that gives a physical
ription (a driver's licence will do),
birth certificate or old passport for
tification, plus the necessary fee.

smallpox vaccination carried out
in the past three years is obligatory
eturn to the USA.

toms Visitors to Italy from Europe
bring in 200 cigarettes or 50 cigars or
gm tobacco; visitors from outside
ope may bring in 400 cigarettes or
valent. US Customs permit duty-free
retail value of purchases per person,
1 quart of liquor per person over 21,
100 cigars per person, regardless of

Electricity in Italian cities is either 125 or
220 volts AC. It is important to check, and
to bring an adaptor for razors *etc* as points
are different from those at home.

Cigarettes British and American cigarettes are obtainable, but they are no
cheaper than at home and are usually
manufactured in Switzerland or Holland.
Of the local brands, *Nazionale* − in various qualities − are quite agreeable.
Cigar-smokers can purchase small, cheap
Avanas or the very strong *Toscanas*, plus
a variety of other local and imported
brands. Tobacconists (*tabaccaia*) are
identified by a large illuminated 'T'.

Postage Stamps may be bought at tobac-.
conists and most other shops where post-
cards and writing paper are sold.

Telephones One can usually telephone
from a bar. One buys a *gettone* (token),
which is inserted in the slot before dial-
ling. In a city of any size there is a central
office, provided with directories covering
the whole of the country, from where one
can make long-distance and international
calls.

Newspapers In any sizeable town or
resort, news stands (*edicole*) at the railway
station or in the more important squares
will carry the best-known newspapers of
other countries. The supply is neither
great nor regular.

Duty-free allowances for UK residents *subject to change*		Goods bought in a duty-free shop	Goods bought in EEC
bacco	Cigarettes	200	300
	or		
	Cigars *small*	100	150
	or		
	Cigars *large*	50	75
	or		
	Pipe tobacco	250 gm	400 gm
cohol	Spirits *over 38.8° proof*	1 litre	1½ litres
	or		
	Fortified or sparkling wine	2 litres	3 litres
	or		
	Table wine	2 litres	3 litres
rfume		50 gm	75 gm
ilet water		¼ litre	⅜ litre
her goods		£10	£50

US customs permit duty-free $300 retail value
of purchases per person, 1 quart of liquor per person over 21,
and 100 cigars per person.

Health As a member of the EEC Britain has an agreement with Italy that medical advice and treatment will be provided on the same basis as for Italian subjects. British visitors must have certificate E111 indicating entitlement to British National Health Service benefits. This certificate is issued by your local Health and Social Security office after you have completed application form CM1. You should ask for leaflet SA28 which gives details of all the EEC health services. If you need medical aid take certificate E111 to the local sickness insurance office (Instituto nazionale per l'assicurazione contro le malattie) INAM. In the provinces of Trento and Bolzano go to the provincial sickness fund (cassa mutua). The INAM office will give you a certificate of entitlement (ask for a list of sickness insurance scheme doctors and dentists). A doctor or dentist will then treat you free of charge. Without the certificate you will have to pay and may have difficulty in obtaining a refund of only part of the costs. Some prescribed medicines are free, others carry a small charge, but you must show form E111 to the chemist.

The doctor will give you a certificate (proposta di ricovero) if you need hospital treatment. This entitles you to free treatment in some hospitals. INAM offices have a list. If you cannot contact the INAM office before going into hospital, show form E111 to the hospital authorities and ask them to contact INAM at once.

American visitors should ensure that their own medical insurance is extended to cover them while abroad. Insurance brokers or travel agents will advise and arrange the additional cover.

Tipping Most hotels and restaurants include a service charge of 10 to 17 per cent. This is generally sufficient, but any special services should be tipped for separately. Usherettes in cinemas and theatres should be tipped 100 lire.

Clothing Great attention is paid to clothing in places of worship. Although there is no longer a strict insistence on a head covering for women, their arms should be covered as far as the elbows, and they should wear a skirt – one· that is not too short. A man should wear trousers rather than shorts.

Papal Audiences Those wishing to participate in a general Papal Audience should apply to the Maèstro di Càmera di Sua Santità, Città del Vaticano, Roma, giving not more than one month's and not less than two days' notice. Roman Catholics are requested to have a letter of introduction from their priest.

Shops are usually open from 08.3 09.00 to 13.00; 15.30 or 16.00 to 19.3 20.00. Socks, stocking and glove size universal, but dresses, shoes *etc* d and it is unwise to purchase a gar without trying it on first.

Public conveniences are few and diffi to find. Use those of filling stations, c bars *etc*. Ladies (*Signore*) may be dist uished from gentlemen (*Signori*) by last letter – 'e' for 'she'.

General behaviour

There has been a considerable slac ing of the one-time rigid standard behaviour, but it is still not consid permissible to wander around chur sightseeing while services are in p ress.

As for queueing, disheartening tho it may be to be shoved aside by a l there is always the hope that one example will prove its worth and we gaze spellbound at orderly queue Italians; till that day dawns, howeve as well to be philosophical about the tom of the country, which does tend 'every man for himself and devil tak hindmost'.

One important thing to rememb that, whatever you may have been ta in your own country, it is courting su to stride blindly and arrogantly acr pedestrian crossing. You must be pared to stand and wait until the accu lation of a fair number of pedestrians signified to the driver of one of the st of passing vehicles that it woul courteous to pause and let the hu walkers cross. If, however, you hav your group a mother with a young your wait will be far shorter.

And now an unpleasant, but necessary, caution: do not carry n money around in your handbag. The *ppo* (bag-snatching) is a popular these days, and those who play i expert and ruthless. If you feel a g tug at your handbag, it is often wiser it go than to enter into combat, unles course, you are a karate champion.

Public holidays

Italy used to be notorious for the nu of public holidays and consequent weekends but, as from 1 January 197 list is as follows: 1 January – Capoda (New Year's Day), Easter Sunday, E Monday, 25 April – Anniversary of eration, 1 May – Festa del La (Labour Day), Pentecost, 15 Augu Assumption of the Virgin, 1 Novemb Ognissanti (All Saints), 8 Decemb Imacolata (Immaculate Conception December – Christmas Day, December – St Steven's Day.

USEFUL ADDRESSES

Britain
ian State Tourist Office, 201 Regent
et, London W1 (01-734 4631).
alia, 251 Regent Street, London W1
734 4040). British Caledonian, Inter-
onal Reservations (01-668 4177).
ish Airways, Dorland Ho., Lower
ent St., London SW1 (01-370 4545).
omobile Association, Fanum House,
more (01-954 7355). Royal
omobile Club, 83-5 Pall Mall, Lon-
SW1 (01-930 4343). British Rail
vel Centre, 4 Lower Regent Street,
don SW1 (01-283 7171).

Italy
ish Consulates: Via XX Settembre
, 00187 Roma (06-4755441); Via San
o 7, 20121, Milano (02-803442);
azzo Castelbarco, Lungarno Corsini
irenze 1-50123 (055-212594); Via
icesco Crispi 122, 1-80122 Nápoli
- 209227); Accademia 1051, Venezia
ers), P.O. Box 679, 30100 Venezia
il), (041-27207).

American Consulates: Lungarno
Amerigo Vespucci 38, Firenze (055-
298276); Banca d'America e d'Italia,
Piazza Portello 6, Génova (010-282741-
5); Piazza della Repubblica 32, Milano
(02-652841); Piazza della Repubblica,
80122 Nápoli (081-660966); Via V. Veneto 119, Roma (06-4674); Via Valdirivo
19A, 4th Floor, Trieste (040-68728); Via
Alfieri 17, Torino (011-543600).

In America
Italian Government Tourist Office, 630
Fifth Avenue, Suite 1565, New York
10020 (CI 5-4822). Alitalia, 666 Fifth
Avenue, New York (JU 2-6500). Ameri-
can Automobile Association, World
Wide Travel Service, 750 Third Avenue,
New York (YU 6-7500).

In Sardegna
Cágliari: Assessorato del Turismo della
Regione Sarda, Viale Trento 69,
Cágliari. ESIT, Ente Sardo Industrie
Turistiche, Via Mameli 95, Cágliari.
EPT, Ente Provinciale per il Turismo,
Piazza Deffenu 9, Cágliari.
Province of Núoro: Ente Provinciale per
il Turismo, Piazza Italia 19, Núoro.
Sássari: Ente Provinciale per il Turismo,
Piazza Italia 19, Sássari.
Oristano: Ente Provinciale per il Turis-
mo, Via Cágliari 125/B.

METRIC CONVERSIONS

CLOTHING

Shoes

Men's	British	6	7	8	9	10
	European	40	41	42	43	44
	USA	6½	7½	8½	9½	10½
Women's	British	4	5	6	7	8
	European	36	37	38	39	40
	USA	5½	6½	7½	8½	9½

Dresses

British	10/32	12/34	14/36	16/38	18/40
European	38	40	42	44	46
USA	8	10	12	14	16

Men's Collar Sizes

British/USA	14	14½	15	15½	16	16½	17
European	36	37	38	39	41	42	43

WEIGHT

	(¼ kg)	(½ kg)	(¾ kg)	(1 kg)
grams	50 100 150 200 250 300	400 500	600 700 750 800 900 1000	
ounces	0 1 2 3 4 6 8 12	16	24	32 36
	(¼ lb) (½ lb)	(1 lb)	(1½ lb)	(2 lb) (2½ lb)

FLUID MEASURES

litres	0 5 10	20	30	40	50
imp. gals	0	5		10	
US gals	0	5	10		

THE LAKES

Italy has many lovely lakes, and sometimes the combination of natural beauty they offer, together with excellent tourist facilities, makes a greater appeal than seaside or mountains.

Starting right up in the Dolomites, to the north of Belluno, is **Lago Misurina,** pine-clad and a trifle austere when the sun is not shining. One comes upon this lake almost unawares; its azure waters, mirroring the surrounding conifers, give it an other-world quality and one wonders whether fairyland is far away. It is only about 13km/10mi from the winter sports centre of Cortina d'Ampezzo, and is excellently equipped for winter and summer entertainment. Swimming and boating are agreeable in summer and fishing yields catches of pink-fleshed trout; in winter there is skiing on the surrounding slopes and skating.

The Dolomites have other attractive lakes. Not far from Trento is **Lévico,** a long, fiord-like stretch of water set among wooded hills. Its transparent greenish waters freeze in winter. Only a kilometre away is the small thermal centre of the same name.

Still in the Dolomites, this time in Val Venosta, very near the **Résia** pass leading from the Engadine Valley, is the lake of the same name, the result of the union of two smaller lakes to form a dam. In addition to the attractions of swimming, boating and fishing there is a photogenic subject in the half-submerged church of one of the villages affected by the building of the dam.

On the way from Résia to Merano one passes through many delightful little villages; a particularly interesting one is Sluderno where stands the Castel Churburg (Castle of Coira), interesting for its frescoed cloisters and ancient paintings and sculpture and for a rich armoury, but also for having once been the seat of the Bishops of Chur, a city now included within the confines of Switzerland.

These are but a few of the many charming lakes to be found in the Dolomites.

Coming now to the region of Lombardia, first of all one arrives at **Lago d'Orta,** only 3½km/2mi long and 1½km/1mi wide, but extremely picturesque. The greenish shade of the water reflecting the surrounding wooded slopes make one think of emeralds. There are many holiday centres in this area. Balzac termed the town of the same name *una perla grigia in uno scrigno verde* (a grey pearl in a green casket).

Almost in the middle of the lake is island of San Giuliano, with a bas. originating from the time when the s himself was living (390 AD). This is St Julian of the Golden Legend.

Eastwards from Lago d'Orta is N**giore,** 54km/33mi long, never more 9½km/6mi wide. It acts as a boun between the regions of Piemonte Lombardia and its northernmost p belongs politically to Switzerland. dark, rocky slopes of the mountains n the northern part grim and almost for ding, but once past the strait betw Cannóbio and Maccagno, the sce. changes; rich green pastureland woods lead westwards to Monte Z and soon come the real jewels of the Stresa and the far-famed Isole Borro (Borromean Islands). Behind Stresa Monte Mottarone, 1491m/4892ft a sea level, from whose peak can be the entire chain of the Alps.

On the eastern shore are numerou tle towns, such as Augera, Arolo, N valle, Cerro and others. In the last-na is the sanctuary of Santa Caterina, a s 17th-century church and convent seem to form part of the high roc which they are built.

On a hill not more than 2km/1 from the town of Arona, near the ba the western shores stands a colo statue of San Carlo Borro (1533–1584). The statue, 23m/75ft h stands on a pedestal 12m/39ft high, the whole is impressive. Those who can climb up inside the statue and em at neck level.

Progressing westwards one comes to **Lago di Varese,** 4km/2½mi from city of the same name, and excelle served by roads to the main centres. little lake is very popular for swimm and bathing, though somewhat shadowed by the nearness of Lag

gano, which has the added attraction
eing a frontier point between Italy and
itzerland. Tourists who wish to take
antage of this must make sure their
sports are valid in both countries.

ago di Como has the form of an
erted Y. 198m/650ft above sea level, it
ne of Italy's loveliest lakes, famous,
, in literature for it was the setting of
nzoni's unforgettable novel *I Promessi
si (The Betrothed)*, which opens with
lendid description of that branch of
lake which turns southward between
uninterrupted chains of mountains,
ving ever higher, and reflected in the
ers.

he town of Lecco stands half-way
n the eastern leg of the Y, and is an
ortant tourist centre. The real pearl of
lake, however, is Bellágio at the tip of
peninsula separating the legs of the Y;
icularly lovely in summer and
mn, it adds splendid scenery to the
e ordinary tourist attractions. Not far
y is the Villa Serbelloni, set in a huge
k and said to be one of the loveliest
s in Italy.

omo is the capital of the region and
a fine Gothic-Renaissance Cathedral
a *broletto* (town hall) which dates

back to the early part of the 13th century.

During the 11th century there originated in Como a privileged group of
master-builders, known as the Magistri
Comacini. Most of the church building
and the characteristic decoration of
churches of that period, not only in Lombardia but in other parts of Italy, were the
inspiration of these clever master-
masons.

Cernóbbio, 5km/3mi away on the western shores, is a well-known resort, with a
pleasantly bland climate even in winter.

A tree-lined avenue links Tremezzo
and Cadenábbia on the western shore,
with views across the water to Bellágio.

These are only a few of the many
enchanting spots on the shores of this
lovely lake.

Lago d'Iseo, between Bergamo and
Bréscia, though small in comparison
with Como, is fourth in size of the northern Italian lakes. Surrounded almost
entirely by mountains, it offers splendid
views, yields a rich harvest of trout, eel
and other fish, and is visited by flights of
wild duck.

Next comes Garda, Italy's largest lake
covering an area over 50km/31mi long
and 17½km/11mi wide, reaching up like

aggio, Lago di Como

a spearhead into the mountains of Trentino-Alto Adige. Its southern shores are relatively flat, but northwards they become steeper and at times rise sheer out of the water.

Around the coast there is such a number and variety of holiday resorts that a whole guide book could be devoted to them.

On the south stands Desenzano, very residential nowadays, a pleasant dormitory town for those who work in Verona and even as far afield as Vicenza and Padova. In spite of a large, modern section, a little area of old, arcaded streets remains, wandering at will and finishing up at the lake shore. One sees gaily painted hand-carts decorated with locally grown oranges and lemons, and in the little, narrow streets are greengrocers' shops where the produce is much fresher than in the modern supermarkets.

Not far away, on a tongue of land to the east, stands the great Rocca Scaligera (Scaliger Castle) of Sirmione (1250).

Beyond it lie the ruins of a Roman known locally as the Grotte di Ca (Grotto of Catullus). It is certain tha poet had a country place at Sir whether at this exact spot or not is a point. But of his beloved Sirmio he w

Of all the islands and of all th almost isles
Which Neptune, God of Water, se among clear lakes
And in the vast seas, you, Sirmio are sole bright gem

(From *Poets in a Landscape,* Ha Hamilton, 1957, p.40, translated by bert Highet).

Standing near the edge of o crowned cliffs on which are the rem of the villa, and looking down at the w washing the vari-coloured rocks be one is inclined to agree with Catu and if, on the way back, one picks a rosemary 'for remembrance', this shr so abundant that one small sprig wil be missed.

If one's feet are protesting after

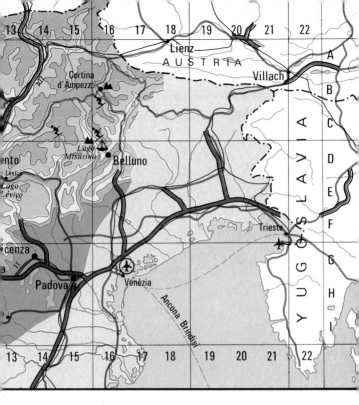

...ab, it is always possible to join the ...dren and return by the little *trenino* ...will deposit one near the Rocca ...igera.

...astwards from Sirmione lies Peschi...once a fortress town and still posses...the great military fortress built in the ...century by the architect Michele ...micheli. Peschiera, together with ...na, Legnago and Mántova consti...d the great Austrian 'Quadrangle'. ...esent-day Peschiera offers excellent ...mming and boating and lives up to its ...e as a good fishing centre.

...orthwards one comes first to Lazise, ...its medieval walls and a castle dating ...to 1024, Garda, Punta San Vigilio, ...e del Benaco, Brenzone and finally ...césine, dominated by the former ...ce of the Captains of the Lake, now ...own hall, and another great Scaliger ...e. Even farther north are Tórbole on ...east and Riva on the west, where the ...ate and vegetation are almost ...iterranean.

All these centres provide excellently for tourists and it is possible to take trips on the lake itself, either by steamer or by the swifter hydrofoil.

Along the western shore there is Salò, from which point the Garda Riviera begins; soon comes Gardone of international fame, offering not only some of the finest views of the lake but, in the months of July and August, open-air theatre and ballet in the grounds of Il Vittoriale, the fantastic estate of the late poet, Gabriele d'Annunzio. This is an estate that has to be seen to be believed, with such strange concepts as a ship on land, a circular burial place with the poet's tomb elevated high above those of his friends and a house filled, one might say crammed, with *objets d'art* which range from the truly beautiful to the utterly worthless.

Working one's way back to Desenzano, every mile or so a fresh expanse of beauty opens up.

(For further information on the lakes, see under regional headings.)

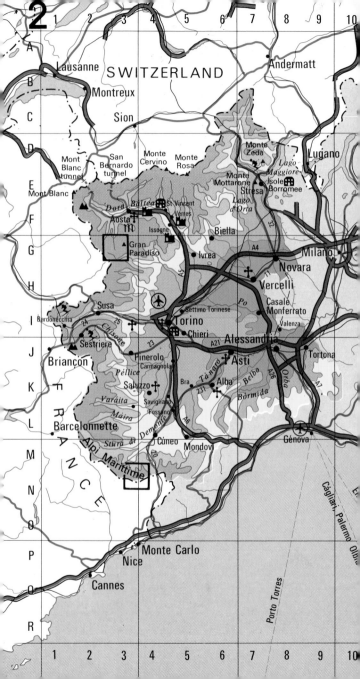

PIEMONTE AND ALLE D'AOSTA

is the name given to the most
westerly region and the largest with
xception of Sicilía. The boundary
:en it and France cuts northwards
gh the Maritime Alps as far as Mont
: (4810m/15,780ft above sea level),
:e Cervino (4478m/14,690ft) and
:e Rosa (4663m/15,300ft), then fol-
the arc of the Swiss Alps until it
:es the western shores of Lago Mag-
and, descending in a series of
:s, arrives at the Ligurian Alps.

D'Aosta, which occupies the
western corner, is one of the
:est valleys in the Alps, ringed
:d by some of the highest peaks in
:pe and including the Parco
:nale (National Park), the Gran
:liso. It has been an autonomous reg-
:nce 10 March 1947.

:ep river valleys alternate with the
:mountains, the principal river being
:)ora Baltea.

:is small area is admirably equipped
:urism. Hotels are excellent, there is
:d system of cable railways, there are
:rous mountain refuges and guides
:vailable for the more hazardous
:is.

:lle d'Aosta also has much to offer to
:interested in archaeology, architec-
:nd art.

:e capital, Aosta, was an important
:1 Roman days and has conspicuous
:1n remains.

:e region is rich in castles, one of the
:impressive being Fénis between
:and St Vincent. Two other
:sting castles are those of Verrès and
:ne, both just off the road from St
:nt to Ivrea.

:onte lies within an arc of high
:tains embracing its northern and
:rn borders, followed by the
:led hills of the Langhe and Mon-
:o, with an oasis of plainland
:d Vercelli and Novara.

:e climate in the mountains is one
:vere winters and mild summers;
:down, though the winters are cold
:considerable rain in spring and
:nn, summers are hot.

:t only is Piemonte a busy industrial
:n, it also has many attractions for
:holiday-maker, from the well-
:ped mountain resorts of Sestriere

and Bardonécchia in the western Alps to
the pleasant western shores of Lago
Maggiore and the exquisite little Lago
d'Orta.

Nor is architectural beauty difficult to
find. There is the 10th century Benedictine abbey, the Sacra San Michele, high
on a rocky crest along the motorway running west from Torino. Several cities
such as Vercelli, Saluzzo and others have
fine Gothic churches and Torino is an
exemplar of splendid baroque architecture with a decidedly French flavour.

Festivals May (first Sunday), Fossano
(near Cúneo) — Festival of San
Giovenale. Portraits or photos of the
town's benefactors are displayed on the
walls, followed by a procession through
the streets. 23 June Torino — Festival of
San Giovanni. Huge wooden construction made in Palazzo Castello; on top is
mounted a papier-maché bull; all set on
fire in the evening. A custom dating from
Longobard days to exorcise the ills of the
city. September (3rd Sunday) Asti —
Palio (horse race) among the various districts of the city, all in costume of the
Middle Ages. 23 October, Alba — Fair of
the white truffles for which the district is
famous, followed by tournament in costume.

Alba   K6

(pop. 27,740) This little city is the seat of
a bishopric in the province of Cúneo.
Situated in the valley of the Tánaro, it
attracts tourists visiting the Langhe. Its
aspect is medieval, even though of recent
years industries have been established
there. It is an important wine-making
centre, its specialities being Barolo, Bar-
baresco, Nebbiolo, Barbera, Dolcetto,
and holds a great attraction for gourmets,
being the centre of a district where white
truffles are found, one of the main attractions of its October Fair.

There is a Gothic cathedral dating

from the end of the 15th century, whose inlaid wooden choir is a fine example of the work of Cidonio (early 16th century).

Aosta   F3

(pop. 36,325) This is the capital city of the region of the same name, and is a charming little city situated in a wide valley among high mountains. It is a much-frequented tourist centre, placed as it is where the great St Bernard and Mont Blanc tunnels converge.

Founded by the Romans, it still preserves fine monuments: the Arch of Augustus, the Porta Prætoria, a theatre and an amphitheatre.

The collegiate church of Sant' Orso is well worth a visit; externally there is a fine *ghimberga* (high cuspid arch) over the main portal and inside are splendid frescoes – in part ruined by time – of the 11th century; there is also an excellent wooden choir.

The cathedral, originally of the 11th to 12th centuries, was rebuilt in the 15th to 16th centuries. The interior is Gothic and there is a fine wooden choir.

Asti   J6

(pop. 76,200) This is the seat of a bishopric, the capital city of the province, and is of patrician aspect, with splendid monuments, some dating back to the Middle Ages.

Lying in the middle valley of the Tánaro, it is the centre of a famous wine-producing area, particularly of the famous Asti spumante. Other industries include the production of modern tapestries, wrought iron, pewter and copper. The cathedral is a massive Romanesque-Gothic edifice, with three ornate portals and circular openings above; the most interesting of the medieval monuments is the baptistery of San Pietro, dating to the 12th century.

Stresa   E7

(pop. 4739) This town lies on the western shore of Lago Maggiore, one of the most enchanting sites on the lake. Once a mere fishing village, Stresa nowadays is a modern town with numerous well-equipped hotels, elegant villas, and every facility; a rack railway connects with the winter sports centre of **Mottarone**. Stresa has boat services to all the lovely **Ísole Borromee**. Although Ísola Madre is the largest, the one which attracts most visitors is Ísola Bella (Beautiful Island), transformed from virgin rock into a splendid garden surrounding the Palace of the Borromeo family. Ísola dei Pescatori (Fishermen's Island) comes next in attractiveness, with its rustic fishermen's houses. Both of these have hotels. *Milano 90km/56mi.*

Torino (Turin)

(pop. 1,100,000) Torino is regarde many as the most French city in much of its culture and many c monuments have a strong Fr flavour. During the Middle Ages it Longobard duchy; during the 16th tury it became the capital of the Fr province of Savoy. It played an exc part in Italy's struggle for independ during the last century, and followin *Risorgimento* was the capital of U Italy from 1861 to 1864.

It is a smart city of gracious squ (166 in all), tree-lined streets and l gardens, with elegant bridges ove river Po and its tributary, the Dora. Via Roma leads from the station t Piazza San Carlo (tourist informa The Palazzo Madama (off Via Roma four turrets, statues on its upper te and an imposing façade. This sple palace is now the home of the M Civico d'Arte Antica. In the Piazza is the Palazzo Reale, erected towar end of the 17th century, from the ba of which Carlo Alberto opened the It War of Independence on March 23, It is now a museum. In the same s the Armeria Reale is celebrated as t second in importance only to that of rid. Nearby is the baroque Palazzo C nano, seat of the Chamber of Dep 1848-59, now the Museum of the *R gimento*. Not far from Palazzo Madar Piazza San Giovanni are the cath and the bell-tower. In a chapel behin cathedral, designed by Guarini, is served the sacred shroud in whicl body of Christ was wrapped after b taken down from the Cross. This re exhibited only on rare occasions an grims come from all parts of the wo participate in the ceremony. Porta P na, near the cathedral, is a relic of Ro days; beyond it lies the sanctuary o Consolata.

On the banks of the Po are the ma cent park and the 17th-century Cas del Valentino and the Borgo Medio (medieval town) erected in 1884 on occasion of the great exhibition o same year. Beyond these, in Corso simo d'Azeglio, stands the huge, mo palace in which are held exhibitions international gatherings. On the side of the Po, visit the hill-top con Monte dei Cappuccini, then take a c or the rack railway to Juvara's ma piece of baroque architecture, Basilica di Superga (1717–31), r decorated and housing the tombs o Kings of Sardegna and the Princ Savoy. *Génova 195km/121mi, M 140km/87mi.*

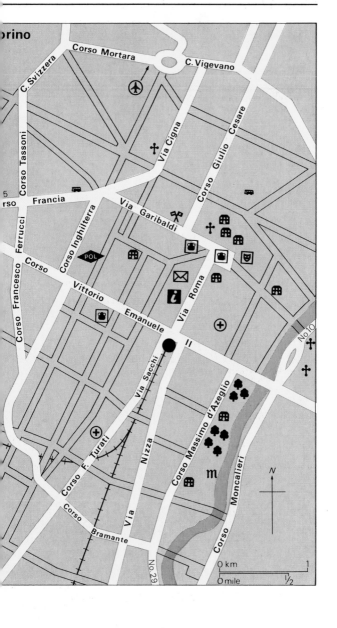

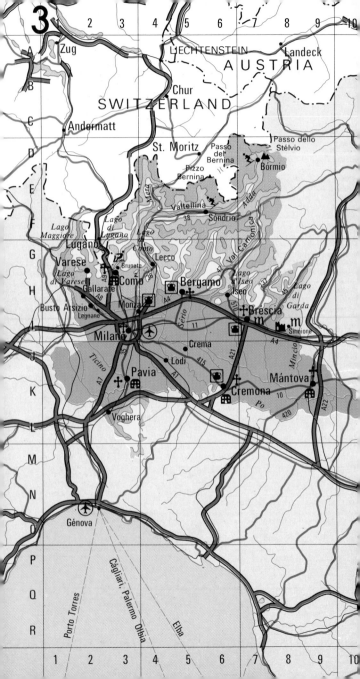

OMBARDIA

e name of this region goes back to the
s of the Longobards, who occupied it
n 568–774 AD, making Pavia their
ital city. It was first mentioned in the
n of King Alboino, in a diploma dated
July 629, as *Longobardia*.
Historical vicissitudes, coupled with
geographical location, have made this
richest and one of the most important
ions of Italy. It has direct road, rail and
communications not only within the
insula, but with the rest of Europe,
is on the main routes between the
diterranean and the Continent.

ts territory includes the middle section
he Po basin, between the River Ticino
he west and the River Mincio on the
t. The southern plain rises to Pre-
s, then northwards to the imposing
in of the Retiche and Lepontine Alps
ch divide it from Switzerland. Many
these mountain peaks are over
0m/9840ft above sea level, Pizzo Ber-
a rising to over 4050m/13,200ft.

he central section, stretching from
monte to the Veneto, is a region of
es: from the eastern shores of Mag-
e, Lugano, Como, Iseo follow in
d succession until the western shores
Garda are reached.

he climate, thanks to the protection
he northern wall of mountains, is
d, particularly in the Pre-Alps. Win-
are cold, but not excessively so,
mers are agreeably hot. On the plain,
ter fogs constitute a driving and flying
ard, and Milano is particularly
cted by these.

both mountains and lakes the scen-
is attractive and hotel accommodation
ellent. The valleys of the Pre-Alps are
ed with charming small towns and
ges; in the higher mountains two of
most popular resorts are Sóndrio in
Bergamasque Alps and Bormio in the
Val Camonica not far from the Stel-
Pass. The lakes of Maggiore, Lugano,
no and Garda are extremely pictur-
e; around their shores Nature has
helped by the hand of man and their
splendid parks, villas and gardens.
is wilder, more unspoiled.

Lombardia is in the forefront for
culture. A great series of irrigation
als criss-crosses the plain, and wheat,
ze, forage, rice and sugar-beet are cul-
ted intensively, aided by the most
dern mechanical means. The vine-
ds of the Pre-Alps produce excellent
es, particularly around Garda and
Valtellina. Mulberry trees flourish in a
few regions where silk is woven.

Industry, helped by rich hydroelectric
resources, is developed at a high level:
much cotton and wool are produced
around Como; metallurgic and mechanical industries flourish in Milano, Bréscia
and several smaller centres; production of
shoes, clothing, hats and rubber is among
the lesser industry of this wealthy, busy
region.

Nor are archaeology, architecture or art
neglected. Val Camonica has rock-
scratched designs depicting life as it was
lived twenty-five centuries ago. In the Po
Valley evidences have been discovered of
terramare – dwellings of a pre-Neolithic
people. Sirmione on Garda has the
imposing remains of a Roman villa;
Bréscia the ruins of the Temple of Vespasian and the ancient jewelled cross of
the Longobard King Desiderio. In the
cathedral museum of Monza is the famous Iron Crown (see page 7).

Italian Romanesque architecture owes
much to Lombardia, and particularly to
Como, from which city came the Magistri
Comacini (master-builders of Como)
who, in the early Middle Ages, greatly
influenced the development of this style
of church building.

Gothic, but of a non-Italian type, is
exemplified in the ornate cathedral of
Milano, begun in 1386, but not completed until 1887.

In Mántova (Mantua) Leon Battista
Alberti's church of Sant'Andrea is a fine
example of Renaissance architecture;
later came a more elaborate note, as witness the Certosa di Pavia and the Cappella Colleoni in upper Bergamo. Finally
comes the neo-classic severity of the
Teatro alla Scala in Milano, and the
glazed Galleria leading from it to the
Piazza del Duomo, in striking contrast to
the city's ultra-modern skyscrapers.

Festivals May (beginning), Bergamo – Amusing rally of 'soap-box' cars. May (last Sunday), Legnano – Procession and race celebrating the victory of the city in 1176 over Frederick II of Swabia. June (early), Milano – Festival dei Navigli (navigable canals). A walk from Piazza del Duomo (or the Arena) for 22km. In 1977 this involved 30,000 spectators and/or contestants. 7 December Milano – Opening Night of La Scala opera season – tickets are eagerly sought after and difficult to come by.

Bergamo   H5
(pop. 113,500) This city is built on two levels. Lower Bergamo offers wide avenues, lined with trees, elegant mansions, and a wealth of Renaissance and baroque churches, with more than one fine museum. The upper city gives one the feeling of having stepped back into the Middle Ages, even though its architecture ranges from pre-Roman to post-Renaissance.

Little is known of Bergamo outside Italy, yet it is a city that really merits a visit. Under Venetian domination for over 350 years, it has absorbed and retained much of the Venetian atmosphere. Sitting at one of the many open-air cafés surrounding Piazza Vecchia one is reminded of Piazza San Marco in Venezia – there is even the omnipresent Lion of St Mark, embedded in the wall of the Palazzo della Ragione.

After you have sat awhile in this lovely square, go through the archway to the left of the stairs that lead up into the Palazzo della Ragione, and you will see two marvellous buildings. To the left is the cathedral, built in the 17th century on the site of an earlier 6th-century church, rich in frescoes, paintings and with a fine choir.

Facing you is the Cappella Colleoni, the work of Giovanni Antonio Amadeo, inside which is the ornate tomb of Colleoni; to your right is a charming little baptistery, while on the left is the church of Santa Maria Maggiore.

Bréscia   I7
(pop. 180,000) What one first notices about Bréscia are its industries, which pollute the air and darken the stone of the buildings. Once famous for the manufacture of weapons of war, it is not surprising that metal-work still features largely among its products.

However, Bréscia has much to offer other than industry and commerce. Look at the Duomo Nuovo (New Cathedral, 17th century), the work of Lantana and rich inside with groups of marble statuary and other works of art. Then proceed to the old cathedral, popularly known as Rotonda from its circular shape; it h very interesting Romanesque cr Nearby stand the Broletto (Court of tice) and the Torre del Popolo (Peop Tower), both Romanesque.

Those who have admired the *Win Victory* at the Louvre in Paris sho make a point of visiting the remains of Temple of Vespasian, in which is Museo Romano, with a splendid bro statue of the *Winged Victory* rivalling in Paris. There is also the Museo C tiano, with the presbytery of the one-t church of Santa Giulia where, am other treasures, one can see the fam gold cross of Desiderio, an example goldsmith's work of the 9th cent breath-taking in its splendour.

Other buildings rewarding to visit the 9th century Basilica di San Salvat the splendid Pinacoteca and the chu of San Giovanni Evangelista.

Como
(pop. 76,914) At the base of the wes fork of the Lago di Como, this delightful spot in which to relax for a days after the hustle and bustle of Mil (43km). It has something of everyth for the visitor: a zoological garden, w sports, fishing, good theatrical en tainments, steamers to other points on lake, pullman coach services to Mil and other centres of the province, a cable railway that in seven minutes veys one to Brunate on the table-l overlooking the city and lake.

It has several interesting buildi including the two Romanesque churc of San Abbondio and San Fedele, cathedral – a jewel of Renaissa Gothic with a splendid façade – Broletto or former seat of the *comune*, the splendid Villa Olmo, adjacent to fine public park. A pleasant walk from town is to the 4th-century Basilica di Carpoforo. *Lugano 31km/19mi.*

Cremona
(pop. 74,275) This might be describe a pilgrimage town for music-lovers, f was once famous for the manufactu Stradivarius violins, and both the M Civico (collection to be moved to Sc di Liuteria in the Palazzo Raimondi) the Palazzo del Comune have fascina collections of 'Stradivariana'. Today city, one of the most absorbing of no ern Italy, is celebrated for a gastronc delicacy – *Mostarda di Cremona* (mona mustard). This concoction whole fruits, cherries, figs, apricots chunks of melon, preserved in a s mustard-flavoured syrup, is delic with boiled meats.

The cathedral is a splendid example of
Lombard Gothic, with a façade that is a
to behold — a lovely rose window,
delicate colonnades and central portico.
Inside there are some fine paintings. The
terrazzo or bell-tower is the tallest in
Italy. Other interesting sights include the
church of Sant'Agata (19th-century
façade and good frescoes), the Loggia dei
Militi and the Palazzo Comunale, (both
pleasant 13th-century buildings).

After having visited the city, it is
rewarding to drive to the church of San
Sismondo on the outskirts. The
church, viewed from the outside, is not
impressive, but inside are frescoes executed by various members of the Campi
family, 17th-century followers of the
great Caracci school. Rich in bright colours, these frescoes present a feast of
Baroque painting at its best.

Mántova (Mantua)　　K9

(pop. 62,000) Mántova is almost entirely
surrounded by the river Mincio which
forms, so to speak, three lakes, Lago
Superiore, Lago di Mezzo and Lago
Inferiore. Originally an Etruscan city, it
has passed through many hands during
the centuries, but its most flourishing
period was during the *signoria* of the great
Gonzaga family, starting in 1328 when
Luigi Gonzaga was elected Capitano del
Popolo, and ending with the death in
1708 of Duke Ferdinand Carlo Gonzaga.
The court of the Gonzagas was an important centre of art and culture, and the
buildings of Mántova testify to the artistic
taste of this great family.

Among the interesting buildings are
the Romanesque Rotonda di San
Lorenzo (1000 AD) and the magnificent
Palazzo Ducale and Castello di San
Giorgio, both of the Gonzaga period. The
cathedral is an example of Lombard
Gothic, but its façade was reconstructed
in the 18th century; nearby is the Cappella dell'Incoronata, while in the church
Sant'Andrea are the tomb of Mantegna
and some valuable frescoes. There are
delightful squares in the city and a
number of other interesting buildings.

Seven km from the city is another
reminder of the great family, the sanctuary of Santa Maria delle Grazie,
founded by Francesco Gonzaga and containing good paintings and a gallery of
votive statues. *Parma 67km/42mi, Ver-
39/24.*

Milano (Milan)　　I3

(pop. 1,471,471) Now Italy's most important commercial city, busy, bustling,
modern, Milano suffered much during the
early barbarian invasions until, with the
arrival of the Longobards, it became the
capital of one of their duchies. With the
fall of the Carolingians and the descent of
Barbarossa in 1152, the city was
destroyed, but rose from the ashes and
from 1279 to 1447 was governed as a *signoria* by the Visconti, followed by the
Sforza to 1533. It again fell under foreign
dominion; Spanish, French, Austrian,
until it was created capital of the Cisal-
pine Republic by Napoleon I, and in 1805
capital of Italy. In 1848 it fell into
Austrian hands, but finally achieved freedom in 1860 when it was united with the
new Italy.

Milano has some splendid examples of
architecture. Probably the finest example
of Italian Gothic is the cathedral (1),
begun in 1386, with its 135 pinnacles,
one over 100 metres high with the famous
gilded *Madonnina* (4 metres high) on top.
The 'mother church' of Lombard-
Romanesque architecture is the lovely
Basilica Sant'Ambrogio (2). In the refectory of the church of Santa Maria delle
Grazie (3) is the famous *Last Supper* of
Leonardo da Vinci, miraculously appearing to extend the length of the room. The
splendid courtyard of the Palazzo di Brera
(4), seat of Milano's fine art gallery, is the
work of the 17th-century architect
Richini; (5) the Castello Sforzesco is
another imposing architectural landmark.

Galleria Vittorio Emanuele (6) by the
Piazza del Duomo is the great meeting,
eating and shopping centre of Milano.

Pavia　　K3

(pop. 67,960) The capital city of the Longobards who invaded Italy in 568 AD and
remained to become absorbed in the
civilization of the country, Pavia is an
agreeable city with some delightful buildings. The Basilica di San Michele in
which the kings of Lombardy were
crowned until the 11th century is a splendid example of Romanesque architecture, its façade decorated with cleverly
grouped windows, blind *loggettas* and
sculpture, and three grand portals,
reminiscent of those seen in some of the
churches of Provence. Two other
interesting churches of the same period
are San Pietro in Ciel d'Oro and San
Teodoro. The Bramante cathedral is very
fine; another church by Bramante is
Santa Maria Canepanova. An ancient
bridge over the Ticino was reconstructed
after World War II; there are many
medieval houses, and some towers
remain from the time when Pavia was
known as the 'City of a Hundred Towers.'
The university is one of the oldest in
Italy, and other interesting buildings are
the Castello Visconteo and the Collegio
Ghislieri.

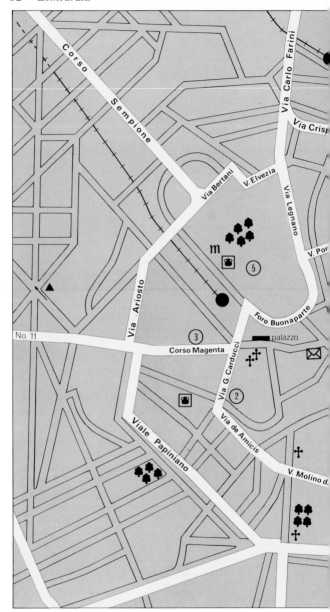

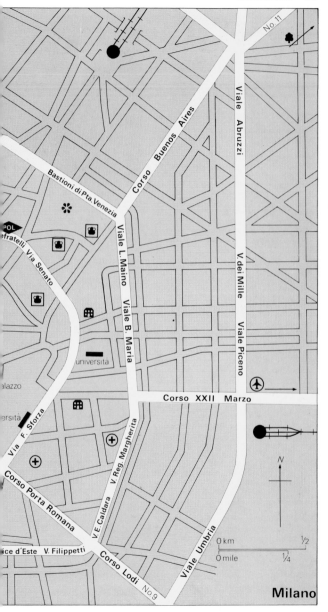

Milano

VENETO

including Trentino/Alto Adige, Friúli/Venezia Giulia

This region occupies the northeastern part of Italy; it is customary to regard the three divisions as individual components of a whole.

Trentino/Alto Adige is the northwestern mountainous region stretching down from the southern Alps to embrace the upper basin of the River Adige and that of the Isarco and Val Sugana on the east.

High mountains alternate with broad, green valleys. The wooded heights favour forestry and cattle-raising. On the less exposed lower slopes are fruit orchards and the vineyards which produce excellent wines. Rich in hydroelectric resources, Trentino-Alto Adige provides about one-fifth of the nation's needs. Paper-making, tobacco-growing, the preserving of fruit and wood-carving are among the industries of the region. Bolzano and Merano have metallurgical and chemical plants. Fishing, too, is important, not only of excellent trout, but in Val Sugana there is considerable salmon-fishing. And one of the great sources of wealth nowadays is tourism, which is well provided for in summer and winter.

The history of Trentino is echoed in its art and architecture. From the time of the Romans it proved a useful passageway between Italy and Germany. The Longobards ousted the Romans and unified the region into the Duchy of Trento, which later became a March under Charlemagne. In the church of San Procolo in Naturno are frescoes dating back to this epoch (8th to 9th century AD). In the year 952 the region passed under Germany, who established ecclesiastical principalities in Trento and Bressanone, from which period remain the Romanesque cathedral of Trento, the abbey of Novacella, the cloisters of the cathedral in Bressanone. At Castel Roncolo near Bolzano, in the imposing 13th-century castle is a fine series of 15th-century frescoes. The cathedrals of Bolzano, Merano and Vipiteno are splendid examples of the following Gothic period, as is the Castello dei Buonconsiglio in Trento with its 15th-century cycle of frescoes of the months of the year. Again near Bolzano, in the little church of Gries, is an imposing altarpiece by Michael Pacher (1471).

Looking at the Renaissance buildings in parts of Trento, one is reminded of the long sitting of the Council of [...] (1545–1563).

The struggle between Austria and [...] continued until in 1810 Trentino [...] declared Italian; but five years [...] under the Treaty of Vienna, it was [...] back to Austria, a bitter pill never [...] pletely digested by Italy. It was ove[...] years before 'Venezia Tridentina' [...] once again recognized as Italian ter[...] following a victory which cost many [...] among them those of three patriot [...] tyrs, Cesare Battisti, Fabio Filzi [...] Damiano Chiesa, remembered tod[...] three flat tombstones in the Ma[...] graveyard at the Castello dei Buonco[...] lio in Trento. This was in 1916; fo[...] ing World War II the region took [...] present name of Trentino-Alto Ad[...]

Festivals There is no set date, but d[...] the grape harvest – in Septemb[...] Merano puts on a colourful parade[...] decorated carts hung with bunch[...] grapes, gaily costumed men and wo[...] music, dancing and an enormous fe[...] the end of a happy day. Again with [...] date, many villages in Val di Ce[...] celebrate the *Canta dei Mesi* – gro[...] youngsters in traditional dress sing [...] to a King and Harlequin in honour [...] various months. And in this region [...] are numerous fine brass bands an[...] song groups, so that music is a fre[...] accompaniment to a mountain hol[...]

The Veneto proper, the middle se[...] occupies roughly the plain betwee[...] rivers Po and Tagliamento, with[...] former providing a natural bounda[...] the south, and on the north the [...] basin of the Piave River and some [...] most spectacular peaks of the Dolo[...] Two isolated groups of hills rise o[...] plain, the Berici near Vicenza an[...] Eugánei not far from Padova (Pad[...]

Forestry and cattle-raising are the [...] activities in the mountainous re[...]

le there is considerable fruit-growing
viniculture on the lower slopes. On
plain the main crops are maize and
ar-beet, with here and there the culti-
on of mulberry trees for the not quite
act silk industry. The Veneto also
duces a considerable quantity of
acco. Fishing is carried on extensively
along the coast and around the
aimed marshes of the Po valley.
ollen and cotton industries are to be
d around Verona and Vicenza;
ghera, near Venezia (Venice), is a
centre for the metal-mechanic
astry.

mong minor industries come the
mics of Bassano, Nove and Este and
goldsmithery of Vicenza.

enezia, with its industrial 'foot on
round' in Mestre, is one of the main
res of commerce, and its port is of
t importance; Verona and Padova
highly industrialized.

ourism plays a very important part,
the Veneto has much to offer, not
in the beauty of the mountains, the
and the coastal strip, but also in art,
itecture and music.

hen, in the year 89 BC, Roma
ted Latin rights to the cities of the
eto, three centuries or more of pros-
y ensued, until the barbaric inva-
s, which finally led to the breaking
y of Venezia. Incidentally, this
ted in the establishment of that city
le great independent power she was
l the rise of Napoleon in the 18th
ury signalled the start of a couple of
uries of slow but certain decadence.
he Veneto is rich in architecture of
Roman period; the Arena in Verona
tstanding, and that city also posses-
Roman theatre and two fine gates.
le Arena gardens in Padova are ves-
of another Arena.

he Veneto went through a period of
ioning into Marches and free cities,
which emerged the free *comunes*
later the *signorias*, so that at the
nning of the 14th century power was
ed in the hands of the Scaligeri of
na, the Carraresi of Padova, the Da
ino of Treviso. This was a period of
t building activity, during which
the great Romanesque churches of
Zeno, San Lorenzo and the early
of the cathedral in Verona.

time this style blended into Gothic
hich examples are to be seen in the
icas of Sant'Antonio in Padova, San
lò in Treviso and Sant'Anastasia in
na, to mention but three of the fine
ches of the period, and the various
halls, such as the Palazzo della
one in Padova, the Palazzo del Tre-

cento in Treviso and the splendid Scaligeri tombs in Verona.

During the 14th century Padova was
enriched by two splendid series of frescoes, those by Giotto in the Cappella
degli Scrovegni, those of Menabuoi in
the baptistery of the cathedral. A century
later Pisanello executed his fine fresco of
St George and the Princess in the church
of Sant'Anastasia in Verona.

The Renaissance left its mark in the
statuary by Donatello in the Basilica di
Sant' Antonio in Padova and the equestrian statue of Erasmo da Narni (The
Gattamelata) outside. Padova was also
fortunate in having a fine series of frescoes by Mantegna in the church of the
Eremitani, unfortunately badly damaged
during World War II; there is a splendid
altarpiece by the same artist in the church
of San Zeno in Verona.

Internal wars and rivalries between
the various *signorias* gave Venezia the
chance to intervene, which she did so
successfully that by 1420 she had seized
and subdued the whole of the Veneto, a
domination which lasted four centuries,
an emblem of which is the Lion of St
Mark to be seen in many cities of the
region. Under the treaty of Campoformio
in 1797 the Veneto was assigned to
Austria, and this was confirmed in the
early 19th century under the Treaty of
Vienna. It was not until 1866 that the
region was declared Italian.

Not surprisingly the Venetian style in
painting spread over the region, which is
rich in works by the Bellinis, Vivarini,
Carpaccio, and later the great Titian himself, Veronese, Tintoretto and others, and
such Renaissance architects as Sansovino, followed soon by the neo-Classic
Palladio. These are but a few of the artists
and architects who have made the Veneto
a treasure-house.

The islands of the Venetian Lagoon   H11

Crossing the long road and rail bridge
that links Venezia with the mainland, one
is approaching not so much a city criss-
crossed by canals, as a group of islands
connected by bridges.

After having explored the principal
ones, those that constitute Venezia as we
know it, it is enjoyable to venture forth to
those more distant.

Crossing to and from Lido, the steamer
passes two hospital islands, San Servilio
and San Clemente. Special permission
has to be obtained in order to visit these.

There are also two 'monastery' islands;
one, San Lazzaro degli Armeni,
approachable by steamer from Riva degli
Schiavoni, is a tiny oasis of the glorious

east once held in fee by Venezia. Formerly an asylum for sick pilgrims, later a hospital for lepers, it was given in 1717 to an Armenian nobleman, Manug de Pietro, who had fled the Turkish invasion of Modone where he had founded a Benedictine monastery. Having arrived at this island, he founded the institute known as I Padri Armeni Mecharisti, and later a college for the education of poor orphans.

Today the island is a serious and severe study centre, with a charming little church, a splendid library and a solemnly cordial welcome to visitors.

To arrive at the other monastery island one goes first to the lace-making island of Burano, and takes a *sandolo* (small type of gondola). The island is tiny, the atmosphere calm but not austere. A mass of cypress trees surrounds the small church and the nearby hermitage with its silent cloisters. Nature has been generous and the beauty and peace of the place give credence to the legend that St Francis of Assisi, on his way back from Soria, put into the island during a great storm, upon which the tempest ceased and the skies cleared. As with many other places visited by Il Poverello (the name by which St Francis was known affectionately), peace and calm have remained as a heritage. The monks living in the island will show you with pride a venerable pine tree said to have originated when St Francis planted his staff of pine wood in the soil.

Murano, Burano and Torcello can be reached by taking an excursion steamer from Riva degli Schiavoni, but it is cheaper and more adventurous to take a steamer from near Piazzale Roma to Murano, from which it is easy to take a boat to the other two. The routes are Circolare Destra and Circolare Sinistra, both following the same route, but in opposite directions.

On the way to Murano the steamer passes the island of San Michele, the cemetery of Venezia, and it is worthwhile spending twenty or thirty minutes between boats to visit the church and the adjoining cloister. There has been a church on the island ever since the 10th century, when San Romualdo, founder of the Camaldolese Order, is said to have lived there. The present edifice dates back to the Renaissance, and was planned in 1469 by Mauro Coducci. It was the first ecclesiastical building constructed in Venezia during that period and is one of the most beautiful.

The cloisters have not always been reserved for religious purposes. During the last century, in the troubled days of the *Risorgimento*, two patriots, Silvio Pel-

lico and Pietro Maroncelli, were im oned there while awaiting trial for h plotted against the Austrian overlo **Murano** is nowadays mainly reno for the production of glassware rar from the extremely beautiful to the g To visit one of the glass factorie watch glass being blown and forme a variety of shapes is rather like tak step back in time to the artisans' shops depicted in ancient prints. W the master as he plunges his iron ro the pan of molten glass in the hear fiery furnace, extracts a blob of the i descent paste and, placing the othe of the rod in his mouth, by sheer power proceeds to convert the blob vase, a bunch of flowers, the figure clown. Lung power and a pair of pi (*borsella*) are the tools of his trade results can be seen in the crowded s room attached to the factory. Watc young apprentices who, while the m is demonstrating his expertise, pic smaller, cooler blobs and with the spatula and pincers fashion them tiny horses or birds, which they then sell to the spectators.

Murano has long been famous f glass-making, as can be seen by exhibits in the Museo dell'Arte Ve (Glass Museum). It had, howeve even more important past, and from 13th century right up to the Fall of ice had its own local government a own Golden Book in which inscribed the names of privileged men; it also coined its own money, a this wealth and prosperity were cl linked with the glass-making indus

Lovers of architecture should m point of visiting the Basilica di Maria e Donato, one of the most im tant Venetian-Byzantine buildings 12th century, nearly as old as San M itself. Externally, it has many fea reminiscent of the architecture of R na; inside, there is a stupendous m floor.

Having done this, pause for a dr wine in one of the many little hoste or a meal at one of several exce eating-houses to be found on the is **Burano** is within easy reach by boat Murano. On the way the boat may at Mazzorbo, which has an intere small Romanesque-Gothic churc convent. One of the bells in the n bell-tower was cast in the year 131

In Burano itself we are in the he the lace-making industry which, b the fall of the Venetian Republic, bro prosperity to the island. Burano mig said to have introduced the art of making to the rest of the world.

nks to the initiative of wealthy, far-
ing people, the art has been revived,
d once again pretty girls are using the
nbolo (the lace-making pillow) in the
e-making school, and one sees women
ting at their cottage doors working at
s delicate task.

Sophistication is far removed from this
sy little island; as you walk around the
row streets bordering the canals, cot-
e doors stand open and there are
mpses of interiors not just scrupu-
sly clean, but gay with the colourful
am of pottery.

On this island one eats well and drinks
l. To accompany the wine special
haped biscuits are made, intended to
ng on the side of one's glass, to be
ped in as one drinks.

Landing from the boat one may have
ticed a group of ancient 'grandfathers'
hered on the quay, one or two of whom
ll have drawn the craft into the correct
oring position. It is customary to
ward them with a small tip, which is
cepted with a charming, old-world
urtesy.

rcello, which one approaches from
rano, might well be regarded as a
radise of peace.

It was to this island that the fugitives
ne to flee the hordes of Attila in 453
. Here they founded a great city.

In the year 638 the Bishop of Altino
nsferred his seat to the island, and up to
14th century Torcello continued to
w. In those days it had a fine woollen
dustry, and was important ecclesiasti-
ly. Then came the scourge of malaria

ezia, showing the Canal Grande

and most of its people moved to what is
now Rialto; as Venezia rose in wealth and
importance, so Torcello declined, its
waters silting up, until it became the
haven of peace we find nowadays,
deserted save for a few little farms and
market gardens.

From the landing, one strolls along the
banks of a lazy little canal and crosses a
bridge into the Piazzetta, on one side of
which stands what were once the seat of
the Council and the palace of the Ar-
chives, now combined as an interesting
Museo dell'Estuario.

On the opposite side of the Piazzetta are
two noble buildings, the church of Santa
Fosca, and the even more imposing
cathedral of Santa Maria Assunta. One
should visit both.

After this it is probably time to think of
something to eat and drink, and in this
connection do not be misled by the humble outward appearance of the *trattoria*
(eating-house) of Cipriani, for the humble exterior leads to a hotel and restaurant
of prime quality. Prices are high, but the
fare is excellent.

Festivals. In the little town of Maróstica
on the last Sunday in May is held the
Cherry Sagra, when the main square is
lined with stalls all displaying and selling
the fine cherries grown in the district.
Padova keeps the name day of its patron
saint, Sant'Antonio, with a solemn
religious procession – June 11th.

One of the great annual festivals is the
annual open-air opera season in the
Arena in Verona, to which come visitors
from far and wide. Opening night in early
August is particularly enchanting, when
all lights are extinguished and the over-
ture is played to the light of literally
thousands of candles in the hands of the
spectators, after which a very blaze of
electricity the opera proper begins. Tickets are hard to get, and very early booking
is advisable.

Again in the little town of Maróstica,
some 7km/4mi west of Bassano, usually
on the first Saturday and Sunday of alternate Septembers, there is a delightful festival: a game of chess played with living
'pieces' in the colourful and elegant
clothes of the 15th century. There are
afternoon and evening performances.

Friúli and Venezia Giulia constitute the
eastern part of the Veneto, stretching
more or less from the Tagliamento River
on the west to the Isonzo on the east, and
reaching down to include a thin tongue of
land as far as the city of Trieste. On the
north the Carnic and Julian Alps close it
off from Austria. The coastal strip is
interspersed with lagoons, and going
inland one finds first a pre-Alpine area

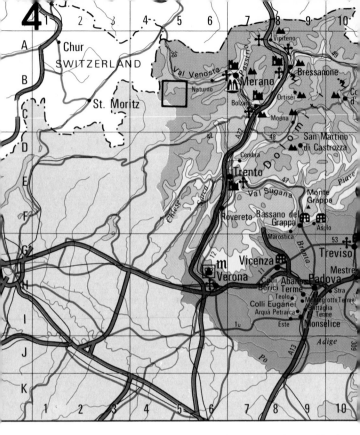

soon rising to the high peaks, which appear like a high protecting wall. It is an area of great caves, Grotta Gigante near Trieste being one of the largest in Europe.

The name of Friúli is known to many since the disastrous earthquakes of 1976 which took a heavy toll of lives and caused the destruction of many historic buildings.

Mainly an agricultural area, cereals, vines and fruit are grown on a commercial scale. Sheep and pigs are raised on the slopes. It is also a busy industrial area; at Monfalcone, near Trieste, are shipyards and Trieste has a fair quota of metal-mechanical industry, oil refineries, cloth mills and distilleries. Other busy industrial towns are Údine, Gorizia and Pordenone. The finest *prosciutto* (raw ham) in Italy comes from the small town of San Daniele, and among minor indus-

tries are the manufacture of furniture woodwork generally.

Tourism, especially along the c and in the mountains, is of great im tance; during the summer season res such as Lignano Sabbiadoro and Gr are crowded, and tourist accommoda is excellent.

Friúli has had an interesting hist ever since its Romanization in the and 1st centuries BC when Aquiléia regarded as the most important city in 10th Region. Traces of Roman days be found in many places – Trieste pos ses a Roman theatre, Concordia Sa taria near Portogruaro offers an inter ing group of paleo-christian tombs basilicas beneath the present cathed but the great treasure-house is the cit Aquiléia which preserves not c Roman houses, but the Via Sacra foll ing the columned remains of the c

...ne port, and other relics (see page 40).
Friúli received the full blast of the
...rbaric invasions, and under the Lon-
...bards was divided into two parts, the
...riúli of the land with its capital at
...ividale, and that of the sea with its
...ntre in Grado.

To this period belongs the Tempietto
...Cividale and various sculptures in the
...thedral of Longobard days.

Before long the Franks superseded
...e Longobards and the authority of the
...triarchs of Aquiléia had increased so
...at, by the 11th century, it had emerged
...the most important ecclesiastic and
...vil principality of northern Italy, with
...ly the most eastern parts of the region
...der the domination of the Counts of
...orizia – a situation which endured
...til the 15th century.

Meanwhile, Venezia had been grow-
...g more and more powerful, so that in
1420 it annexed Friúli. Up to the advent
of Napoleon the region was divided between Venezia and Austria, with Trieste
in 1719 declared a free port. In 1815 the
whole region passed under Austria and
it was not until 1866 that the province of
Údine was free to call itself Italian; the
rest of the territory had to wait until
1918.

Once it had fallen under Venetian
domination, Friúli adopted the Venetian style in art and architecture, a striking example of which is to be seen in the
main square in Údine.

Festivals. Epiphany, Cividale –
heralds a celebratory Mass in the cathedral, the Mass of the Great Sword, during which a deacon, wearing a plumed
helmet, faces the congregation and,
holding an ancient Gospel in his left
hand, makes the Sign of the Cross with a
huge sword held in his right.

Again at Epiphany, Tarcento celebrates the festival of the *pignarui*, an affair of bonfires on the mountain peaks, accompanied by almost pagan rites.

Sacile, on the first Sunday after 14 August, holds the *Sagra degli Osei,* a bird show which attracts ornithologists from far and near.

Abano Terme   H9

(pop. 11,000) This great thermal centre, about 12km/7mi from Padova, lies at the edge of the friendly little group of hills known as the Eugánei. It is one of the best-known and most frequented spas in Europe for the cure of rheumatic and arthritic complaints. The fame of its curative powers goes back to Roman days.

Huge modern hotels line its streets, many with splendid gardens, several with luxurious swimming pools. Walking along the streets of Abano one notices houses and luxury shops alternating with clouds of acrid-smelling water vapour rising from one or another of the pools of bubbling, gurgling mud.

Like most spas, it is a moneyed town and presents an appearance of comfortable well-being.

Its nearness to Padova makes it possible to visit that city easily; apart from private means of transport, there are three frequent and swift local bus services between this town and the railway station in Padova.

Abano is growing at such a rate that the nearby smaller town of Montegrotto, also a spa town, almost joins it.

Walks and drives into the nearby hills are among the attractions, and a meal in one of the many restaurants or *trattorias* scattered among them is a gastronomic experience not to be missed. The hills are not only beautiful, but friendly, and they have given shelter to more than one famous person in the past centuries. The poet Petrarca lived out the last years of his life in the tiny village of Arquá Petrarca, where you may still visit his cottage; Shelley and Byron once spent a year in the city of **Este**, an event marked by a commemorative plaque on the wall of the Villa Kunkler where they stayed. Abano provides the means for many an excursion into these little hills, and one should not miss the opportunity of visiting such interesting little places as **Este**, **Monsélice**, **Teolo**, **Battaglia Terme** and many others.

Aquiléia   F14

(pop. 3500). This is nowadays a village, not far from Údine, the capital of Friúli, but it has had a rich past and is a place to be visited if one happens to be in the near vicinity.

Once an important city and river p‹…› under the Roman emperor Augustus, the Middle Ages it became a patriarcha‹…› There is a lovely Romanesque basili‹…› originally built around the year 10‹…› which possesses some of the most wo‹…› derful mosaic floors in the wor‹…› Aquiléia is rich in memories of Rom‹…› days; there is a Roman cemetery; one c‹…› still walk along what used to be the ban‹…› of the river port and a visit to the Mus‹…› Archeologico is exciting. Anyone stayi‹…› in Údine or holidaying in Grado or L‹…› nano Sabbiadoro should not fail to devo‹…› a day to this unexpectedly lovely plac‹…›

Bassano del Grappa   F‹…›

(pop. 35,200). This charming little tow‹…› lying on the banks of the Brenta not ‹…› from Vicenza, is linked with the name ‹…› Monte Grappa and the campaigns of t‹…› Great War.

It is situated in a picturesque positio‹…› characterized by ancient winding stre‹…› with porticoes, a number of fresco‹…› houses and an Alpine bridge spanni‹…› the river.

It is the centre of a flourishing ceram‹…› industry, and the streets leading to t‹…› famous bridge vie with each other in wi‹…› dow displays of the characteristic potte‹…› and also of another Bassano speciality‹…› *grappa,* the fire-water of the Veneto ‹…› and, in the proper season, mushroom‹…› The asparagus of Bassano is al‹…› renowned, and in spring one sees gr‹…› displays of this succulent vegetable.

The cathedral rises within the encl‹…› sure of the one-time castle of the Ezzeli‹…› family.

One of the best views is to be obtain‹…› by turning left at the entry to the cover‹…› bridge and walking along the Viale d‹…› Martiri, where every tree bears a memo‹…› ial plaque of one of the Alpine soldiers ‹…› the city fallen during the Great War.

Within easy reach of such pretty litt‹…› centres as **Ásolo**, and the **Villa Mas**‹…› (frescoes by Paolo Veronese), Bassa‹…› can be recommended for a weekend vis‹…›

Bolzano   C‹…›

(pop. 90,000) 262m/860ft above sea lev‹…› Not only is this a busy industrial city, b‹…› it is a holiday city much frequented ‹…› mountain lovers, and a base for all kin‹…› of truly magnificent excursions to t‹…› many mountain centres in the vicinity.‹…› is an elegant city with much in its aspe‹…› that reminds one of Austria, which is n‹…› surprising when one realizes that for 4‹…› years, until the end of World War I, B‹…› zano was under Austrian rule.

It has a network of enchanting arcad‹…› streets, shopping facilities are excelle‹…› and its open-air fruit market is colour‹…› and appetizing.

Its 13th-century cathedral is well worth
siting, and a bus or tram ride to the
burb of Gries is truly rewarding for
ere one can see a splendid altarpiece by
e Bressanone painter Michel Pacher
5th to 16th century). During winter this
urch is not used for religious services,
d permission to view can be obtained
om the caretaker in a cottage nearby.

These are but two of the interesting
ildings of Bolzano; walking around the
y you will see others, but it is quite
ssible that you will prefer to spend your
ne exploring the outskirts of the city,
d taking some of the many panoramic
alks or drives.

Hotel accommodation is plentiful and
od, and the tourist feels welcome.

ressanone   A8

p. 14,000) 559m/1834ft above sea
vel. Here we have a lovely mountain
ty in the upper reaches of Alto Adige, an
cellent winter sports centre and with
merous architectural beauties such as
e 13th-century Romanesque cathedral,
scoed by the Unterberger family, with
o bell-towers and a beautifully frescoed
oister. The castle of the Bishop-Princes
as built during the 13th and 14th cen-
ries, and the church of San Giovanni
attista is also worth visiting.

Not far from Bressanone is the 12th-
ntury convent of **Novacella**, a very
portant group of buildings with a most
teresting chapel, that of San Vittore.
The monks of Novacella are great
ne-makers and their wines are deser-
dly popular. One can taste samples,
rved by the monks, in a cellar whose
n pervading light gives one the impres-
on of having stepped into a painting by
vercamp. It is a truly fascinating place
visit.

aorle   G13

p. 11,500). This was originally merely
little agricultural and fishing village,
t the modern trend for seaside holidays
d its fine stretch of sandy beach have
mbined to turn Cáorle of recent years
to a flourishing resort with numerous
cellent hotels and restaurants to suit all
stes.

Cáorle is thought to have been origi-
lly a part of the one-time Roman city of
oncordia Sagittaria.

There are two seashores at Cáorle, the
stern and the western, divided one from
e other by a dyke on which stands the
tle church of the Madonna dell'Angelo.
ar the apse of this church a sandbank
ts off a part of the eastern shore that
eeps around in a curve, and there one
n see the characteristic *bragozzi*, the
hing boats of the Venetian lagoon.
arby is a small harbour with accom-

modation for about 800 tourist craft.

The old part of the town is fascinating
and is dominated by a lovely 11th-century
cathedral which has a cylindrical bell-
tower, one of only two examples in the
Veneto, of the type found in Ravenna.

Cáorle has good road and rail communications with Venezia and the inland
towns and is altogether an excellent
centre for a holiday.

Cividale   E14

(pop. 10,790) This little city, within easy
reach by road or rail from Udine, is one
of the most interesting in Friúli; at present a busy commercial and agricultural
centre, in the past it was the seat of one
of the duchies of the Longobards and
capital of Friúli.

Lying in a picturesque position on the
banks of the swift river Natisone, its central square, Piazza del Duomo, was once
the forum of the city in Roman days.
The cathedral, in Venetian Gothic style,
was begun in 1457 by the architect Bartolomeo delle Cisterne, and completed
in the 16th century by P. Lombardo. It is
rich in treasures; in the chapel of San
Donato is the *Last Supper* by Palma the
Younger, and an *Annunciation* by Amal-
teo. Over the main altar is a fine embos-
sed silver altarpiece of the early 13th
century; in the Chapel of the Holy Sacrament *Noli mi tangere* by Pordenone
and the *Martyrdom of Santo Stéfano* by
Palma the Younger.

From the right-hand nave one enters
the part now used as a museum of
objects connected with Christianity,
one of the great treasures of which is the
octagonal baptistery of Callisto, and
another the altar of Duke Ratchis (both
of the 8th century). There is also a pat-
riarchal chair and there are frescoes
from the Longobard temple.

The Tempietto (Little Temple)
stands in the medieval part of the city, on
the edge of the steep banks of the River
Natisone, and is a most interesting
monument with a barrel vaulted roof,
Byzantine style frescoes, Gothic choir
stalls and stuccoes of the 8th century –
something not to be missed.

While in Cividale one should not fail
to taste the typical spiced bread of the
region, *gubana*, made throughout
Friúli, but at its best in its native city of
Cividale.

Cortina d'Ampezzo   B10

(pop. 6967) One of the busiest tourist
and winter sports centres in the Dolomites and one of the loveliest. The
Winter Olympics of 1956 prompted the
building of the huge Olympic Ice
Stadium, with two enormous skating
rinks. For the winter sports enthusiast,

Cortina offers every facility, but in summer it is equally delightful. There is a wide range of accommodation; restaurants, tea shops and coffee bars abound. Excursions to several interesting centres are available and one of the most attractive is to the lovely **Lago Misurina,** an hour's drive away, lying in a crown of the Dolomites. *Venezia 160km/99mi.*

Grado   G14

(pop. 10,000). This is a favourite holiday resort, standing on one of the islands in the Golfo di Venezia, linked to the mainland by a traffic bridge 5km/3mi in length. It has a long stretch of sandy beach and a considerable number of excellent hotels.

The modern part of Grado has a fine array of public parks and gardens and bathing establishments. Fishing and nautical sports are well catered for.

The older quarter is typical of Veneto marine centres, but also offers treasures for lovers of architecture and ancient history, for back in Roman days, Grado was the fortified outpost of the once-famous river port of Aquiléia, and when in the 5th century AD Aquiléia fell, Grado inherited much of that city's importance.

The 5th-century church of Santa Maria delle Grazie is in the form of a basilica and is built largely of material from Roman and Byzantine buildings. The cathedral is even earlier, 4th century, and its treasures are a splendid mosaic floor, a fine pulpit and some valuable frescoes. The 6th-century baptistery has a very interesting font.

From Grado one may make an excursion by boat to the small island of **Barbana,** where there is a Byzantine Madonna in wood. Pilgrims visit this little shrine in July and in mid-August.

Lido di Jésolo   H12

(pop. 4500). This resort, a bare 30km/19mi from Venezia, situated between the Port of Cortellazzo and the mouth of the River Sile, with a long, wide stretch of fine, white sand and excellent communications by land and sea, is popular not only with Italians of the north, but also with English, German and other visitors.

Excellently equipped with hotels and with a wide variety of restaurants to suit all tastes and pockets, it seems to offer everything needful for a really wonderful seaside holiday.

Be a little careful when booking a holiday here, and impress upon your agent that you would prefer one end or the other – preferably the end nearer to Punta Sabbione – rather than the middle section,

for, among Jésolo's entertainments f tourists, the centre proliferates with tho of the noisier kind. You have bee warned; if you take notice of the warnir you may expect to spend a truly marve ous holiday here, and you will sufficiently near to Venezia to visit more than once.

Lignano Sabbiadoro   G1

(pop. 1180). This deservedly popul resort lies at the tip of a promontory ju ting out into the Laguna di Maran almost midway between Cáorle ar Grado, and is linked with Lignano Pine and Lignano Riviera, the three makir one large and very lovely expanse of se side holiday terrain. Within easy road ar rail reach of Venezia and Trieste, they a all excellently equipped with hotels ar restaurants to suit numerous tourists varying tastes.

There is a large dock at Sabbiador well-protected, and able to accommoda a considerable number of all kinds boats.

In the pinewoods are little cottages an bungalows which can be rented, an where one can feel really in touch wi lovely nature.

Lignano Riviera has a spa open f cures from June to September.

Merano   B

(pop. 29,850) 323m/1060ft above s level. This is one of Italy's strikingly pi turesque cities, gifted with a perfect c mate for holidays both in summer and winter, and wonderfully well-equipped the way of accommodation and places eat.

A tributary of the River Adige ru through Merano, crossed by sever bridges and with delightful walks either side.

Standing at the head of the lovely V Venosta, the surrounding mountai make a lovely frame for a charming cit Although of ancient origin, its gre development as a holiday and therm centre began during the last century, a so the 'new' town has an air of elega dignity and unity.

In the medieval part stands the ancie castle of the 15th century, the 14t century cathedral where one finds a cur ing nave, reminiscent of that of Quimp in Brittany, said by some to be the resu of an architectural miscalculation, b thought by many others to have bee intentional and to represent the bowe form of the crucified Christ.

There are characteristic little streets this older part, and famous walks, tl *Tappeiner* and *d'estate* and *d'inverno.*

A city of lovely public and private ga dens and of enticing shops, Merano al

...fers hunting in the nearby hills and ...hing in the Passirio and Adige Rivers. ...here are many enticing excursions to be ...ken, and whether one fancies an ...ergetic or a lazy, relaxing holiday, ...erano provides for both, and moreover ...fers good camping facilities. There is a ...ell-patronized racecourse and horse-...cing is one of the many popular sports.

Frequent folklore spectacles take place and altogether Merano seems to offer something of everything enjoyable.

Padova (Padua)   H9

(pop. 194,706) Padova has the second oldest university in Italy, nicknamed Il Bo, founded in 1222. This was where Galileo Galilei held the chair in Mathematics (1592–1610), where the

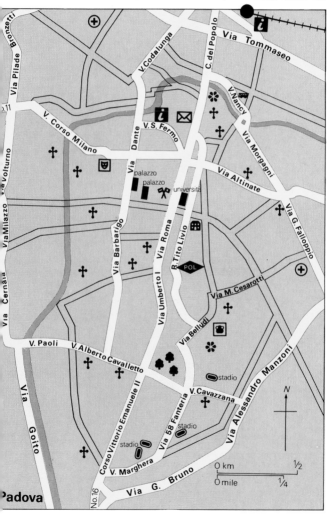

poet Tasso studied law and the playwright Goldoni took his degree in jurisprudence, where even Oliver Goldsmith spent a little time during his wanderings. For Catholics Padova holds a magnetic attraction in the huge Basilica dedicated to Sant'Antonio of Padova, whose tomb is the object of many pilgrimages. This magnificent basilica (off Via M. Cesarotti) is a treasure-house of sculpture and painting – Donatello, Sansovino, Menabuòi are but three of many artists whose work is to be found there. Externally it presents a striking aspect with its ornate façade and its minarets and domes reminiscent of a mosque rather than a European church. At its side, in a huge square, is the famous equestrian statue of Gattamelata, the work of the Florentine sculptor Donatello. Nearby are the Oratorio di San Giorgio with fine frescoes by Altichieri and Avanzo, and the Museo Civico where are to be found paintings by Bellini, Titian, Giorgione.

Take Via Belludi from the Piazza del Santo to another huge open space, Prato della Valle, in the centre of which is a patch of green, shaded by trees and surrounded by a circular moat crossed by four stone bridges, then surrounded again by a circle of statues of men who have been famous in the history of the city. On the wall of a palace is a plaque bearing a sonnet by the poet d'Annunzio lauding its quiet and peace – times have changed. In a corner of this huge square is the church of Santa Giustina (14th century) which has an interesting altar picture by Paolo Veronese, and the tomb of St Luke the Evangelist. To the north (near the post office) is the Cappella degli Scrovegni, with a series of incomparable frescoes by Giotto. The series was painted 1303–1305: of particular beauty are the *Flight into Egypt*, *Kiss of Judas*, and the huge *Last Judgment* which covers the entire end wall. The nearby church of the Eremitani (hermits) possesses all that remains of a splendid series of frescoes by Mantegna (1431–1506) – the rest were destroyed in World War II.

Of the three market squares (between Via Dante and Via Roma), the large busy Piazza delle'Erbe, with a corner devoted to flowers and a delightful fountain, and the remainder filled with stalls of fresh vegetables, is the most absorbing. The enormous Sala della Ragione, a huge hall decorated with frescoes, houses at one end a large wooden statue reminiscent of the Gattamelata that stands outside the Basilica. At one end of the Piazza dei Signori stands the Palazzo del Capitano, with an interesting and ancient clock which tells not only the hours but the

date. If you are in Padova long enough drive along the road to **Teolo** or any of t towns in the charming Euganean Hil visit the **abbey of Praglia**. The monks a pleased to show one over, and a pleasa liqueur is brewed there; honey may a be purchased.

Trento

(pop. 91,700). This city, capital Trentino-Alto Adige, is a city of tr noble aspect. The River Adige ru through it, and high mountains surrou it. Seat of a bishopric, it was the scene the famous Council of Trent, whi lasted from 1545–63.

The cathedral, a severe example Romanesque-Gothic architecture, pre ides over the monumental centre of t city, Piazza Duomo. Nearby is t Palazzo Pretorio, the Torre Civica a two picturesque frescoed houses.

Via Belzani, which leads off Piaz Duomo, is one of the city's lovelie streets, rich in Renaissance houses wit strongly Venetian air.

The Castello dei Buonconsiglio was ancient times the residence of t Bishop-Princes. Surrounded by a w with here and there low towers, it consi of several different edifices. To the no is the cylindrical Great Tower, the b tlemented Castelvecchio; in the cen rises the portion known as Giunta Alb tina, dating from the 17th century, to t south the Renaissance Magno Palaz erected in 1526 to the order of the bish Bernardo Clesio.

There is much to see in the compl forming the castle, and one sight not to missed is the splendid series of frescoes the months in the Torre dell'Aquila. one enters the castle one passes near t tombstones marking the graves of t three martyred patriots, Cesare Batti Damiano Chiesa and Fabio Filzi w met their death in 1916.

Across the river, on a height which c be reached by a *funivia*, stands t memorial erected in honour of Cesa Battisti; from that point there is als splendid view of the city.

Treviso

(pop. 91,000). This charming little c merits a visit from anyone spending holiday in the Veneto or in Venezia itse It is city of many waters; the River S laps its walls and there are numero canals. It has many interesting mo ments of medieval and Renaissar origin.

Piazza dei Signori is in the centre of t city and is very medieval in aspect w the huge Palazzo del Trecento whi dates back to the beginning of the 1 century, the Palazzo del Podestà with t

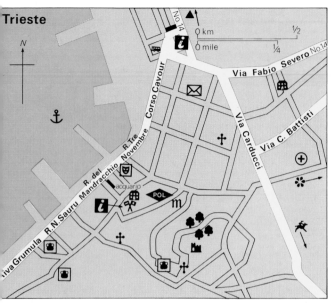

igh tower and, on the west side, the ncient Palazzo Pretorio.

The cathedral, originally medieval, has ad many restorations, even to an elegant neoclassic entrance porch. Less remodelled is the Romanesque baptistery n the left.

There is a fine *Annunciation* by Titian , the Chapel of the Annunciation, and ere are various examples of the Renaissance sculpture of the Lombardo family. he crypt of the 11th and 12th centuries, ith its forest of supporting columns, is ell worth a visit.

The church of San Nicolò is a large othic edifice of the 13th and 14th centuries, all in brickwork, with extremely ll single-mullioned windows along the des and in the three apses.

Inside there is a fine organ, and an teresting, very large 15th-century esco of St Christopher. The Onigo mb is also of considerable interest, the ulpture being the work of Antonio Riz-, the painted sections by Lorenzo Lotto.

The severely plain church of San rancesco is interesting from a literary int of view, for here are buried Fransca, daughter of the poet Petrarch, and etro, son of Dante Alighieri.

The gates of the city are beautiful, in rticular that of San Tomaso.

Another interesting point of the little city is the Peschiera, the little island which is the scene of a lively fish market; nearby is one of the old-time hostelries, La Colonna (in Piazza Rinaldo), where it is still possible to drink the rough local wine, Clinto, which is drunk from a cup without a handle, *not* a glass.

Trieste   G16

(pop. 282,776) Trieste is off the beaten track, but it is a delightful city, and during one's drive from Venezia (150km/ 93mi) it is worthwhile branching off at Cervignano to **Aquiléia** (see page 40).

From 1382 Trieste formed a part of Austria, returning to Italy only in 1954, and its way of life offers a mixture of Austrian and Italian customs. There is good bathing and pleasant walks in and around the city. The Arco di Riccardo dates back to the time of the Emperor Augustus. The cathedral (near the castle), an amalgamation of two 11th-century buildings – the Basilica dell'Assunta and the little church of San Giusto – is a fine example of Romanesque art, with 14th-century frescoes, a 9th-century font and a painting by Carpaccio. Other interesting churches are Santa Maria Maggiore and Sant'Antonio. The palaces of the *Comune* and the *Governo*, and the *Palazzo della Borsa* all merit a visit. A spacious square near the Stazione Marittima is the Piazza dell' Unita. On the left of this square is the Peschiera, with a fine aquarium. About 7km/4mi back along the coast is the beautifully situated castle **Miramare**, where there are *son et lumière* performances in summer. *Údine 75km/46mi.*

Údine   E14
(pop. 100,770). This seat of a bishopric is also the capital of Friúli, a peaceful city with many fine monuments. In olden days it was the capital of the patriarchy of Aquiléia and as such assumed great importance, until the subjugation by Venezia in 1420.

The Castello, which from a height towers over the city, rises on the remains of the earlier castle of the bishops of Aquiléia. At present it houses the local Galleria d'Arte Antica e d'Arte Moderna and the Museo Civico, with many fine exhibits.

The city centre is to be found in the monumental Piazza della Liberta at the foot of the hill on which stands the castle. Surrounded by elegant buildings, it is strongly reminiscent of Venetian architecture, a remark which applies particularly to the Palazzo del Comune, known as the Loggia del Lionello, a fine building erected in the 15th century to the design of the architect Lionello.

The cathedral preserves part of its 14th-century Gothic Romanesque structure, but was modified in the 18th century.

On the 1st altar to the right, and the 2nd and 4th on the same side are fine altarpieces by Tiepolo.

Other frescoes by G. B. Tiepolo are to be found in the 18th-century Oratorio della Purità on the right of the cathedral.

An interesting excursion from Údine is to **Passariano** to visit the most splendid villa in all Friúli, the **Villa Manin**, which belonged to the last Doge of Venezia, Ludovico Manin, and where Napoleon stayed in 1797 for the period of the signing of the Peace of Campoformio, which marked the end of the Venetian Republic.

Venezia (Venice)   H11
(pop. 346,735) A city founded on fear. When the Huns of Attila came storming into northeastern Italy in the 5th century, many of the inhabitants fled to the lagoon for greater safety. Their first place of refuge was Torcello, where they established a thriving colony and built an imposing cathedral with wonderful mosaics and the octagonal church of Santa Fosca. Then came malaria, Torcello was deserted, and only the now two churches, a handful of houses and now Cipriani's, the restaurant beloved of

Gondolier

Hemingway, remain. The inhabita moved to the Rialto district, and from t small nucleus Venezia grew a developed into a powerful coastal c Separated from the rest of Italy until building of the causeway across wh road and rail traffic now travel, it was v much a city apart, prosperous, indepe dent, elegant, more than slightly easte in some aspects. During the Midd Ages, indeed, Venezia was a bridge tween east and west, and during Crusades she established small mari colonies along the Dalmatian coast a even farther afield. The head of the c was the Doge; later came the Gr Council who nominated a smaller Co cil of Ten which worked in secret. One their organs was the group of th Inquisitors of the State, denunciation whom could mean death. The yawni letter box into which secret denunc tions were dropped can still be seen in Palazzo Ducale (1). The might and pow of the city declined after the discovery America, but Venezia remained rich, c ourful, gay, a city of extravagance of ev kind.

The great houses along the Ca Grande, Ca' d'Oro (2), built in 1421 the Contarini family, Ca' Rezzonico where Robert Browning lived (now a f museum), Palazzo Ducale (15th-cent Gothic with a Renaissance courtyard Rizzo), and other Renaissance buildin such as the Palazzo Vendramin (4), churches of San Zaccaria (5) and S Michele in Isola, Sansovino's Palaz Corner (6) and lovely *loggetta* of the L reria of San Marco, all testify to t wealth and extravagant taste of the c The Basilica di San Marco (7) holds curious blend of Byzantine a Romanesque art. It became the treasu house of the city, as can be observed fro its wonderful mosaics, the celebra Pala d'Oro and the two twisted ser transparent columns behind the Pa which are said to have formed part of So omon's Temple. The four bronze hors the terrace above the façade of the asilica came from Constantinople, but ome believe that they were originally art of the statuary group of which only he *Charioteer* remains at Delphi in reece. The spacious and elegant Piazza an Marco has been called 'the finest rawing-room in Europe'. The Torre ell'Orologio (8), the two Moors striking ie hours, appears in many an 18th-:ntury painting, but the bell-tower is a ithful copy of the original, which col-psed in 1902.

If one stands on the embankment in ont of Piazza San Marco one's eye is aught by the splendidly ornate church of anta Maria della Salute (9), on the oppo-te bank of the Canal Grande. This iurch, consecrated in 1687, was built to ommemorate the end of a plague pidemic. During the *Festa della Salute* 1 Nov.), a bridge of boats is cast across ie Canal Grande and worshippers walk ack and forth to pay their respects to the aint. Farther across the lagoon can be een the austere beauty of the church of an Giorgio Maggiore (10), built by Pal-dio in the 16th century, and if one cros-s to the island and proceeds back along ie embankment one comes to another alladian church, that of Il Redentore. n July 16 a bridge of boats is built from ie Zattere embankment to this church. here are also colourful regattas at the nd of June and early in September when ie Canal Grande is cleared of traffic to iake room for gondola races, the crews 1 period costume.

Venezia's eastern connections are flected in the floridity and richness of er painting. Canaletto and Guardi give ne a faithful picture of what the city and s life were like in the 18th century but olours glow almost like mosaics in itian's great series of paintings in the iurch of Santa Maria Gloriosa dei Frari .1), in the Accademia delle Belle Arti .2) and the Palazzo Ducale. Colours low richly, too, in the Tintorettos in the cuola di San Rocco (13), and what a irror of 16th-century Venetian life are ie splendid paintings of Paolo Veronese 1 the Accademia, in San Giorgio Mag-iore, in the Anti-Collegio and the Sala el Collegio in the Palazzo Ducale. mong other treasures in the upper floors f Ca' Rezzonico is a series of charming aintings of Venetian 18th-century life by ie younger Tiepolo.

Apart from the **Lido** – crowded but xcellent beach, and one of Venezia's two isinos – visit the islands of **Murano** (the land of fire), and **Burano**. The former is a number of glass factories where one an see the molten glass blown and fashioned into intriguing shapes and where there is a fine 7th-century basilica with a precious mosaic pavement. The latter is famous for its lace. Another pleasant trip is by boat to **Chioggia**, a picturesque fishing town. Buses leave from Piazzale Roma for **Padova** and **Stra**, one of the many lovely villas on the Brenta, set in a charming park, with twin spiral stairways leading to a belvedere overlooking the road, a maze and a lake.

Verona   H6

(pop. 232,280) This is not just an agricultural and industrial centre, but a city that has much to offer by way of art and architecture and cultural attractions. Driving from Vicenza to Verona one sees in the hills the two castles of Montecchio and Cappelletti, where, according to the legend, lived the families whose history gave rise to the story of Romeo and Juliet. In Verona one can visit Juliet's tomb, her balcony, Romeo's house; if one is fortunate enough to be in the city during July or August, one may very well see a performance of *Romeo and Juliet* in the huge Roman Theatre.

The River Adige describes a double loop in its passage through Verona, on one of which stands the impressive Castelvecchio (1354–75), now the home of the Museo Civico with a fine collection of paintings by Veronese, Tiepolo, Guardi, the Bellinis, Titian and other artists of the Veneto. From this castle the Ponte Scaligero crosses the river; it has been rebuilt in its original form, following its destruction in World War II. Nearby are the 16th-century Palazzo Canossa and the 12th-century church of San Lorenzo. In the Corso Cavour which runs northeast from the castle are the Palazzo Bevilacqua and the 1st-century Porta dei Borsari; at the end is the picturesque Piazza delle Erbe, with its market column and fountain, where sellers of fruit and vegetables protect their wares under huge, colourful umbrellas. Verona rose to great importance during the Middle Ages under the *Signoria* of the Scaligeri. Near Piazza delle Erbe in Piazza dei Signori are the impressive tombs of the Scaligeri, the Loggia del Consiglio, and a monument to Dante who dedicated *Il Paradiso* to the Scaligeri. Still in the same district are the 17th-century Palazzo Maffei and the Palazzo Emilei (now the home of the Galleria d'Arte Moderna and the Museo del Risorgimento), and the church of Sant'Anastasia with paintings by Mantegna and Pisanello and two interesting holy water stoups supported by dwarfs. The 12th-century Romanesque cathedral has a fine Titian. Across the river are two other churches, the 12th-century Santo

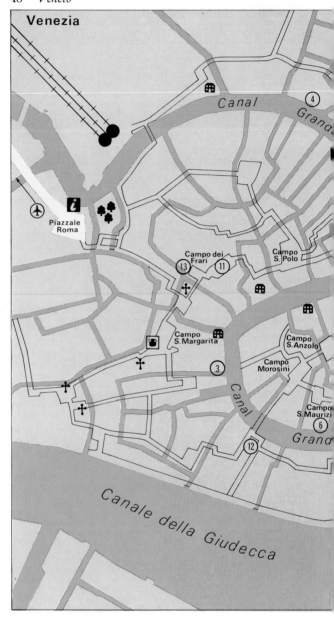

Venezia

Canal Grande

Piazzale Roma

Campo dei Frari

Campo S. Polo

Campo S. Margarita

Campo S. Anzolo

Campo Morosini

Campo S. Maurizi

Canal Grande

Canale della Giudecca

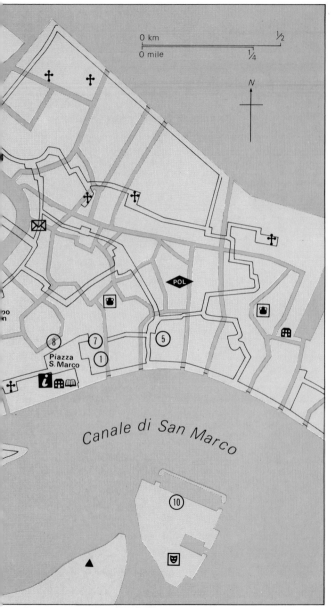

0 km   ½
0 mile   ¼

N

POL

⑧   ⑦   ⑤

Piazza
S. Marco

①

Canale di San Marco

⑩

▲

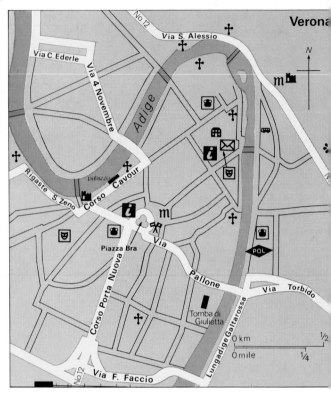

Stefano, and the 15th-century San Giorgio in Braida, which contains paintings by Tintoretto and Veronese.

The church of San Zeno is a fairish walk from Piazza Bra along Via Roma and Rigaste San Zeno. This 12th-century Romanesque church has a delightful façade with bronze doors dating from 1100, illustrating in their many panels the Old and New Testaments and the story of the Patron Saint. Inside, the church has a wooden ceiling in the form of the reversed keel of a boat, and slender columns alternating with robust pilasters. There is a precious altarpiece by Mantegna and a charming statue of the smiling Saint.

Vicenza   G8

(pop. 102,670). The two great architects of the late 16th and early 17th century in this part of Italy were Palladio and Scamozzi, and Vicenza has many examples of their work, the most famous be the Teatro Olimpico, said to have b the first covered theatre in Europe whe was built in 1580–82, and still use this day. Its stage is a masterpiece of spective. The Palazzo della Ragio (1549–1614), the Loggia del Capita the Palazzo Festa, the house of Palla himself, the Palazzo Chiericati (15 now the museum with some fine pa ings, are only a few of the many lov buildings to be seen in this city. On outskirts are the Villa Valmarana, wi splendid series of frescoes by Tiep and the Villa Rotonda (1570) begun Palladio and finished by Scamozzi. Basilica del Monte Berico stands high a hill as one approaches the city from south. In the church are a 15th-cent statue of the Madonna and a *Pietà* (15 by Montagna. *Padova 31km/19mi, V ona 51/32.*

LIGURIA

art from the Valle d'Aosta, this is the allest of the regions of Italy. It consists n arc of mountains, the Maritime and urian Alps, framing the bay of nova (Genoa) and stretching from the uth of the River Magra on the east to e Mortola on the west. The hills rise sharply from the sea, leaving only a row coastal strip. Liguria is noted for wonderful land- and sea-scapes, to ich this sudden contrast of sea and untain contributes.

he city of Génova forms a point of sion between the two Rivieras, ante and Ponente, and both together stitute one of the most popular tourist as in Italy. All along this coast hotels liferate and are mostly excellently ipped; there are also several good ping sites.

egetation is semitropical – mimosa oms around Christmas-time, followed n afterwards by bougainvillea; aloes the coastal roads. From San Remo tward there is intensive cultivation of ers, mainly carnations, which are to the markets of all Europe. Olives vines grow well.

énova is Italy's most active port for 1 passenger ships and freighters; La zia is one of Italy's two naval bases, other being Táranto in Púglia.

he arc of mountains protects the coast n the bitter north winds and conse- ntly winters are agreeably mild, her element which attracts visitors. ishing is carried on all along the st, and excellent oysters, mussels and eri di mare (similar to mussels) are to ad in the area around Portovénere.

here is considerable industry carried n Liguria, particularly in large cities 1 as Génova, Savona and La Spezia.

thabited in ancient times by the uri, the region fell under Roman ination in the 1st century BC. The gobards occupied it during the Mid- Ages, followed by the Franks.

entimiglia near the French border Luni near Sarzana possess the finest nan remains in Liguria. Paleochris- art is manifest in the baptistery at enga.

nder feudalism, Liguria was split up various counties and marches. It n to make itself felt as a sea power the 11th century onwards, but it was until the end of the 14th century that iova gained control of the whole re-. Wars ensued between Venezia and ova for supremacy at sea, then later

the region became subject first to France and later to Spain. In 1528 the great Admiral Andrea Doria succeeded in re-establishing its independence.

Architecturally, the period which has left most examples is that of Romanesque-Gothic (11th to 14th cen-turies); then, towards the end of the 16th century, the influence of baroque is observed. Albenga, San Fruttuoso, Génova, Portofino and Lavagna are among the centres where examples of this style may be seen.

The early period of the Renaissance is exemplified in the work of sculptors such as Gaggini and Civitali, particu-larly in the chapel of San Giovanni in the cathedral of Génova.

In the 16th century Génova was in the vanguard of the world of art, and exer-cised considerable influence over the art and architecture of the rest of the region.

Under Napoleon, Liguria fell under French domination in 1805 but in 1814, after the Congress of Vienna, it was added to Piemonte.

It must not be forgotten that the dis-covery of America owed much to Chris-topher Columbus, born in Génova in 1451.

During the *Risorgimento*, two men who played leading parts, Mazzini and Garibaldi, were both Ligurians.

The region has always attracted many English and American visitors, among them the poet Shelley, who met his tragic death by drowning in the Bay of Spezia in the year 1822. Another was the late Ernest Hemingway, who spent much time in Alássio.

Festivals Good Friday, Savona – A solemn procession through the city in which huge groups of wooden sculpture exemplifying the Passion of Christ are borne through the streets. May (2nd Sunday), Camogli – The festival of

fish; immense quantities of fish are
ght and then fried in *Il Padellone*, a
e frying pan, then distributed to the
tators. August, Alassio – This is
month of the *Muretto*, which is a wall
d with porcelain tiles bearing the
atures of illustrious visitors to the
e Roma; during August this *Muretto*
ue scene of popular beauty contests.

ssio J3

. 11,000) This resort has for years
n beloved by English visitors, and
bines excellent hotel accommoda-
and restaurants with an air of great
ance. It possesses a fine esplanade
h splendid sands, lovely gardens, and
n Alássio one can take walks around
richly cultivated hills that rise
nd and around it. It attracts tourists
l types, not stopping short of 'jet set'
ionaires.

uring *Ferragosto* (the Italian mid-
ust holiday) it is the scene of
nerous festivities, and for this period
ocal traffic police are supplanted by
most glamorous bathing girls who
ulate traffic, duly equipped with
nets and batons.

he tower of Adelassia at **Vegliasco**,
/2½mi away, has an amusing legend
hed to it. It takes its name from
lassia, the charming, beautiful, but,
, greedy wife of Aleramo, the First
quis of Monferrato. This good lady,
ng betrayed her spouse, was impris-
d in the tower. Bored with her
rced confinement, she gave herself
to an over-indulgence in the plea-
s of the table. One day came an
ortunity to escape, and Adelassia
ded to take advantage of it, but
ortunately, she had by this time
me so fat from over-eating that she
k in the doorway. Her husband took
on her, and not only eased her out of
door, but took her back as his
oted wife, and also named after her
town we now recognize as Alássio.
e or false, if you look at the coat-of-
s of Alássio, you will observe the
ce of a tower with a barred door.

mong the more recent visitors to
ssio were the late Sir Winston Chur-
l and the late Ernest Hemingway,
it is still a favourite spot for such
ent-day notabilities as the Italian
Eugenio Montale and the actress
nia Loren.

iles reproducing the signature of
n notabilities are set into a famous
e wall in Alássio – the *Muretto*.

estivals and sporting events prolifer-
here, and among its gastronomic
cacies are little pastries known as
(kisses) of Alássio.

Albenga I3

(pop. 16,000) Albenga is one of the
many lovely seaside resorts fringing the
coast of the Italian Riviera, a city with
many facilities for the delight of tourists
who want sea air, bathing and boating,
but also an important agricultural centre
for the surrounding fertile hills, rich in
the cultivation of flowers and fruit
which go to supply the markets of the
north.

The little city has ancient roots, going
back even before written history, into
the era of mythology – it is said to have
been founded by Albion, son of the sea-
god Poseidon.

Back in the 6th century BC it was the
capital of a tribe of navigators, the
Liguri Ingauni, subdued only after a
long and bloody war fought against
them by the Roman Consul, L. Emilio
Paolo, in the year 181 BC. First a Roman
and later a Byzantine city, Albenga was
destroyed in the 5th century AD by the
barbarian hordes, and later re-built by
the Longobards. In the 12th century it
became an independent marine city and
the seat of a bishopric, and its inhabitants
sent war ships to take part in the
Crusades. It had excellent commercial
dealings with the Florentines, until Pisa
became allied with Génova and Albenga
was attacked and destroyed. Late in the
12th century we see Albenga under the
domination of Génova. In 1863 it
was incorporated in the province of
Savona.

Not surprisingly, the historical centre
of the city has a wealth of interesting
monuments. The cathedral of San
Michele dates back to the 5th century
AD, as does the adjoining bell-tower.
But even older are the Roman aqueduct
and the remains of the Roman
Amphitheatre. In the 5th-century baptistery are wonderful mosaics and the
remains of a font in which baptism by
total immersion was practised.

The Museo Navale Romano has a
rich collection, including a considerable number of amphora, bronze helmets
and other military equipment recovered
from the bed of the sea by the ship *Artig-
lio* as recently as the year 1950. Divers
still make explorations in the waters
offshore hoping to recover further treasures.

There are numerous medieval houses
still standing in the historical centre,
and many lovely mansions.

Those who care to climb the tall,
14th-century tower of the Palazzo Vecchio del Comune will be repaid by the
stupendous view from its summit.

The privately-owned island of **Gallinara,** 1500 metres offshore, can be visited by boat. Once the site of an early Benedictine monastery; only a single tower remains to mark the site. On the same island it is possible to visit the Grotto of St Martin, where the saint is said to have sought refuge from Arian persecution back in the 4th century, when he was Bishop of Tours.

The modern part of Albenga is well-equipped with tourist facilities, and altogether it is a town worth visiting.

Bordighera   K1
(pop. 10,949) Celebrated even on the Riviera for the mildness of its climate, for its lovely and abundant Mediterranean vegetation, for its palms. The palm leaves which are blessed in San Pietro in Vaticano on Palm Sunday come from Bordighera. And there is a reason for this 'concession'. In the days of Pope Sixtus V, in the year 1586, the great obelisk was being raised in Piazza San Pietro in Roma, when the ropes heated from friction and seemed about to burst into flame. It was a man from Bordighera, a certain Bresca, who saved the situation by shouting *Acqua alle corde* ('throw water on the ropes'). In gratitude the Pope granted to him and his family in perpetuity the privilege of supplying these emblems of Palm Sunday.

The old city, high above the sea, dominates the bay of Ospedaletti on the one side, while on the other the view extends almost to Monte Carlo.

Coming down to modern Bordighera from this old part of the town one sees the tiny church of Sant' Ampeglia, built over the cave in which the saint once lived. The church is at the beginning of the modern town itself, which is reached along a lovely esplanade stretching far beyond the centre of Bordighera almost to **Vallecrosia,** where, incidentally, there is a delightful Flower Show around the beginning of the year.

Many famous people have lived in Bordighera. One can still see the villa of Queen Margaret of Savoy, to whom a monument has been erected; another interesting villa is that of Garnier, architect of the Opera House in Paris and the Casino of Monte Carlo. Walking towards Ospedaletti, one passes the little house where Katherine Mansfield lived. Bordighera has all the usual Riviera facilities. *Monte Carlo 25km/16mi, San Remo 17/11.*

Camogli   H7
(pop. 9000) Camogli is justly regarded as one of the pearls of the Ligurian coast. Situated in the curve of an enchanting bay, it has a tradition as a fishing centre

that goes back to the Middle Ages. houses here seem to rise sheer out o water; olives and citrus fruits flouris

It is said that the mariners of Cam taught the art of sailing to the who Europe. Be that as it may, King L Philippe hired the fleet of Camogli w he proceeded to conquer Algiers, much more than a hundred years ago sailing fleet of this little town was la than that of Hamburg. Then came employment of steam-powered ves and the importance of Camogli decli so that the medieval city, with its cha ing little port and its 17th-century qua now just a fishing village, thoug important one.

In spite of its decline, Camogli be the most important Nautical Institut Italy, the Cristoforo Colombo.

Picturesque   and   other-wor Camogli is a delightful holiday centr has several hotels of various grades, some excellent little restaurants w freshly caught fish can be enjoye offers opportunities for many plea walks, strenuous or not-so-strenuou nearby **Portofino, San Fruttuoso Punta Chiappa.**

Chiavari
(pop. 24,000) Chiavari lies across pleasant River Entella from the pop seaside resort of Lavagna, and is on direct railway line between Génova La Spezia. It is a city of considerable ture, a fact that is suggested as soon as approaches it by its neatly arranged, streets, the flower beds bordering its avenues.

Behind it rise slopes where luxur orchards vie with acres of hothouse pride of place.

Chiavari has a long tradition of we and prosperity. Many of its families trace the source of their fortune to c ings with South America, with whicl town has had close links in the pas was a Chiavari family who built the ways of Peru. In the museum in Chia can be seen a collection of priceless re of Inca civilization, for it was that s family who, during the last century, i gated investigations into the origin that far-off civilization.

Chiavari was the birthplace of fathers of two great Italians, Mazzini Garibaldi.

Through the centuries the town given great encouragement to art an erature. In 1791 was founded Economic Society, the aims of wl were the promotion of industry, agri ture and knowledge. Every two y there is an Industries Fair.

Furniture-making is the princ

ustry, and a close second is slate carv-

Walking around this elegant little
n, one gets an impression of the
racter of its inhabitants, industrious,
gant and interested in the aesthetic
gs of life.

he Citadel, behind which lies the old
n distinguished by its narrow arcaded
ets, was built in the 13th century. In
square in front is a monument in
mory of Mazzini, and if we go along
arcaded Via Vittorio Emanuele II as
as Piazza XX Settembre, we find that
cted in memory of Garibaldi.

he cathedral, originally built in 1613,
a neoclassic façade in imitation of
Pantheon in Roma. In the parish

church of San Giovanni Battista are
interesting frescoes by the Carlone family, Coppola and Pinelli.

Accommodation is good in Chiavari,
and there are numerous restaurants
where one eats well. It is not, however, a
town where one can expect to spend an
inexpensive holiday.

Génova (Genoa)   H6

(pop. 819,500) Génova, the great port of
Italy, and an important industrial and
commercial centre, is the scene of many
trade fairs. In October is held the Nicolò
Paganini Violin Competition, for the
celebrated violinist (1784–1840) was a
native of the city and his violin is preserved in the Palazzo Doria Tursi.
Génova is best approached by sea, for it

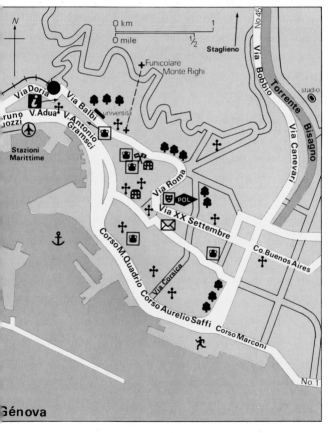

Génova

occupies a delightful position on the Golfo di Génova and is within easy reach of the many charming resorts of the Riviera.

In Roman days it was a flourishing municipality, and it has continued to grow in importance through the centuries. During the Crusades its power expanded throughout the Mediterranean; it became a free *comune*, then a marine republic until 1805 when it was annexed by France. Ten years later, under the Treaty of Vienna, it became part of the Kingdom of Sardegna. It was the home of Christopher Columbus who is honoured by a striking monument in a square near the main railway station. Off Via Corsica is the church of Santa Maria Assunta in Carignano, from whose dome one has a splendid panoramic view over the city and its surroundings. Two of the great figures of the *Risorgimento* – Mazzini, who was born in Génova in 1805, and Garibaldi, who set forth for Sicília with 1000 Redshirts in 1860, an expedition which was to lead to the conquest of Nápoli and the south – testify the independent spirit of the city.

The older part of Génova, west of the central Piazza de Ferrari (junction of Via Roma and Via XX Settembre), dates back to the Middle Ages. Here is the cathedral of San Lorenzo, consecrated in 1118, with three impressive Gothic doors. Here, too, are the churches of San Donato, of Santo Stefano where Columbus was baptized, San Matteo and Sant' Agostino, and the mansions of the famous mercantile families of the Middle Ages, the Doria, the Spinola and the Grimaldi, many constructed in the black and white marble typical of Genoese architecture. In the newer part, slightly farther north, are impressive Renaissance palaces such as the Palazzo Doria Tursi now the seat of the *comune* of Génova, the Palazzo Bianco (1565) and the Palazzo Rosso (1677), both now picture galleries with splendid collections of paintings by Veronese, Rubens, Dürer, Teniers, Caravaggio.

Local specialities include *trenette col pesto* (spaghetti served with a sauce that includes garlic, basil, Sardinian cheese and olive oil), exquisite candied fruit and a rich, fruity bread (*pan dolce*). Information offices at the main station and 11/14 Via Roma.

One visit that is essential is to the impressive cemetery of **Staglieno**, easily reached by local transport, and lying on a hillside with a charming view. The statuary in this vast cemetery is stupendous, and among the interesting tombs is that of Mazzini. Another fine view is from

Monte Righi (cable railway), from wh[ich] one can also see the system of defen[sive] forts on the surrounding hills. *La Sp[ezia] 112km/70mi Savona 46/28*

Impéria

(pop. 36,500) This city, with ne[ar] **Oneglia**, is yet another city of the Ital[ian] Riviera that merits a visit. The [two] centres are linked by the extrem[ely] panoramic Corso Matteotti. The R[iver] Impero which divides them gave its na[me] to the present city.

San Maurizio, slightly to the w[est] knew its moment of fame under [the] Benedictines in the 10th century. It [has] the characteristics of many of the pr[imi]tive Ligurian towns and is presided [over] by an ancient castle.

The famous Admiral Andrea D[oria] was born here in Oneglia in the [year] 1466, as was Edmondo de Am[icis] (1848–1909) the author of *Cuore* (*[The] Heart*) a story beloved by Italians [who] were children in the early part of [this] century.

The walk up the slope from the vil[lage] of San Maurizio to its neocla[ssical] cathedral is rewarding for the numbe[r of] splendid views one can see en route[.]

The idea of uniting San Maurizio [and] Oneglia to form the present Impéria ca[me] from Mussolini, but the name, as m[en]tioned earlier, came from that of the ri[ver].

Not only is Impéria the chief tow[n of] the rich district surrounding it, it is [said] to be the chief producer of the spaghet[ti] beloved of Italians.

Like most towns along this co[ast] Impéria is well equipped to provide [for] tourists, and offers also cam[ping] facilities.

La Spezia

(pop. 125,925) La Spezia lies on a [large] bay, backed by hills, and with excel[lent] communications by road, land and se[a;] offers a particularly pleasant climate, [with] delightful scenery. The city stret[ches] along the sea with lovely gardens, ric[h in] palm trees, pines and plants of m[any] kinds. It also has a busy mercantile [port] and is a naval base. The city was foun[ded] in the 12th century and has an interes[ting] cathedral, with a splendid terra cott[a by] Andrea della Robbia; there is a fine [lib]rary with an excellent collection [of] illuminated manuscripts. La Spezia [is a] good centre for walks into the hills o[r to] the remote villages of the Cinquet[erre.] One worthwhile excursion is to L[erici] along the coast for memories of the [poet] Shelley. *Génova 112km/70mi.*

Lavagna

(pop. 11,000) Lavagna, lying alm[ost] mid-way between Génova and La Sp[ezia,]

rtunate in possessing a long stretch of
dy beach, which for many years has
acted visitors. Recently it has
rged considerably its port facilities
private yachts, and seems bent on
acting even more holiday-makers.
. is well equipped to deal with tourists,
in addition to a number of good
els has camping facilities.
avagna has the added advantage of
g easily accessible by road or rail
n Génova. It is within easy walking
ance of the next town, Chiavari, and
nd Lavagna rise hills dotted with
ll, picturesque settlements. One very
arding walk is up to the little village of
orno, the centre of the slate-
rrying industries from which
agna takes its name, *lavagna* being
ian for blackboard and, as we know,
he best blackboards used to be made
ate.
rom the town below one can see the
interesting little church of Cogorno,
of San Salvatore, Romanesque and
resting to visit.
the town itself stands a really impos-
church of the 18th century, with twin
towers and an elaborate double flight
teps typical of the somewhat preten-
s architecture of the period.
he old part of Lavagna offers many a
sant stroll.
you are in Lavagna on 14 August you
be able to enjoy the festival of the
ta Fieschi, which ends in a splendid
de and the distribution to all around
lices from an immense cake said to
gh 15 quintals (well over a ton). One
ders where such a cake might be
d.

Cinque Terre (The Five
nds).   **I8**

veen Portovénere at the western
emity of the bay of Spezia, and the
ide towns of Sestri Levante, Lavagna
the city of Chiavari, nestle the five
: fishing villages of Monterosso,
naggiore, Vernazza, Corniglia and
arola.
til very recent years the only means
pproach to these enchanting little
s was by sea, train, or very cautiously
g an extremely poor road. Gradually
gs are improving for travellers by car,
alas, one can see the day coming
n these may have developed into just
more of the many tourist resorts of
.
he villages are dotted along about
n/9mi of rugged, rocky coastline, so
that even the birds seem to find
ulty in flying over the towering
. Barren in appearance, these rocky
s are terraced in vineyards and the

light wine of Le Cinque Terre has been
highly esteemed through the centuries;
even Boccaccio, in the 14th century,
praised it in his lyrics. Often, when it is
time to harvest the grapes, it is necessary
for the harvesters to be let down the cliff-
side on ropes.

Wine and fishing constitute the means
of livelihood here.

Now and again one comes across
streets so steep as to be interspersed with
flights of steps. In the microscopic
squares in the centre of each little town,
women sit outside their rough medieval
cottages, their lives punctuated by the
comings and goings of the fishing fleets.

Monterosso is the largest and the one
that, in addition to the old medieval
houses high above the level of the sea, has
some attractive modern dwellings on the
shore. On a neighbouring hill stands an
ancient Capuchin monastery; there is a
13th-century black and white church,
there are the remains of a 16th-century
fortress, a splendid view, and nothing
more, save for a beauty of atmosphere
rarely encountered in modern times.

Monterosso is the birthplace of the
Italian poet, Eugenio Montale.

Next comes **Vernazza** with 2000
inhabitants, rugged and medieval with no
concessions to modernity. Until it was
destroyed during World War II, there
used to be a medieval castle; now only a
couple of fortresses remain, high on the
cliffs above. Here, too, there is a
Capuchin monastery, and westward of it,
a 14th-century dark stone church.

Corniglia, with its fine Romanesque
church, stands perched on a plateau, the
sides of which rise sheer from the sea; this
is the only one of Le Cinque Terre not
actually washed by the waters of the sea.

Hotels are lacking, but nearby there is a
tourist village of about 30 pre-fabricated
bungalows and with a restaurant.

Manarola, with only 900 inhabitants,
consists of a handful of dark little cottages
perched on a cliff of dizzy height. If you
live in Manarola, your only means of contact with the less-secluded world is along
a little cliff path, *Via d'Amore,* leading
down to **Riomaggiore** (3000 inhabitants),
which is built around the mouth of a
mountain torrent that rushes into the sea
at this point. Houses rise in tiers on either
side of the main – and only – street, and
on the heights above are the ruins of a
14th-century castle, now transformed
into what can only be termed a 'filing
cabinet' cemetery, where the graves rise
one above another.

There are no big hotels, no smart
restaurants in Le Cinque Terre, but at
most you will find one or two small

eating-houses where a risotto of seafood, or *gamberoni* (larger than the largest Dublin Bay prawns or scampi) are excellent, washed down with some of the local wine. This makes an excellent finish to a day spent in somewhere approaching fairyland.

Lérici   I9

(pop. 13,600) This little town has particular associations for English visitors, for it was near here that the poet Shelley lived in 1822, the year of his death. It was on the beach at Lérici that his body was washed ashore a few days after his boat had overturned during a squall in the Bay of Spezia, and here on the beach was held the ceremony of his cremation, in the presence of his friends the poet Bryon and the novelist Trelawney.

Lérici today is a popular seaside resort, well equipped with hotels and restaurants, and with good bathing facilities.

The town is dominated by the huge pentagonal castle of the 13th century, and the beach below is noted for its ivory-white fine sand.

Legend has it that one of the houses in Piazza Garibaldi is haunted by unquiet spirits from the past; as hauntings are not frequent in Italy this is a novelty.

The hills surrounding Lérici are dotted with elegant villas. Nearby are less well-known beaches such as **Fiascherine** (3km/2mi) and **Tellaro** (4½km/3mi), which is picturesque with its church rising on a tall cliff that dominates the little seashore village.

Another interesting excursion is to **Sarzana**, 11km/7mi away, from which it is a short distance to the remains of the Roman city of **Luni** (see SARZANA).

Portofino

Portofino

(pop. 1035) Portofino, lying on a prom tory jutting out into the Golfo di Gén is not only beautiful but has an agree mild climate throughout the year. T is a small natural harbour with a col ful little square, and on each side tinted old houses. There are deligh walks as far as **Punta del Faro** and ex sions to **Portofino Vetta** (possibly finest viewpoint of all Liguria) and trips to the enchanting village of **Fruttuoso.**

Accommodation is varied and go

A development of modern hotels villas has been proposed for Portofinc at the time of writing, this has not l implemented. Hopefully, Portofino remain as charming and unspoiled as today.

Portovénere

(pop. 5300) On the western edge of bay of Spezia and about 13km/10mi f that city lies the interesting seaside t of Portovénere. Its origin goes back n centuries; not surprisingly it was on favourite haunt of pirates; today its r industry is fishing.

Its ancient buildings are sited in a turesque position on the high cliff a far end of the town, where stands church of San Pietro, dating back tc 13th century, behind which is a tiny i with the Grotto Arpaia, known local Byron's Cave, from which it is said poet used to bathe.

The whole town is inviting, wit tall, multicoloured houses around th tle port.

It is possible from Portovénere to boat trips to the nearby islands of **mária, Tino** and **Tinetto,** and to the so-near **Cinque Terre.** The scenery unfolds before one's eyes as the churns onward is charming; rocky clad slopes rise out of the water, and not unusual for passengers to be er tained by the frolics of a passing sho dolphins.

The local food is appetizing interesting; try, for example, the far 'Sea Date Soup' — you won't regret choice.

Rapallo

(pop. 20,000) Rapallo is beauti situated. An enchanting little delightful walks in the town and in surrounding hills, and all the organization necessary to make a sea holiday a joy, account for its popula The Collegiata dei Santi Gervasio e tasio with an interesting bell-tower, the 16th-century church of San F cesco in which are paintings by Borz

rtist of the district, and a picturesque
-century castle, enhance its attrac-
s. Among excursions is a visit to the
ctuary of Montallegro, by road or by
e railway; another to the picturesque
of **San Michele di Pagana** where, in
parish church, is a painting by Van
k. *Génova 33km/20mi.*

Remo   **J2**
. 60,000) San Remo, capital of the
era of Flowers, is one of the most
ous tourist resorts of Europe, with
200 hotels and pensions, numerous
ly villas and delightful walks. Just
ide the city is the Pian di Poma,
re every year there are international
ting competitions; on the left is the
leading to the racecourse; then
es the famous promenade which pas-
ound the north of the city, presenting
ramas of great beauty, and passing
ugh parks and gardens. In the 15th-
ury sanctuary of the Madonna della
a are paintings by Fiasella and sculp-
by Maragliano, and the old town is a
of narrow streets full of interest. The
r great promenade is that of the
ress, along the sea front, flanked by
t palms. Here is the Russian church,
gnizable by its dome and its gilded
s. There are elegant shops, and many
esting buildings to be visited. From
centre of the city a cable railway
es for **Monte Bignone**, crossing the
18-hole golf course in Liguria. *Ven-*
lia 17km/10mi.

zana   **I10**
17,000) Going inland, at a distance
km/4mi from Lérici lies the interest-
city of Sarzana, rich in interesting
dings such as the *pieve* (parish
ch) of Sant' Andrea, mentioned in
ry as far back as the 12th century, the
ieval fortress of a famous soldier of
ne, Castruccio Castracani, the
century cathedral and the church of
Francesco.

here is a tradition in Sarzana that dur-
religious processions the figure of
st is borne facing backwards, which
given rise to a not very complimen-
rhyme on the part of those who dwell
e nearby section of Falcinello, to the
t that the inhabitants of Sarzana can
no fear of God since they carry his
ge backwards in processions.

radition apart, Sarzana offers other
ests; it is an important commercial
re, and every year holds an exhibition
all antiques.

earby can be seen the ruins of the
ent Roman city of **Luni.**

hose who have visited Lucca will
ably have seen there in the cathedral
the very ancient wooden statue of Christ,
which is carried through the streets every
year on the occasion of the festival of the
Volto Santo (Holy Face). It was the old
city of Luni that set up a counter claim for
possession of this image when it was first
observed floating in the sea, and the
choice of Lucca as its eventual resting-
place was determined by placing the
statue on a cart drawn by a team of oxen,
and leaving to the beasts themselves the
choice between Luni and Lucca – as we
know, Lucca was the favoured city.

Ventimiglia   K1
(pop. 23,000) Here we have the gateway
to France and many of the advantages
(and disadvantages) of a frontier town,
the Customs offices, to mention but one.

Buses ply through Ventimiglia on
their twice- or thrice- daily regular journey to Monte Carlo and Nice; the journey is along the coastal road and reveals
lovely panoramas with every turn.

We are on the Floral Coast, and the
hillsides are lined with greenhouses in
which grow the carnations and other
lovely flowers which go to enrich the
markets of northern cities. The Flower
Market in Ventimiglia is universally
well-known; the 'Battle of the Flowers'
that takes place each year on the second
Sunday in June is colourful and exciting.

The wide mouth of the River Roja
divides the newer part of the city from
the old, perched on a hillside and
reached across a bridge. At the mouth of
the Nervia, the city's other river, is the
well-preserved Roman theatre dating
back to the 2nd century AD.

In the village of **Mortola** (300 inhabitants), just before one reaches the French
border, is the once-famous Giardino
Hanbury (garden), at one time among
the loveliest in Europe. Reduced to a
ghost of its former splendour, it still
repays a visit. In the grounds can be seen
a stone plaque bearing Dante Alighieri's
words (true to this day) about the stretch
of the old Aurelian Way that borders part
of the garden, and the steep course it
follows.

Down at sea level are what are known
locally as *I Balzi Rossi*, a sinister group
of nine caves in which have been found
Paleolithic remains, animal bones of the
Neanderthal epoch and statuettes
thought to have been the work of men of
the Cro-Magnon era.

For the holiday maker, Ventimiglia
has many attractions, and is also a good
starting-point for many interesting
excursions. It has numerous good hotels
and some excellent restaurants.

EMÍLIA-ROMAGNA

These two territories, always associated, form one of the largest regions in Italy, bordered on the north by the River Po, on the east by the Adriatic, on the south and west by the Apennines. The Roman-constructed Via Emília, running northwest from Rímini through Forli, Faenza, Bologna, Modena, Réggio nell' Emília and Parma to Piacenza, divides the region neatly into plainland to the northeast, mountains to the southwest. On the plain lie Ferrara, Ravenna and the reclaimed marshes and wet valleys culminating in the low-lying city of Comácchio.

In one of the rich, green valleys of the Parma Apennines are the much-frequented thermal spas of Salsomaggiore and Tabiano whose various mineral waters are effective in the treatment of arthritis, bronchitis and other ills. Not far away is the hill town of Castell'Arquato, a charming medieval enclave in the modern world.

From Comácchio to Rímini seaside resorts follow one another so closely as to seem one uninterrupted stretch of fine sand, offering excellent bathing and hotel accommodation to suit all pockets. Between Ravenna and the coast is one of the best-known pinewoods of coastal

Italy, much visited by holiday-mak

Agriculturally this is a wealthy ion. The high mountains are given largely to forestry and pasturage; the vines cultivated at a lower level the pleasant wines of Lambrusco, giovene and others. Tomatoes here in even greater quantity than i south. The plain produces wheat, h sugar-beet and fruit, especially the ries of Vignola. Large numbers of and cattle are raised, giving rise t dairy and delicatessen products which Emília-Romagna is noted. T a region where it is considered no s 'live to eat'!

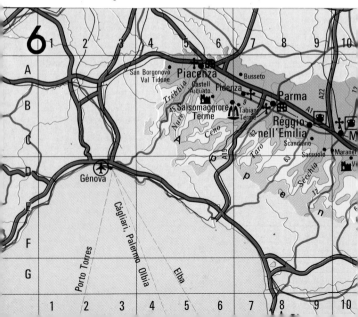

The area is rich in methane and there also deposits of oil.

The Ferrari and Maserati luxury cars built at Maranello near Modena. venna, apart from its history and saics, is well known for the produc-n of synthetic rubber, Faenza and ola for ceramics, and in particular the e faience. Parma is noted not only for splendid cheese and ham, but also for perfume of Parma violets, still pro-ced in large quantities.

n Emília Romagna the march of his-y is signalized by many monuments. The Museo Archeologico Nazionale Spina (on the main floor of the azzo di Ludovico il Moro) in Ferrara uses a valuable collection of treasures m Spina, one of the necropolises of Etruscans who dominated and ught prosperity to the region from 6th to the 4th century BC.

The end of the second Punic War saw arrival of the Romans who, among er achievements, built the Via ilia and left conspicuous monu-nts, such as the Arco d'Augusto and Ponte d'Augusto in Rímini.

Jnder the Romans Ravenna became important city; then followed periods der the Ostrogoths and the Byzantines, r which Ravenna sank more or less o obscurity.

Following the Longobard and Frank asions, the rest of the region was under episcopal domination until the 12th cen-tury and the epoch of the prosperous free *comunes*. Early in the 13th century the University of Bologna was officially founded. Now came the building of the great cathedrals of Modena, Parma, Fidenza, Piacenza, Ferrara and the Abbey of Pomposa, linked with such names as Lanfranc and Wiligelmo in Modena, Antelami in Parma. To this period belongs the Castello Estense in Ferrara. Examples of the Gothic that followed are to be seen in the Palazzo del Comune in Piacenza, the church of San Petronio in Bologna.

By the 14th century the *comunes* had given place to the *signorias,* the overlord-ship of great families, the Este in Ferrara, Modena, Réggio nell' Emília, the Malatesta in Rímini, the Farnese in Parma and Piacenza, the Bentivoglio in Bologna, until by the second half of the 16th century the region was divided up into three great states, the Farnese, the Este and the Church. In this period of Renaissance splendour Leon Battista Alberti designed the Tempio Malates-tiano (see page 68) in Rimini, Rossetti the Palazzo di Schifanoia, the Palazzo dei Diamanti, the Palazzo di Ludovico il Moro in Ferrara, Laureti the Fontana del Nettuno in Bologna, Giambologna the bronze statue of Neptune which adorns it.

In more recent days came the Napoleonic campaign, and on his defeat

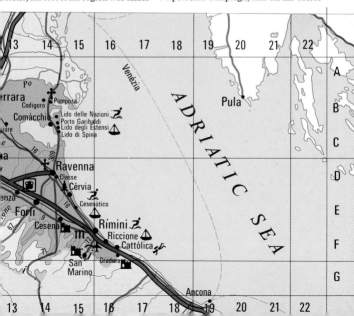

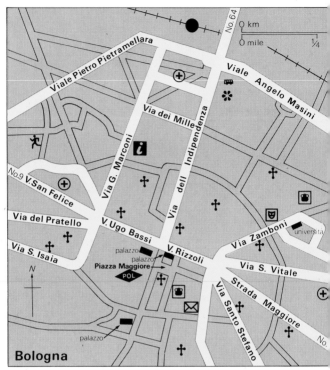

Bologna

Parma and Piacenza were ceded to his widow, Maria Luigia, who in her 32 years as Grand Duchess of Parma did much for that city, including the building of the Teatro Regio, still regarded as a testing-ground for opera singers the world over.

Emília-Romagna has produced many great figures. The end of the 14th century saw Bologna and Ferrara vying with each other in the world of art. In the former the influence of the brothers Caracci was great on painters such as Guido Reni, Guercino and others; Costa left evidence of his talent in the frescoes decorating the Palazzo di Schifanoia in Ferrara. Correggio and Parmigianino both worked in Parma. In our own days, Minguzzi, sculptor of the last of the bronze doors of San Pietro in Vaticano in Roma, was born in Ímola.

Verdi was a native of Busseto, near Parma; Toscanini is another whose name is linked with that city. Marconi was born in Bologna in 1874.

The Italian poets Ariosto and Tasso spent much of their time at the cour the Este in Ferrara, Carducci and Pas in turn held the Chair of Literatur Bologna University.

These are but a few of the men monuments whose names have brou honour to this region.

Festivals last Sunday in June, Faenz *Festa del Niballo* — a tournamen 'knights' who attack the image of Saracen, which is later burnt.

Cesena (no set date) banquets in hon of *Il Passatore* (The Ferryman) who to rob the rich to aid the poor.

Bologna   D

(pop. 441,145) This Etruscan and su quently Roman city has long been on the most important towns of northern ly. During the Middle Ages it was a th ing *comune*, memories of which linge two of its great buildings, the Palazzo Podesta and the Palazzo Comun which now houses an interesting col tion of pictures. Early in the 13th cen the University of Bologna, the oldes

rope, was officially established;
ogna had been recognized as an
ortant seat of learning for a consider-
e time prior to this.

here is an air of prosperous efficiency
ut Bologna, the gastronomic capital of
ly. Strings of sausages − *mortadella,
ami* and a thousand others − cheeses
a variety that beats description, tempt
e from the numerous delicatessen
ps. As one walks through the por-
ed streets one gazes in amazement at
icacies being consumed to the accom-
iment of coffee or an apéritif: a simple
nita (frozen black coffee, chipped,
ed into a dish and topped with thick
ipped cream) becomes a dish for the
ls in Bologna.

Architecturally the city has much to
er. Two leaning towers in the Piazza di
ta Ravegnana (junction of Via Rizzoli
I Via Zamboni, *etc*) make a useful focal
nt. Nearby is the Gothic church of San
ronio, facing the Piazza Maggiore and
zza Nettuno. Michelangelo worked on
ronze statue of Pope Julius II for this
rch, but this was unfortunately
troyed. In one of the chapels off the
th aisle is a modern statue by Manzù
ich is well worth pausing to admire,
on the pilasters of the main door are
e interesting reliefs by Jacopo della
ercia. Also near the towers is the
azzo della Mercanzia, a building of the
e 14th century, and three tiny
rches, all that remain of the former
up of seven known as the Basilica di
to Stefano in Via Santo Stefano. The
acoteca (Picture Gallery) near the
versity has a fine collection of paint-
s by Titian, Tintoretto, Giotto,
hael and others, and the city also con-
s several interesting churches.

stell'Arquato   B6

o. about 6000) A turning off the motor
l leading from Piacenza to Fidenza
gs us to a little hill town that is
emely interesting from an architec-
l point of view, and moreover very
oramic.

t goes back to the 8th century AD, but
special interest lies in the tiny square
the buildings around it, the *collegiata*
legiate church), an early Romanesque
ic of the beginning of the 12th cen-
, with interesting frescoes of the 15th
17th century and a 14th century clois-
which houses a fine collection of
tings and embroidery. There is a
n hall of the late 13th century and the
conti stronghold of the 14th century −
hing more, but all arranged around
square in such a way as to offer
itectural perfection, and when one
enjoyed this and the view to the full,

there is a welcoming little bar where one
may stop before going down the hill once
again to more level ground.

Cattólica   F16

(pop. 12,000) This is a busy commercial
and fishing centre but also, thanks to its
position along the sandy shores of the
Adriatic, it is a thriving and well-
equipped holiday resort. It stands on a
charming bay, surrounded by hills.

The beach of clean velvet-smooth sand
is 3km/2mi in length and slopes gently
into the sea. During the season, which
extends from April to October, there are
numerous entertainments, cultural, artistic and sporting.

Excellently served by road and rail, one
is within easy distance of the mountain
republic of **San Marino**, and of two other
hill towns, Gradara with its legendary
castle in which was enacted the tragic
love story of Paolo and Francesca, and
San Leo, the impregnable fortress where
for a time the arch-imposter, Cagliostro,
was imprisoned.

Among the many entertainments Cattólica provides for visitors is the Sea Carnival held on 15 August of every year,
which attracts visitors from far and wide.

Cérvia   D15

(pop. 20,000) This has been a popular
resort since it was founded in the 17th
century. It has an excellent climate, a fine
beach and pinewoods, and is well equipped with hotels and holiday attractions.

The town itself is interesting; the
cathedral and the Bishop's Palace merit a
visit. A pretty little canal runs through the
town, and one can, if one wishes, be fer-
ried across this.

There are many pleasant walks around
Cérvia, and altogether it is an agreeable
place for a holiday.

Cesenatico   E15

(pop. 16,000) This is another of the many
popular seaside resorts along the Adriatic
coastline. It lies midway between Rímini
and Ravenna, road and rail services are
excellent, and the town is well equipped
with hotels and diversions for holiday-
makers.

Back in the 14th century, Cesenatico
was the port for the city of Cesena.

It is possible to take interesting walks
in the area and among the attractions held
out to tourists are pigeon-shooting,
mini-golf, fishing and, naturally, sea-
bathing.

Cesena   E14

(pop. 86,000) This busy commercial
centre situated in the heart of Romagna is
the seat of a bishopric, and during the
15th century was the seat of the *signoria*
of the Malatesta family.

One of the most interesting buildings is the Biblioteca Malatestiana, the oldest and best preserved of all the convent libraries of the era of Humanism. It was erected thanks to the munificence of Novello Malatesta in the convent of the Franciscans in 1451; as a building it is of great interest, its contents, however, are even more worthy of a visit from all who love books, illuminated manuscripts and the like.

The Malatestian stronghold, Rocca Malatestiana, can be reached via the picturesque Piazza del Popolo, and is a fine example of a 15th-century fortified dwelling.

Comácchio   B14
(pop. 16,883) This interesting little town is built on a group of 13 islands intersected by canals and bridges. A peculiarity is the 16th-century *treponti*, a construction of five flights of steps forming an arch over the intersection of various canals.

There is an interesting 17th-century cathedral, with an uncompleted baroque bell-tower.

The town is a centre of eel-fishing, which is carried on in the hinterland of salt marshes.

Not more than 6km/4mi away is the necropolis of **Spina**, a city first of all Pelasgic, then Etruscan and finally Roman, before it became buried by the silting up of the marshes. Excavations, begun in 1922 and still going on, have revealed several thousand tombs from the 6th to the 4th century BC, and in the Museo Archeologico in Ferrara it is possible to see numerous vases and other treasures brought to light during these excavations.

Comácchio is very near the stretch of coast known as the Lido di Ferrara, 20km/12mi east and north of the Valli di Comácchio and lying partly in luxuriant pinewoods. Of fairly recent formation the seven lidos (**Lido di Spina, Lido degli Estensi** (the best-equipped), **Porto Garibaldi, Lido degli Scacchi, Lido di Pomposa, Lido delle Nazioni** and **Lido di Volano**) offer possibilities for a delightful seaside holiday within easy reach of such interesting places as **Ravenna** and **Ferrara** and the **abbey of Pomposa** (see under Ferrara).

Faenza   D13
(pop. 50,830) This is a place that should be visited by anyone interested in ceramics, for this is the city once so famous for its majolica that it gave its name to the faience so particularly sought after and highly valued in the 15th and 16th centuries. The industry is still kept alive, thanks to able craftsmen and the activities

of the Museo Internazionale Ceramiche (Ceramic Museum), other interested organizations. Faen still of great importance in the wor ceramics and is the seat of the an International Show of Ceramics of temporary Art, with an annual com tion open from the end of July to the of September.

The Museum should certainly be ited.

The Renaissance cathedral (147 early 16th century) was designed Giulio da Maiano.

In the Pinacoteca are painting artists of Romagna from the 14th to century; there is also a fine wooden st of San Girolamo by Donatello and a ble bust of San Giovannino by A. Ro lino.

Ferrara
(pop. 153,393) This is an industrial c the Po valley, but it is also a city strong literary associations. Founde the Romans, the city became a l gobard duchy after the Longob invaded northern Italy. It was su quently part of the Church State, the 13th century it became the seat o great Este family, who establishe influential court in the huge moated tle that still dominates the city. Ludo Ariosto (1474–1533) was at one time retary to Cardinal Ippolito d'Este, bu Cardinal travelled far too much for secretary's liking, and he eventu returned to Ferrara, bought a mo house, which can still be visited, there wrote one of Italy's great work literature, *Orlando Furioso*. A genera or so later, Torquato Tasso, the auth *Jerusalem Delivered*, another of glories of Italian literature, was unde protection first of Cardinal Luigi d' and later of Duke Alfonso II d'Este.

The cathedral of Ferrara has a stri façade, that merits much more th casual glance. Inside there is a Byzar baptismal font, and valuable painti among the treasures in the adja museum are some particularly fine s carvings representing the months o year, the work of an unknown century sculptor. The picture galle housed in the Palazzo dei Diamanti includes works by Carpaccio and painters. The Museo Archeolo Nazionale has several Etruscan exh In the Chiesa del Corpus Domini a be found the tombs of the Este family that of Lucrezia Borgia. Ferrara is n for its excellent bread, and it specializes in a semi-spherical brown cake with an unusual choco nutty flavour, Panpepato.

About 40km/25mi east on the estuary of the Po, near the small town of Codigo, is the magnificent **abbey of Pompo-** with a fascinating basilica of 8th- to -century origin and an elegant 11th-ntury bell-tower. The nearby monas-y has chapter-house and refectory corated with frescoes of the Bolognese hool, and there is an 11th-century Sala lla Ragione (Hall of Justice).

idenza   B7
p. 20,370) Within 10km/6mi of the rmal resorts of Salsomaggiore and biano lies this important agricultural d industrial city, which merits a visit its very lovely Gothic-Romanesque hedral, its majestic façade flanked by o imposing towers, and with three eresting portals.

Internally the cathedral is in three ves and there is a fine series of 14th-ntury frescoes representing the Last dgement.

Fifteen km/9mi away to the northeast is little town of **Busseto**, where it is pos-le to visit the house where the com-ser Giuseppe Verdi lived.

rli   E14
p. 104,900) This is one of the principal tres of the province of Romagna, lying the plain and along the Via Emilia, rounded by a richly agricultural re-n. It is not only an agricultural centre also a busy industrial and commercial .

Originally Roman, it became a free une in the Middle Ages, then fell der Church domination until its inte-tion within the Kingdom of Italy dur-the last century.

The cathedral, of medieval origin, was uilt in the 19th century. It should be ited for the sake of two interesting pels, that of the Holy Sacrament in right-hand nave and that of the donna del Fuoco in the left. There is a fine Romanesque crucifix.

n the 12th-century church of San rcuriale, with its bell-tower of the e epoch, is the fine sculptured tomb of rbara Manfredi.

The local Pinacoteca has paintings by lozzo da Forli, Guercino and others. There is also the Rocca di Ravaldino, stronghold wherein Caterina Sforza osed a strong resistance to the aults of the notorious Cesare Borgia.

odena   C10
p. about 130,000) This busy agricul-al and commercial centre is said to e been originally Ligurian. In the year BC it became a Roman colony and w a period of great prosperity, which a temporary lull during the Barbaric

invasions of northern Italy. In the 9th century AD, however, it became powerful once again, and so it remained through the centuries right up until the French Revolution, after which, in the general share-out of northern Italy, it was ceded to Austria. In 1859 it became a part of the newly united Italy.

Apart from agriculture and commerce, Modena is rich in art and architecture. Its cathedral is one of the outstanding Romanesque edifices of Italy. There had been two previous cathedrals on the same site, but the building we see today goes back to the end of the 11th century, when the Countess Matilda of Canossa − a great and important lady in her day − approved the idea of building this great temple, worthy to receive the remains of Geminiano, the patron saint of the city.

Lanfranc, the greatest architect of the times, was commissioned to design and supervise the building; the stone carvings are the work of Wiligelmo.

At the side of the cathedral rises a famous bell-tower, Torre Ghirlandina, partly Romanesque, partly Gothic, in which is housed a famous household article, a bucket, which, stolen from Bologna in 1325, sparked off an inter-city war and has been rendered immortal to Italians by the celebrated poem by Tassoni, *La Secchia Rapita (The Stolen Bucket)*.

Walking around Modena one encounters smartly attired students, the scholars of the Accademia Militare, housed in the 17th-century former ducal palace. In the Palazzo dei Musei, the Galleria Estense has a fine collection of paintings by such masters as Tintoretto, Veronese, Velasquez, Correggio and others.

There are other fine and interesting churches, such as San Giovanni Battista where one sees other terracotta statuary groups by Begarelli.

Altogether a fascinating provincial city and, moreover, one where to eat is a pleasure, and where the local sparkling red wine, Lambrusco, gives a satisfactory fillip to the excellent food.

Parma   B8
(pop. 155,000) Parma is a provincial city situated in a fertile plain; a busy agricultural centre, it is also an industrial town.

It is of ancient origin and was one of the northern Italian provincial centres that in the year 183AD became a Roman province. The Barbaric invasions brought about a temporary break in its prosperity, but in the 11th and 12th centuries it was a flourishing *comune*, and in 1303 began various periods of splendour and importance under, successively, the Da Correggio, the Visconti and the Sforza families. From 1545 to 1860 it was the capital of the independent duchy of Parma and Piacenza. After the fall of Napoleon, his widow, Marie Louise (Maria Luigia to the Parmesans), was given this duchy, and established herself in the Farnese palace (*La Pilotta*), with a summer court in nearby Colorno, which formed the setting for Stendahl's novel *La Chartreuse de Parme*.

In spite of her reputation of being rather too fond of the opposite sex, it was Maria Luigia who did much for the city, building roads and bridges, orphanages and other public institutions. She it was who founded the picture gallery that one sees today in *La Pilotta*. This gallery, and the private theatre of the Farnese family, are well worth a visit. Incidentally, the Farnese palace was known by this nickname because in Renaissance days the game of pilotta – which resembles tennis – was played in its courtyard.

But the name of Parma is familiar to us for things other than Napoleonic associations. Our grandmothers valued highly the perfume made from its famous violets, which is evidently still one of the city's best-selling tourist products, though nowadays the faint, musky odour of violets is less popular. And, coming to another of the five senses, there is the famous Parmesan cheese.

One of Parma's glories is the Romanesque cathedral and its baptistery.

The baptistery is the work of Benedetto Antelami, who was not only the architect but the sculptor of the reliefs one admires inside and outside the building. This building, of the late 12th century, merits a lengthy visit, but the cathedral, too, is a treasure-house, for here we are looking at the architecture of the 11th-century Comacine master-builders; then, adding beauty to beauty, here and in the church of San Giovanni Evangelista are frescoes by Correggio, while the work of Parmigianino is to be seen in the nearby church of Santa Maria della Steccata.

Incidentally, behind the cathedral is a fascinating old-time chemist's shop, and if one wants to take home the fragrance of Parma violets, a little shop to the left of the cathedral is well stocked with the perfume.

In Parma one can eat excellently, and the hard, sharp-flavoured cheese is at its best. Don't regard this cheese as merely something to be grated over pasta, eat a chunk of it as you would eat other cheese – you will enjoy it.

A worthwhile trip from Parma is to the nearby town of **Fidenza**, 20km/12mi distant, where stands yet another splendid Romanesque cathedral.

Piacenza

(pop. 84,500) This busy agricultur industrial and commercial city is situat in a fertile plain. In its earliest days inhabitants were successively the Ligu the Etruscans and the Gauls. Its situati made it an important colony for Rom and the rectangular streets of the cen echo Roman town planning. Later car the Goths, the Byzantines and the Lo gobards, followed by the Franks, a around the year 1000 the city ranked as free *comune* – the twisting narrow stre one finds between the heart of the city a the 16th-century bastions, and the sple did Gothic town hall of the 13th centu stand as reminders of that period. Vario *signorias* followed the *comunes* then, 200 years, the city became a duchy und the Farnese. After this it passed to Ma Luigia, wife of Napoleon, and later to t Bourbons, forming a part of the Gra Duchy of Parma. In 1859 it became p of the United Kingdom of Italy.

The cathedral (1122–1233) was d signed by the Comacine master-builde who had considerable influence ov Lombard-Romanesque architectu The bell-tower is of the 14th centu The interior of the dome was frescoed Guercino in the 17th century. The 11 century church of Sant' Eufemia merit visit, as does the richly frescoed sanctua of the Madonna di Campagna and t 11th-century church of Sant'Antonio, the side of which is a Gothic atriu (1350) known as *Il Paradiso*, a attached to which is an interesting lit museum of illuminated manuscripts a church vestments.

The splendid Palazzo Farnese is of t late Renaissance (1558), begun by t architect Paciotti and from 1564 onwar continued by Vignola. Nearby are t remains of the 14th-century Visco stronghold.

Interesting excursions can be made the **Collegio Alberoni,** which possesse fine collection of tapestries, and to **S Borgonovo Val Tidone,** where the c legiate church of Santa Maria Assur has a fine polychrome wood altarpiec

Ravenna

(pop. 120,000) An important Roman c as early as 90 BC, Ravenna rose to mu eminence during the great days of Empire, becoming in 404 AD the capi of the western Roman empire with Clas – now several km inland – as its po Then came the Ostrogoth invasions, a in 476 AD Ravenna became their capi under Odoacer and Theodoric. In 5 Justinian, emperor of the eastern Rom empire with its capital at Byzantiu (Istanbul), declared war and in 20 yea

ove out the Ostrogoths; Ravenna once
ain became a Roman capital, under the
gis of the Byzantine empire. In 568 the
ngobards invaded northern Italy and
tablished Pavia as their capital.
avenna sank to the level of a provincial
y, but its magnificent buildings with
:ir unique mosaics recall its former
ry.

One of the earliest is the 5th-century
ausoleo di Galla Placidia, one of the
st romantic and powerful of Roman
trons, at whose death a long funeral
:tège travelled the width of Italy, from
·r name is remembered today not only
the mausoleum but also in the nearby
e forest. The Orthodox baptistery was
·cted a little later; in both the mosaics
zzle with their rich and varied colour-
. In the time of Theodoric, the
silica di Sant' Apollinare Nuovo was
Arian church, but after the Ostrogoths
d been destroyed, it became a Catholic
urch dedicated to San Martino; in the
century the relics of Sant' Apollinare
re transferred to it from their previous
ting place, Sant' Apollinare in Classe.
e basilica is one of the most striking in
venna with a broad central nave and
rinthian columns; the apse is semicir-
ar inside, but covered by a polygonal
:ll; the 6th-century mosaics of the nave
»ict the Procession of Virgins on the
·, that of the Martyrs on the right; above
windows, other mosaics show the
·y of Christ.

aic, church of San Vitale

The greatest complex of architecture
and mosaics is the octagonal church of
San Vitale, consecrated in 547 AD by
Archbishop Maximian. The decorative
capitals of the columns, the marble *trans-
enna* (low partition dividing the presbytery from the body of the church), the
matroneo (ladies' gallery), and above all
the splendid mosaics showing scenes
from the Old Testament and the Courts
of Justinian and Empress Theodora are
incredibly beautiful. Visit also the
strange and impressive Mausoleo di
Teodorico (Tomb of Theodoric), its
cupola a monolith brought from Istria,
and the tomb of Dante, who, exiled from
Firenze, died in Ravenna in 1321. The
6th-century **Basilica di Sant'Apollinare
in Classe** (5km/3mi) stands in open country and again has magnificent mosaics.
The surrounding pinewoods and the
Corsini Canal, which starts in Ravenna,
are additional attractions for this town so
close to many Adriatic Resorts. *Rimini
52km/32mi, Ferrara 74/46.*

Réggio Nell'Emília C9

(pop. 128,844) This is an important
industrial and agricultural centre, with
narrow streets in the centre that betray
not only its medieval importance but, by
their rectilinear plan, the city planning of
the earlier Romans who established the
city in the 2nd century BC.

Among its many monuments of artistic
value is the Romanesque cathedral, originally erected during the 11th century,
then rebuilt in the 13th century.

The church of the Madonna della
Ghiara, in late Renaissance style, has
frescoes by Guercino and others.

The 18th-century Palazzo del Comune
is imposing, and going around the city
one notices statues erected in honour of
Boiardo and Ariosto (born in Réggio in
1474), both highly regarded at the court of
the Este *signoria* in Ferrara.

The Museo Civico has a fine collection
of mementos of the *Risorgimento,* and in
the civic gallery are interesting collections of jewellery, costumes of foreign
countries, paintings, sculpture and furniture.

In the public gardens can be seen a
Roman tomb.

3km/2mi away stands the **Villa
Mauriziano** where the poet Ariosto lived
for some years.

Riccione F16

(pop. 23,000) This large holiday resort on
the popular Adriatic coast of Italy has
grown up within the past fifty years
around a one-time tiny village, a mere
halting place for pilgrims before crossing
the high mountains on their way to
Roma.

There is no sport beloved of seaside visitors that Riccione does not provide for. There is an airport at nearby Miramare, and between Riccione and the equally popular Rímini there is a regular trolley bus service.

In addition to numerous hotels there is a good camping site, and food, as everywhere in Romagna, is excellent, as are the wines – Albana, Sangiovese and Vino Santo.

Small wonder that this town attracts visitors from far and wide.

Philatelists should put Riccione on their list of places to visit, for every August an exhibition of stamps takes place here.

Rímini   F16

(pop. 98,675) This is not only a vast tourist centre, with hotels and *pensions* stretching far and wide along the coast, but also a busy agricultural and commercial centre. It has a splendid beach, and an excellent climate, but apart from its seaside attractions, there is much of interest in the older part of the city. From Roman days it has the impressive Arco d'Augusto, the Ponte d'Augusto, completed by Tiberius, and the ruins of an amphitheatre; but one of Rímini's richest treasures is the Renaissance Tempio Malatestiano, a masterpiece of the architect Leon Battista Alberti, reminiscent, on the outside, of Roman triumphal arches, and with internal decorations by Agostino di Duccio. In the choir of the church of Sant' Agostino are charming frescoes by an unknown 14th-century artist. In the church of San Giuliano is a painting by Veronese, and the city possesses a fine art gallery, housed in the Biblioteca Gambalunga, with works by Giovanni Bellini, Ghirlandaio and many others. *Ravenna 52km/32mi, San Marino 24/15.*

Salsomaggiore and Tabiano Terme   B6, B7

(pop. 17,300) and (pop. 1000) These two well-known and very beautiful thermal centres, both 160m/525ft above sea level, lie in a green, hilly region, 30km/19mi or so from Parma.

Let us look first at Salsomaggiore, renowned for the curative properties of its saline springs. Splendidly equipped as a holiday centre, not only for those 'taking the cure', it provides – particularly in the panoramic section known as Poggio Diana, every kind of amusement one could wish for, including a good theatre and a ballroom.

Nearby Tabiano Terme is frequented particularly by those suffering from bronchial ailments, its waters being strongly sulphuric. Around the thermal zone protective belt of trees has been planted a type that do not bear pollen-lad flowers so distressing to those suffer from hay fever.

From both these centres it is possible take delightful walks, short or lo depending on the walker's wish a capabilities.

Vignola   D

(pop. 14,500) Vignola is a tiny provinc city, but one worthy of a half-day visi one is in nearby Modena, especially one's visit takes place at 'cherry bloss time' for Vignola is the heart of a cher growing district, and its firm, sweet fr (*duroni*) are in great demand. At bloss time (La Fioritura) folks come from and wide to enjoy the spectacle of ac and acres of flower-decked trees.

The city is the birthplace of architect, Jacopo Barozzi (1507–157 known as 'Vignola'. His one-time ho is now converted into a bar and billia parlour, but beyond the bar one con upon a splendid helical staircase.

Vignola also boasts a castle of the 1 century and a charming parish chur and here, as in nearby Modena, it is p sible to enjoy that delicious, sparkling wine, Lambrusco.

SAN MARINO

San Marino, a mountain city of 3500 p ple, is the capital of an ancient indep dent republic. It has its own governme army, coinage and stamps, and preser diplomatic relations with several Eu pean countries and with America. It is earliest republic in the world, going ba it is said, to the 4th century AD. Its e liest statutes date from 1263.

In 1797 Napoleon recognized independence of San Marino; later it w confirmed at the Congress of Vienna 1815.

The ruling body, the Great and G eral Council, consists of 60 membe renewed at each sitting of the legislatu The two Reigning Captains have mandate of representation and are elec every six months.

The picturesque little city climbs u hill and down, then up and down aga and has marvellous views all arou There are three fortresses, Guaita, Fra and Montale, and in the Basilica di S Marino are the niches where the sa used to sleep. San Marino's lovely sit tion and its Ruritanian air attract good visitors. There are several good hote and countless small restaurants a souvenir shops. *Rímini 26km/16mi.*

OSCANA

scana extends over the northwestern
tion of the peninsula, the Apennines
ming its northern and eastern bound-
:s, the Tyrrhenian Sea marking its
g, southwestern coastline. The two
in chains of the Apennines are divided
a series of natural basins — those of the
gra, the Garfagnana, the Mugello and
Casentino. Mainly hilly, the region is
eved by a series of lovely valleys, Val
Chiana and that of Chianti. There is
le real plainland, and that mainly
ng the coastal strip. Off the coast lie
very popular island of Elba and the
ser islands of Gíglio and Montecristo.
The highest regions of the interior and
mountains around Monte Amiata in
south are thickly wooded, with a pre-
aderance of chestnut groves; here, too,
umple pasturage for cattle and sheep.
e lower hills produce olives and vines,
n the latter of which come some of the
t-known wines of Italy, in particular
ianti; other areas famous for vinicul-
e lie around Val d'Elsa, Siena, Mon-
ulciano, the Mugello and Val di Sieve.
eals and forage are the main products
he plains.
The soil is rich in minerals. The iron
es of Elba have been famous since
uscan days; around Grosseto iron
ites is mined; Monte Amiata is rich in
osits of mercury; Volterra specializes
he mining and working of alabaster;
marble quarries of Carrara, from
ch Michelangelo personally selected
ble for some of his finest sculpture,
n inexhaustible.
There is a fair amount of chemical
ustry, particularly at San Giovanni
darno, Arezzo and Pistóia; Prato has
g been renowned for cloth weaving,
Tuscan products in straw have
ld-wide fame. Another peculiarly
scan craft is the working of leather.
This region has long had a magnetic
raction for tourists, be their interests in
oric cities, art and architecture, or just
enjoyment of natural beauty as pro-
:d by hills and coastline. Not surpris-
ly, provision for tourists has reached a
h level, though Toscana is so popular
: early booking of accommodation is
ential.
As far back as the 9th century BC Tos-
a was occupied by the Etruscans, and
n then was highly civilized and well
anized, so that when, in the 3rd cen-
BC, the Romans came and added it to
their 7th Region under Augustus, the
ground was already prepared for adminis-
trative unity.

There are many evidences of Etruscan
civilization. The stretch of land between
Cortona and Chiusi is rich in tombs, and
both have fine museums; Volterra has an
Etruscan arch and possibly the finest
Etruscan museum in the peninsula, and
these are merely the best-known centres
of that civilization.

The Romans left a fine theatre at
Fiésole, amphitheatres in Arezzo and
Lucca.

Like other regions, Toscana suffered
under the Barbaric invasions, until the
arrival of the Longobards, under whom
Lucca became the centre of a duchy, then
later, under the Franks, first a county and
then a march.

The *comunes* came into being during
the 11th century, and for a time there was
bitter inter-city rivalry involving Pisa,
Lucca, Pistóia, Siena, Volterra, Firenze
and Arezzo, during which time Pisa
assumed importance as a naval power.

Throughout this period Firenze had
more or less taken the lead, gradually
asserting its superiority over Pisa, Arezzo
and Pistóia. Later, when the great Medici
family had taken over the reins of the
signoria, we see the conquest of the proud
city of Siena (1570).

During the 18th and 19th centuries
Toscana made enormous progress
economically and in the field of art, for
after the fall of Constantinople in 1453,
the Greek scholars who had fled persecution found a ready welcome awaiting
them in Firenze, where the Renaissance
and the doctrines of Humanism knew a
flowering that no other city enjoyed.

This period of brilliance was inter-
rupted only slightly under Napoleon, and
when the *Risorgimento* movement took
over, once again Toscana was in the

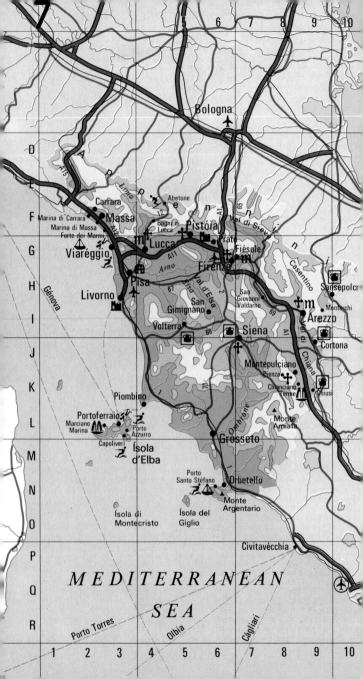

efront. When, in 1860, it was joined to
e Kingdom of Italy it was a keypoint of
onomic progress, and from 1865 to
71 Firenze enjoyed the honour of being
e capital.

From the 11th century onward, Tos-
na vied with the Veneto in Romanes-
e architecture, of which Toscana has a
ecial, easily recognizable variety, with
ack and white or coloured marbles
ernating, sometimes in stripes, some-
nes in geometrical designs. Examples
n be seen in the cathedral in Firenze,
pped by Brunelleschi's famous cupola,
d the cathedrals in Lucca and Pistóia.
the Piazza del Duomo (or dei Miracoli)
Pisa there is a complex of Tuscan-
manesque at its best, with many-
lleried façades and elegant decoration.
ring this period Toscana had a galaxy
fine sculptors; Arnolfo di Cambio,
drea Pisano and the famous father and
n, Nicola and Giovanni Pisano, who
re responsible for the splendid pulpits
Pisa and Pistóia. It was in Toscana that
great family of the Della Robbia
stly produced their statuary in glazed
racotta. In the period of the Renais-
ce the architects of Toscana were
nowned, and their work remains in the
ny fine palaces we see in and around
enze today. Brunelleschi, Leon Bat-
a Alberti, Rossellino, Michelozzo
re among them. In painting, too, Tos-
na took the lead, with the works of
ccio and the Lorenzettis in Siena,
nabue, Giotto and a host of others.
scana in general, and Firenze in par-
lar, was rich in all that has to do with
and architecture. Possibly the greatest
lptor of all time, Michelangelo,
rted his training as a lad under the
ronage of Lorenzo de'Medici.

Nor did literature lag behind: the three
eats' of the 13th century, Dante
ghieri, Francesco Petrarca and
ovanni Boccaccio, were all Tuscans.

ba   L3

oa is the largest island of the
hipelago off the coast of Toscana. It
s an area of 224sq km/86sq mi and a
pulation of nearly 30,000. Its nearest
nt is only 10km/6mi from the main-
d, and so it is easily reached from
mbino by steamer (70 minutes) or
rofoil (20 minutes), which in the high
son furnish 25 daily sailings. There is
o a daily ferry service from **Livorno**
ghorn).

To the British the island is familiar
ause of its Napoleonic associations.
ough he spent only one year there,
14–1815), he left many memories,
d the Palazzina dei Mulni where
lived, and his summer residence,

San Martino, are both now museums.

Elba was well known long before the
days of Napoleon. The Greeks named it
Athalia; later on the Etruscans knew and
valued it for its iron deposits. When war
raged between Pisa and the Florentine
Medici family, it belonged first to one side
and then to the other. The town we now
know as Portoferraio was founded by
Cosimo I of the Medici, who gave it its
original name of Cosmopoli.

There is an excellent network of roads,
over 170km/106mi asphalted, 90km/56mi
macadamized. There are regular bus services and numerous good hotels. There
are no fewer than 40 swimming pools,
three 9-hole golf courses, 16 mini-golf
courses, sailing schools, riding schools, a
wealth of fine, sandy shore and an equ-
able, mild climate.

Portoferraio on the northern side is the
principal town, with many attractions and
within easy reach of other centres. In Portoferraio make a point of visiting the old
Medicean forts.

For those wishing to combine a holiday
with some form of thermal treatment,
there is an excellent thermal institute at
San Giovanni, very near Portoferraio,
where mud and seaweed therapy are said
to be highly efficacious in the treatment
of skin diseases, rheumatic and arthritic
complaints and even cellulitis.

Marciana, also on the north coast, is a
good centre and not far from the **Poggio
thermal centre** for curative waters; it also
has an excellent archaeological museum.

Porto Azzurro on the southern coast
has good beaches and offers fine views.

Campo nell'Elba is very near the one
airport and so is convenient for those
wishing to make the short journey by air.
It has many tourist attractions and good
hotels, and is a good central point from
which to reach smaller centres.

Those who have a passion for Pisan-
Romanesque architecture will find many
examples on the island, for example, the
church of San Giovanni e San Nicola at
San Piero not far from Campo nell'Elba,
San Michele at Capoliveri on the southeastern peninsula, San Lorenzo at Marciana and Santo Stefano alle Trane in
Portoferraio.

Food is excellent, the wines of Elba are
justly popular and hotels are geared to
welcome tourists.

Festivals Easter Sunday in Firenze: the
Scoppio del carro, when an artificial dove,
set alight, traverses a wire leading to the
carro, a decorated float surrounded by
popping fireworks. 1 May, also in
Firenze, the *Calendimaggio*, when gar-
lands are placed on monuments and
around the necks of pretty girls. 24 and 28

June in the Piazza dei Signori in Firenze there is a rough-and-tumble football game in medieval costumes. July 2 and August 16 are important dates in Siena, for then is held the world-famous *Palio*, a horse race around the main square, all in costume and preceded by a parade of costumed dignitaries of the many *contradas* (divisions) of the city. In Arezzo on September 4, the *Giostra del Saracino*, a colourful tournament dating back to the 13th century. In Lucca on September 13 comes the *Festa del Volto Santo*, a solemn religious procession when the image of the Holy Face is taken from its place in a chapel in the cathedral and paraded round the city accompanied by priests and choristers.

Abetone   E4

(pop. 831) 1388m/4554ft above sea level. When one thinks of winter sports, one tends to think of the high mountains of the north, but there are quite a few centres in the Apennines where skiing and other winter sports are provided for. One such is Abetone, halfway between Modena and Lucca, in a splendidly panoramic position on the borders of Toscana and Romagna.

Extremely well-equipped with hotels, ski-lifts, a ski-school and a swimming pool of Olympic dimensions, it also offers excellent possibilities for interesting walks and for hunting.

Arezzo   I9

(pop. 73,176) Arezzo is of Etruscan origin; in the Middle Ages it was a flourishing *comune*, and it is now the economic centre of a large area of the province. It is rich in works of art, and one of Italy's greatest poets, Francesco Petrarca, was born here in 1304.

From the station, walk up Via Guido Monaco, turn right into Via Cavour, then left into Via dei Pileati, to reach the delightful Piazza Grande in which stands one of the town's most spectacular churches, Santa Maria della Pieve, constructed in the Romanesque style peculiar to Arezzo and the surrounding area. The façade is embellished with three tiers of columns which remind one of the pipes of a mighty organ; the bell-tower, set right into the façade, seems to float on its 40 double arches. As you enter the main door look up at the decorations of the barrel vault, representations of the 12 months of the year, a very common form of ornamentation of churches of this period (12th century); at the extreme right-hand end is a particularly brutal carving of December, showing a farmer killing a pig. Over the main altar is a delightful polyptych by the Sienese painter Lorenzetti (1320).

From the Piazza Grande behind church, one has a splendid view of exterior, the apse decorated with two r of columns. This square is a treas house of architecture. Near Santa Ma is the fine Palazzo della Fraternità Laici, the lower part featuring h 14th-century arches; the upper part 15th-century, the work of the Ren sance architect Rossellino. The arched Loggia is by Vasari, another fa ous citizen of the city, and around other two sides of the square stand a ra of tall medieval houses.

Continue up the Via dei Pileati past Palazzo del Capitano on the left, and house where Petrarca was born wh has, alas, been almost entirely rebuilt. the right is the large public park Il Pr with the remains of a former fortress the Medici family; on the left is cathedral with a Gothic façade, inter ing frescoes and a striking marble al said to be the work of Giovanni Pisa To the left of the altar is a funeral mo ment to a former Archbishop by unknown Sienese artist, and near monument is the famous *Mador Tricolore* by Piero della Francesca. one of the chapels, divided from the n by fine wrought-iron gates, are interesting terracottas, said to be De Robbias.

Returning to the city centre by Cesalpino, one passes the Palazzo Comune, farther down the Well Tofano, mentioned by Boccaccio in *Decameron*, and farther down again, house of Guido d'Arezzo, who inven the tonic sol-fa, and who is remembe annually in August at a Polyphonic C gress held in the Petrarch Theatre.

At the junction of Via Cesalpino a Via Cavour, turn right to the great chu of San Francesco, in the main chapel which is the splendid series of frescoes the Tuscan artist Piero della Frances painted between 1452 and 1464, and c sidered to be one of the three most imp tant works of art in Italy − the other t are the Sistine Chapel in the Vatica and the Cappella degli Scrovegni, Pa va. One can gaze at these frescoes sp bound, then go away and return not o but many times, finding always sor thing new, something of particular bea ty. Of special interest are the *Meetin the Queen of Sheba with Solomon*, *Death of Adam*, and the *Dream of C stantine*.

In **Sansepolcro** (39km/24mi) are ot works by della Francesca, notably *Madonna della Misericordia*, and fresco of the Resurrection. Also in S sepolcro is the painter's house, remir at in miniature of the architecture of Palazzo Ducale at Urbino. In the little village of **Monterchi** on the way (route) is the famous and unusual fresco of *Madonna del Parto*.

Early in September Arezzo becomes y gay with the annual *Giostra del racino*, a colourful pageant held in the azza Grande. The *Buca San Francesco* the Piazza San Francesco serves licious and rich Arezzo specialities, ably pork and lamb. *Firenze 85km/ ni, Perúgia 85/53.*

ianciano Terme K8

p. 540) 540m/1772ft above sea level. y is famous for its many spas and rmal centres, one of the most frented of which is Chianciano Terme Toscana, not more than 30km/19mi n Lago Trasimeno, and reached along ood road through the very pleasant brian and Tuscan countryside.

ts waters are recommended for those ering from liver and biliary complaints, and it is a common sight to see ients strolling back from the thermal tre, bearing their own special glass or g of the curative water.

The high season for such cures is from l-April to the end of October, and during this period there is a fine programme ntertainments to relieve the tedium of cure.

The old nucleus of the town is of uscan origin, for Chianciano lies in a t of Italy rich in Etruscan findings.

The Romanesque collegiate church s some fine decorations and sculpture artists of the Siennese school, and in small church of the Misericordia is a sco said to be the work of Luca Signelli.

An interesting excursion is to the town **Chiusi** where there is a splendid Etrus-a museum, the Museo Nazionale usco, and from which one can visit some very interesting underground tombs, having obtained permission from the museum authorities.

Also nearby is the little town of **Pienza,** planned by Pope Pius II.

Cortona J9

(pop. 26,720) This city, high on the hills above the station of **Terontola**, was of extreme importance in Etruscan days, and possesses a fine Etruscan museum, the Museo dell'Accademia Etrusca.

After a period of Roman occupation it was occupied in the 5th century by the Goths, and later followed the fate of the rest of Toscana.

In the Museo Diocesano is one of the finest Annunciations of Beato Angelico.

In the church of Santa Margherita, who died in Cortona, is the Gothic tomb of the saint (1362).

The cathedral still preserves traces of the original church of the 11th century, but has been many times restored.

A little way down the hill from the main city is the interesting church of La Madonna del Calcinaio, designed in 1485 by Francesco di Giorgio Martini; it was built on that spot as a result of the miraculous injunction of the Madonna, despite the fact that the site is that of a landslide and therefore presents architectural difficulties, even at the present day.

The views from Cortona, apart from its architectural beauties, make a visit worthwhile.

Firenze (Florence) G6

(pop.428,955) The most important city of Toscana, Firenze spreads itself along both sides of the River Arno.

Founded by the Romans in the 1st century BC, it did not really expand until Carolingian days, developing between the 12th and 15th centuries into the greatest cultural centre of Europe. Despite internal strife between Guelphs and Ghibellines, despite disputes with

te Vecchio, Firenze

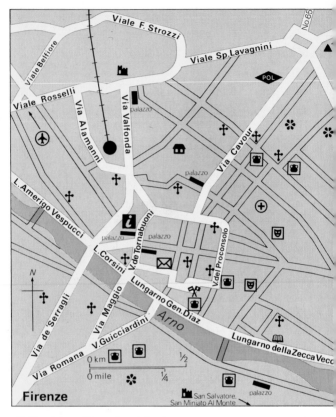

Firenze

the Church state, Firenze forged ahead as a free *comune*. In the 15th century she enjoyed even greater prosperity under the *signoria* of the great Medici family, wealthy bankers who eventually became the Grand Dukes of Toscana. Around the Court of Lorenzo de' Medici (the Magnificent) were such figures as Michelangelo, Raphael, Leonardo da Vinci. Lorenzo himself was a poet of no mean talent, and a great organizer of the spectacles and carnivals which were a feature of the age. During the late Middle Ages and the Renaissance Cimabue and Giotto (two of the earliest masters of Italian painting), Brunelleschi, Donatello, Masaccio, Ghiberti, Beato Angelico, Filippo Lippi, Paolo Uccello, the Della Robbias, Verocchio, Pollaiolo and Botticelli were among the many painters,

sculptors and architects working in a around Firenze, and today the city i living monument to their lives and wo

The damage done by the floods of 1 has still not been fully assessed, but major works have been saved.

Benvenuto Cellini developed the ar the sculptor in bronze and silver to a h level. In the Galleria degli Uffizi, Palazzo Pitti, the Bargello, the Conve di San Marco, the Accademia and Medici Chapels and many otl museums and palaces are housed tre ures that testify to the genius of this c as do the buildings themselves. See Palazzo Vecchio, the nearby Uf (designed by Vasari), the Palazzo Stro the cathedral with Brunelleschi's cupo Giotto's bell-tower and the octago baptistery with its world-famous bro

ors, and the many churches – San
iniato al Monte, Santa Croce and the
ppella dei Pazzi among them.

Even the Italian language was born in
renze at the end of the 13th century
en Dante began writing in *Volgare*
e language of the common people);
mans declare that the purest Italian is
gua toscana in bocca romana* (Tuscan
oken by Romans); Florentines con-
t with the first part of the phrase.
Today the city still plays a leading role
art and culture. May in Firenze is the
nth of musical events; at Easter, in
mory of the victory of the First
usade, the ceremony of the *Scoppio del
rro* is held in the cathedral square, a
ne of fireworks and great excitement;
May and June football games in
dieval costume are held in the Piazza
la Signoria, preceded by a medieval
geant – football games which have to
seen to be believed. Shoppers find
enze a paradise for leather goods, fine
broideries, and articles made of straw,
her in the many elegant shops in such
eets as Via de Tornabuoni, or in the
nous Straw Market just off Via Cal-
uoli.
Here only the surface of Firenze can be
iched; there is much more to see and to
; there are visits to **Fiésole** up on the
l, to **Pistóia, Lucca** and **Pisa**. Informa-
n is obtainable from the Azienda
tonoma di Turismo, Via Tornabuoni
by the Ponte S. Trinita or from the
urist Information Offices inside the
ntral Station. *Bologna 104km/65mi,
a 91/57, Rímini 158/98.*

rte dei Marmi   F3

p. 9120) This is a lovely seaside resort
hin easy reach of **Pisa** (46km/28mi)
l **Lucca** (44/27). It enjoys a splendid
mate, protected as it is by the Apuan
ps, on the lower slopes of which are
ve trees and pines. It has a large beach
sand, and the many villas and the well
t and beautiful gardens along the
re give it an attractive appearance. It
s good bathing, all kinds of water
rts, fishing, boating, and there are
ightful walks to be taken in the
ewoods.
n view of the town's excellence as a
ring centre and resort, accommoda-
n should be booked early.

vorno (Leghorn)   H3

p. 165,000) Livorno is an agreeable
ort lying in a fertile plain between hills
l the sea. The promenade stretches for
r 8km/5mi and in the bay is a modern
nstruction of the 14th-century light-
se. The Medici fortress, the Fortezza
cchia, was erected in the 14th century
und a 9th-century building and was

later (1521–30) reinforced by the
architect Sangallo. It is now being transformed into conference rooms and
restaurants. Everything in Livorno seems
to be on a larger scale than normal: the
statue of Ferdinando I de'Medici, erected
to celebrate a victory over the pirates who
once were the scourge of the Mediterranean; the extra-wide streets and spacious
piazzas. The cathedral has been almost
completely reconstructed since World
War II, but preserves some fine paintings
from the original edifice. Livorno's
unique charm, its nearness to **Pisa**
(21km/13mi), **Lucca** (42/26), and such
seaside resorts as **Viaréggio**, suggest a
stay of several days, possibly in combination with a week in Firenze (95km/59mi).

Lucca   G4

(pop. 88,428) Lucca is a charming little
city with some splendid Tuscan-
Romanesque architecture. Not far away
are several villas which are numbered
among the most beautiful in Italy, such as
the **Villa Mansi**, and the **Villa di Marlia**,
with charming gardens and fountains.
About 17km/10mi to the north is the
peaceful holiday resort of **Bagni di Lucca**,
with lovely walks among the hills and
along the banks of the river Lima, where
there is a thermal establishment for the
cure of arthritis. Lucca is pre-Roman, but
it enjoyed its period of greatest splendour
during the 12th and 13th centuries when
it was a free *comune*. It is surrounded by
ancient walls along the top of which is a
pleasant tree-shaded drive. From a point
in this drive can be seen the garden of a
house described by Charles Morgan in
his novel *Sparkenbroke*.
The cathedral of San Martino is a
splendid example of Tuscan art and
architecture, with the columned *loggettas*
of its façade and its graceful bell-tower.
Inside is a statue of the patron saint on
horseback and a beggar, a group that was
originally outside the cathedral but
which has been moved inside to protect it
from the weather. Also in the cathedral is
the tomb of Ilaria del Carretto, the work of
Jacopo della Quercia – notice particularly Ilaria's faithful small dog, lying at
her feet. In the Cappella del Volto Santo
(Chapel of the Holy Face), a highly ven-
erated wooden statue of Christ is kept.
Early in September every year is the *Festa
del Volto Santo*. Services are held in the
cathedral and during the evening the
statue, arrayed in elaborate robes, is carried through streets, lit only by candle-
light and torches, accompanied by a long
procession of priests and choirs.
The church of San Michele houses a
precious terracotta by Andrea della Robbia and a painting by Filippino Lippi. In

the church of San Frediano, distinguished by a fine external mosaic, is the tomb of San Riccardo Ré d'Inghilterra, an English king of the 7th or 8th century who relinquished his right to the throne to become a saint. There is also a chapel devoted to Santa Zita, the patron saint of domestic servants, and a delightful baptismal font, the work of the 12th-century sculptor, Roberto.

Marina di Carrara
Marina di Massa   F2

(both pop. 12,000) These two well-appointed holiday resorts are within 7km/4mi of each other. Both have fine esplanades along a sandy shore and here and there little plantations of umbrella pines for those who prefer the shade to the blazing sun.

Behind them rise the Apuan Alps, white here and there, not with snow, but with the fine, white Carrara marble, which is exported from this area.

It is an easy bus or car journey up the mountain to Carrara itself; the city itself is a mere 80m/262ft above sea level, but the road continues upward beyond it until it reaches the quarries, and these are the same quarries which were visited by Michelangelo when he wished to select personally the particularly fine white marble he wanted for his sculpture. These quarries have been worked for centuries, and there is still abundant marble. Along the way up the mountain one passes here and there small establishments where local craftsmen fashion small statues, ashtrays and other small objects.

There are camping facilities at both Marinas, and Marina di Massa has also a youth hostel; there are facilities for all kinds of marine activities, bathing is good, and the vegetation is lush and almost African in type.

Not far from **La Spezia, Lérici** or **Viaréggio**, either of these towns would make an excellent holiday base.

Pienza   K8

(pop. about 3500) This tiny but charming little city is well worth visiting if one is in the region of Chianciano, Montepulciano or Siena. It is a small, but exquisite, model of a purely Renaissance city, owing its beauty to the efforts of Pope Pius II, born here with the name Enea Silvio Piccolomini in 1405. On being elevated to the Papacy in 1458, it was his wish to transform the place of his birth into a model city, and for this purpose he engaged the Florentine architect Bernardo Rossellino, giving him a free hand. The project was carried out in three years (1459–1462) and still stands although, once Pius II had died, it was no longer the

chosen 'off duty' residence of Popes. buildings calling for special no include the cathedral, a very typic Renaissance edifice. On the timpanur the façade will be noticed the crest of Piccolomini family. The interior divided into three naves of equal heig with a polygonal apse. In the crypt baptismal font, also the work of Ros lino. After the cathedral, Palazzo I colomini calls for attention, mode largely on Alberti's Palazzo Rucellai Firenze.

The mansions one sees along Co Rossellino were the dwelling places the dignitaries of the Papacy.

The little town today is an agricultu centre where, among other products, possible to buy excellent cheeses.

The Campanile, Pisa

Pisa

(pop. 96,545) Pisa possesses one of loveliest architectural groupings Europe, in the Piazza del Duomo (or Miracoli), in which are to be seen only the famous Campanile (Lean Tower) and the cathedral, but the bap tery and the Campo Santo (bu ground), each a masterpiece of sculpt and architecture. The cathedral begun in the 11th century, to the des of the architect Buscheto; it was co pleted in the following century, the or pipe façade the work of another fam architect, Rainaldo. Among the treasu

ide are the pulpit by Giovanni Pisano,
e lamp on which Galileo Galilei based
s theory of the swing of the pendulum,
e splendid bronze doors of Ranieri, and
ne valuable paintings. The baptistery
s an interesting cupola, which in fact
nsists of two: an inner one in the form
a cone which projects through the
ter one – an idea taken from Arabian
hitecture. Because of its sea traffic dur-
g the Middle Ages, Pisa was in close
uch with the Orient, and there is more
n a flavour of the east in the architec-
e of the city. The decoration of the
ors is particularly interesting, and the
lpit here is one of the last works of
cola Pisano, father of Giovanni. The
mpanile, work of Bonanno, was aban-
ned for 90 years when the slope was
t noticed, but was eventually com-
ted in the middle of the 14th century.
the nearby Campo Santo are famous

frescoes by Gozzoli, Traini and Orcagno.

Pisa is a graceful city and the embankment of the Arno makes a particularly
agreeable walk. Near the Ponte Solferino
is another delightful little church, Santa
Maria della Spina, jutting out right into
the street; another veritable treasure-
house is the church of Santo Stefano dei
Cavalieri. *Firenze 18km/11mi, Livorno
19/12.*

Pistóia   F5

(pop. 82,425) A little Tuscan city, within
easy reach of Firenze and well worth a
visit for those interested in sculpture and
architecture.

The church of San Giovanni Fuor-
civitas (12th century) is an interesting
example of Pisan Romanesque, with a
fine marble pulpit by Fra Guglielmo of
Pisa. The cathedral (12th century) is also
in similar style and has a fine bell-tower;
it houses a famous *dossale* of San Jacopo,

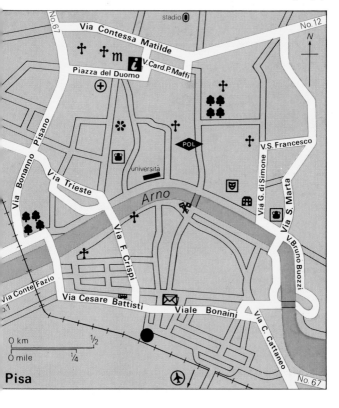

Pisa

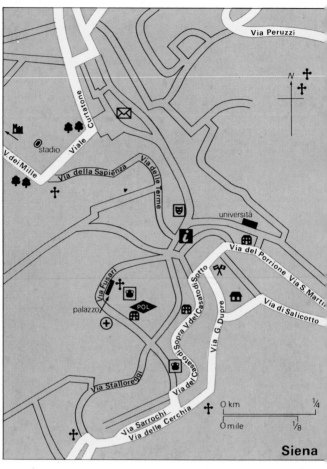

Siena

a fresco by Lorenzo di Credi and a baptismal font of the end of the 15th century. The Ospedale del Ceppo, founded in the 13th century, has a magnificent coloured frieze, the work of Giovanni della Robbia, while in the church of Sant'Andrea is an exquisite pulpit by Giovanni Pisano.

Porto Santo Stéfano   N6

(pop. 8500) This is one of the more recent of holiday resorts to spring into popularity. Lying on the western coast of Toscana, its nearest railway station is Orbetello.

Originally a small fishing village, its wide, lovely bay and splendid san beaches have of late years attrac numerous tourists. Its buildings largely post-World War II, as during th conflict the original village was co pletely destroyed. Because of its excell port and good facilities for the repair fitting-out of all kinds of sea craft, attracts travellers by sea as well as by la

In the season steamers ply easily a quickly to the nearby **Ísola del Gíglio** pleasant day's excursion.

The central point of the peninsula which stands Santo Stéfano is **Mo**

rgentario, which provides some
teresting, though somewhat strenuous,
alks.
Porto Santo Stéfano has all the charm
a small fishing village, combined with
xcellent modern facilities, including
ood eating-places.

rato   G6
op. 121,200) Known to the woollen
ade for its manufacture of cloth, this city
s also several very famous monuments.
ithin easy distance of Firenze, it
erits a visit of half a day if not more.
The cathedral (8th century, but
larged in the early 14th century) has an
egant façade at the right-hand corner of
hich is the famous pulpit (pergamo del
cro Cingolo) by Donatello, decorated
th splendid reliefs. The choir is deco-
ted by Filippo Lippi and the splendid
te leading to the chapel of the Sacro
ingolo dates back to the 15th century.
n the fine altar (1478) is an exquisite
atuette by Giovanni Pisano.
The battlemented castle is interesting,
d another fine church is that of Santa
aria delle Carceri, a splendid example
Renaissance architecture.

an Gimignano   I6
op. 10,060) In medieval days, to have a
wer to one's house was not only a
eans of defence, but also a status sym-
l. This little city is one of the few still
ssessing a fair number of the ancient
wers that used to rise like tall trees
ove the horizon. Old prints show a ver-
ble forest of towers, but nowadays the
mber is reduced to a dozen or so;
vertheless, approaching the city by
ad, the effect is still unusual. The main
uare, the Piazza della Cisterna, is sur-
unded by interesting palaces of the 13th
d 14th century. The Palazzo del
desta and the Palazzo Comunale (now
e home of the civic museum with valu-
le paintings by Lippi, Pinturicchio and
hers) are both interesting, and in the
omanesque church known as the
uomo are examples of the work of
iuliano and Benedetto Maiano, Jacopo
lla Quercia and a fresco of Santa Fina
the patron saint of the city — by Ghir-
ndaio.

iena   I7
op. 62,954) Siena is famous for its art
d architecture, and noted for one of
aly's most colourful pageants, the *Palio*,
e most tumultuous horse race in the
orld.
The Gothic cathedral (off Via Fusari,
iginally planned to be much greater
an its present size, has a splendid pave-
ent, a fine pulpit by Nicola Pisano and
embers of his famous school of sculp-

ture and, in the Libreria Piccolomini, a
series of frescoes by Pinturicchio. In the
main square is the impressive Town
Hall, and nearby the graceful Torre del
Mangia, with the one-handed clock that
used to sound the hour of *mangiare* (to
eat), and the charming Cappella di Piazza.
The Loggia della Mercanzia, the
church of San Martino, and the church of
Santa Maria di Provenzano are fine
examples of Renaissance architecture, as
is the Palazzo Piccolomini delle Papesse,
designed by Rossellino. The 13th-
century Gothic church of San Domenico
is also interesting. The Museo dell'
Opera del Duomo should be visited if
only to see the famous *Maestà*, the *Noli
me tangere* and *Gesù in Emmaus* by Duccio di Buoninsegna. Other works by
Duccio, and by Dürer, Lorenzetti, Pinturicchio are to be found in the
Pinacoteca in the Palazzo Buonsignori.
The Casa di Santa Caterina, who wrote
admonitory letters to the Popes during
their residence in Avignon, is now a sanctuary.

Viaréggio   G3
(pop. 50,415) Viaréggio is an extremely
popular seaside resort, surrounded by
pinewoods and backed by the Apuan
Alps, with a splendid beach. In February
a Carnival is held, in which wonderfully
decorated floats take part, with fireworks
and similar attractions. Among its
interesting buildings are the church of
the Annunciation, the Palazzo Bel-
luomini, and a 16th-century tower in the
market square. *Livorno 40km/25mi,
Lucca 24/15.*

Volterra   I5
(pop. 17,137) By far the most dramatic
approach to this ancient town is by road,
when one has the sensation of almost
flying over the eroded valleys that surround it. The picture gallery is housed in
the 13th-century Palazzo dei Priori, decorated on the outside with numerous
coats-of-arms. In the Pisan-Romanesque
cathedral is a fine baptismal font by Sansovino and an exquisite *Deposition* carved
in wood. The museum, with its fine collection of Etruscan funerary urns and
other relics is a joy, as are the Etruscan
walls and the Porta all' Arco close to the
cathedral. In Via Buonparenti are some
interesting tall, narrow medieval houses.
A pleasant walk through the town brings
one to the grim fortress erected in 1472 by
Lorenzo de'Medici, and now used as a
prison for those condemned to life sen-
tences. Volterra is famous for its alabaster
ornaments, and a visit to the various
workshops is entertaining. *Firenze
78km/48mi, Siena 50/31mi.*

MARCHE

Occupying a position on the Adriatic side of the Apennines, the region consists of a series of high slopes parallel to the coast, decreasing gradually in height as they near the sea. The rivers run perpendicularly to the coast and are of a torrential nature, partly utilized for the production of electricity. The coast itself is rich in seaside resorts.

Wheat is grown, and there is considerable pasturage for cattle, pigs and sheep; tomatoes and cauliflowers are among the vegetable products, and there are numerous vineyards. Fishing is carried on all along the coast, the principal centre of this activity being San Benedetto del Tronto.

Around Pésaro sulphur is mined. The main industry is that of paper-making, centred on the city of Fabriano. Ceramics are made around Urbino, and Castelfidardo is famous for the manufacture of accordions.

All along the coast, tourists are well provided for in the many seaside resorts.

One still sees ox-carts in use in this region, a relic of the long-distant Etruscan days.

In its earliest days the region was divided between the Gauls and the Piceni, and Romanization did not begin until the 3rd century BC, when it was first of all divided between the 5th and 6th Regions of Augustus and later united.

There are a fair number of Roman remains all over the area; the splendid Arco di Traiano in Ancona and Augustan arches in Fano and other cities.

The Longobards later dominated the part south of Ancona, while the northern part came under the Exarchate of Ravenna, and later under the Pope, who received it as a gift from the Franks. The word *marca* (march) was not used until the 10th century.

Feudalism and the ecclesiastical authority were both powerful until in the late 12th and early 13th centuries came the rise of free *comunes*, followed shortly by the *signorias*, which again wielded great power, as is seen in the history of the Montefeltro family of Urbino, the Malatesta in Rímini. Meanwhile the Church was striving to maintain and even to reinforce its one-time authority, in fact, under Cardinal Albornoz in the 14th century, many castles and cities fell under its domination. Little by little, following the short-lived rule of first the Sforza and later the Valentino dynasties from middle of the 15th to the beginning of 16th century, we see the Church ruli the entire area, except for the sh Napoleonic era, until 1860, wh Marche became a part of the Kingdom Italy.

Building activity was considerab from the 11th to 13th century, and there an attractive blending of Romanesc with Byzantine styles as, for example, the dramatically-sited church of Sar Maria at Portonovo near Ancona, or t cathedral in Ancona itself, badly da aged during the recent wars and by earthquake, but faithfully restored.

The Gothic period left evidences Ancona, showing signs of strong Ver tian influence, as in the Loggia dei M canti in that city and in the church of S Nicola at Tolentino, a church well wor a visit not only for its architecture but a fine series of frescoes reminiscent Giotto and for a 15th century portal Nanni di Bartolo.

For Renaissance architecture at finest one cannot do better than vi Urbino with its splendid Palazzo Duca and the sanctuary town of Loreto whe in the Santuario della Santa Casa a examples of the work of some of the fin sculptors of the period: Braman Laurana, Pontelli and Sansovino. The cities possess priceless paintings by Pie della Francesca, Melozzo da Forli, S norelli and others. The Museo Nazion in Ancona has paintings by the Veneti Crivelli and in the Palazzo Comunale Recanati is a fine Lotto.

The minor arts find expression in majolica to be seen at Urbino, Pésaro a other centres. The town of Castelfidar is noted not merely for two great victori that of Rodolfo da Varano against Ghibellines in 1355 and that of Gene Cialdini in 1860 against the Papal troo

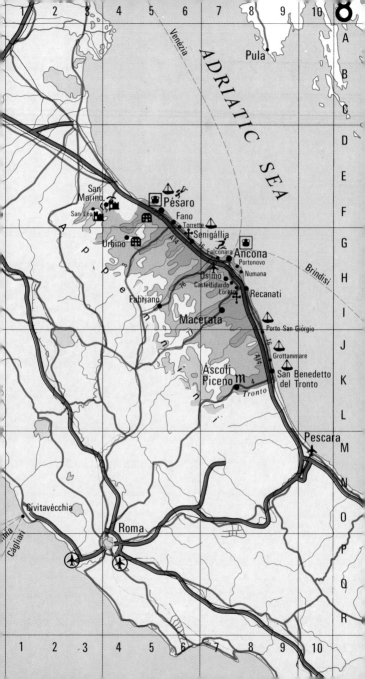

but also for the manufacture of accordions.

Literature owes a debt to Marche, for in the little town of Recanati was born the poet Giacomo Leopardi (1798–1837), a near-contemporary of Keats and Shelley. **Festivals** The first Sunday in August sees the colourful *Quintana* (a tournament in costume) in Ascoli Piceno. There is a parade through the streets, headed by the Mayor, after which cavaliers from every quarter of the town present themselves to their ladies to receive the traditional handkerchief to bring them good fortune, before engaging in combat to defeat the figure of a Moor. Fireworks follow in the evening, and all ends with the singing of a triumphal hymn in honour of the winner. In Fano at the beginning of August is the summer carnival, with a long file of allegorical carts, song, dancing and a Pantagruelian feast, ending with a huge bonfire in which the *Pupo*, representing the spirit of Carnival, is burnt.

Ancona   G7
(pop. 98,175) This busy Adriatic port is one of the most interesting cities of Marche. Its origins go back to 400 BC. First Greek, then Roman, at the fall of the Roman empire it became one of the five marine cities dependent on the Byzantine overlords of Ravenna. It then fell under the domination of the Church state, was in turn besieged by Frederick Barbarossa and occupied by the Malatestas, once again became a part of the Church state, and was finally united with the Kingdom of Italy in 1860.

The city rises sharply from sea level, and though it suffered grave damage during World War II, it is well endowed with pleasant squares – Piazza Cavour and Piazza Roma – and the streets in the new part are spacious and well planned. The really interesting part of the city is, however, the older section, over towards the headland from the heights of which the Romanesque cathedral looks down upon a tangle of narrow, twisted, cobbled streets. Here hide the Palazzo degli Anziani (the University, with a fine *Virgin and Child* by Titian and another by Crivelli); the Museo Nazionale, rich in treasures of antiquity; the church of San Domenico with a Titian *Crucifixion*; the quite charming church of Santa Maria della Piazza, a mixture of early Christian and Romanesque architecture that is well worth a visit; and in a nearby street the elaborate façade of the 15th-century Loggia dei Mercanti. Ancona has three interesting arches, the Arco Traiano and Arco Clementino below the cathedral, and the baroque Porta Pia nearer the har-

bour. In the harbour, too, is the fla rectangular Lazaretto (seamen's hospita designed by the 18th-century archite Vanvitelli who also designed the Arc Clementino.

Ancona is an excellent centre fro which to visit the inland towns **Recanati** – birthplace of the po Leopardi and the singer Gigli – the p grimage town of **Loreto**, and **Osimo, Ca telfidardo, Macerata**, all charming h towns rising from the fertile tableland Those preferring seaside amusemen may go by steamer to the nearby beach of **Passetto, Portonovo** and **Numan** while motor coaches travel south alor the Via Adria to the more distant reso of **Porto San Giórgio, Grottammare** an **San Benedetto del Tronto** (excelle camping facilities; 90km/56mi). Near beaches to the north are at **Torrett Palombina** and **Falconara,** the airport fo Ancona. *Pésaro 63km/39mi, Pescar 152/94.*

San Leo

Ascoli Piceno   K
(pop. 51,600) This is a pleasant ci situated on the plain where the Rive Tronto and Castellano converge; it is centre that attracts lovers of Roma remains and medieval monumen There is a charming little Roman ga Porta Gemina, dating back possibly the 1st century BC. Beyond it can be se a portion of the Roman wall.

Piazza Arringo is interesting for he stands the cathedral, the 16th-centu Bishops' Palace, and the Palazzo Con unale, behind the baroque façade which are the former palaces of the Con une and of the Arringo. Here is hous the local picture gallery which has pair ings by Titian, Giordano, Reni, Ma nasco and others.

oreto H8

(p. 8565) This pilgrimage town is ut 28km/17mi from Ancona. Its great erest for visitors is the Santuario della nta Casa, the alleged house of the donna which, according to the legend, s brought to Loreto by angels. The ctuary rises at the end of a lovely are in the centre of which is a fine h-century fountain. The façade is late naissance, and the three bronze doors r splendid reliefs; inside the church is eritable museum of works by Signorel-Sansovino, Raffaello da Montelupo d many others, while the Palazzo Apos-ico, the work of Sangallo and San-ino, houses a museum. There are a mber of hotels, but, as Loreto is a pil-nage town, accommodation is not y to find and is apt to be expensive.

esaro F5

(p. 70,500) This is another of the popu-seaside resorts along the Adriatic st, but it is also a busy centre of com-rce, which, after having been a Roman ony in its early days, was burned to the und during the Gothic invasions, then e to eminence again under the sig-ias of the Malatesta, Della Rovere and rza families.

Not surprisingly, with this historical kground, Pésaro has many interesting dings. The 15th-century Palazzo cale is among them, as is the church of Francesco and a fine Romanesque hedral of the 13th century. The Musei ici, including a collection of majolica d to be the finest in Italy, are housed in Palazzo Toschi-Mosca and are very l worth visiting. In addition to these, e is a fine picture gallery.

The music lyceum, the Conservatorio ssini, bears the name of the composer, o was a native of the city. His house l stands and holds a small museum. e theatre (1637) also bears his name. The splendid esplanade at Pésaro ends for 3km/2mi along the shore, and nd there are many panoramic walks to taken.

Pésaro is well-served by road and rail vices, and has numerous good hotels.

n Leo F3

Leo occupies a commanding posi-n on a height in the Apennines, about m/7mi southwest of San Marino. It is wned by a fortress, built originally in dieval days but enlarged in the 15th tury by Franceso di Giorgio Martini. e famous prisoner in this fortress was Palermitan Giuseppe Balsamo, better wn to the world as Cagliostro, one of world's best-known 'confidence men'. e he was imprisoned and here he died

in 1795. It is possible to visit his grim prison where there is a museum of arms and a small gallery of pictures.

The cathedral, said to have been erected on the ruins of a Roman temple, is a fine Romanesque-Gothic edifice.

The view from San Leo is extensive and very interesting.

Senigállia G6

(pop. 36,500) This agricultural, commercial and industrial city, 15km/9mi north of Ancona on the Adriatic coast, combines the industry of shipbuilding with that of tourism, fishing and all the possibilities of amusement that make for a splendid seaside holiday. It has a long stretch of sandy beach that slopes gently to meet the Adriatic.

Founded originally by the Gauls, later it became a Roman colony, passing into the possession of the Longobards when they invaded Italy. Later for some time it was a free *comune*, after which it passed under the *signoria* of the Malatesta family, and from that, under the jurisdiction of the Papacy.

There are some fine paintings to be seen in the 18th-century cathedral, and in the church of Santa Croce.

A pleasant excursion takes one to the church of Santa Maria delle Grazie, where there is a fine painting by the Umbrian painter Perugino.

Senigállia is becoming extremely popular with tourists, and there are numerous good hotels as well as camping facilities.

Urbino G4

(pop. 20,550) The great Palazzo Ducale, the 'city in the form of a palace', was begun in the year 1444. In 1468 the architect Luciano Laurana took charge of the work for the illustrious *signore*, Federico da Montefeltro who founded there one of the greatest cultural centres of his time. The palace rises on a hill and the two tall towers of its façade look down over the valley in truly ducal fashion. The interior courtyard is simple and elegant, and the whole palace is a series of splendid halls and rooms in which are displayed art treasures of great beauty and considerable value, for the palace now houses the Galleria Nazionale delle Marche and has works by Raphael, Piero della Francesca, Titian and many others. A whole morning or afternoon is barely sufficient to see and savour everything.

The 14th-century church of San Domenico boasts a fine terracotta by Luca della Robbia in the lunette of the main portal, and the 15th-century house of Raphael, the Casa di Raffaello, can also be visited. *Pésaro 36km/22mi.*

UMBRIA

Umbria, Holy Umbria, the green heart of Italy, is one of the favourite regions for Italians as well as for foreign visitors. Situated in the centre, it is the only peninsular region entirely surrounded by land. Largely mountainous, bordered on the east by the Apennines, its main watercourses are the upper basin of the Tévere (Tiber) and the Nera. In the northwest lies Lago Trasimeno, the largest of Italy's peninsular lakes, famous in history as being the site of Hannibal's defeat of the Romans in 217 BC, familiar to art-lovers as appearing in the background of many paintings by Perugino and other Umbrian painters.

There are three islands on Trasimeno: Maggiore, rich in memories of St Francis of Assisi, Minore and Polvese. Steamers ply across the lake from Passignano to Castiglione del Lago, touching Maggiore en route. It is a pleasant day's outing to cross the lake mid-morning, visiting the church at Castiglione del Lago, where hangs a reputed Raphael of the Madonna with the Christ-child, then taking lunch in a *trattoria*, or eating a *tosto* at a bar before making the return journey.

Not far from the industrial city of Terni in the south of the region is the spectacular Cascata delle Marmore (waterfall), the harnessing of which has proved a rich source of hydroelectric power.

Umbria was Etruscan before it was Roman and both civilizations have left their mark; Perúgia has no fewer than three Etruscan arches, Orvieto boasts Etruscan tombs, and Roman remains are to be seen in such unexpected spots as the little hill town of Spello, as well as in such better-known cities as Gúbbio, Spoleto, Nórcia.

It is said that more than twenty thousand saints have been born in Umbria; three at least are outstanding, San Benedetto of Nórcia and his twin sister Scolastica, born in 480 AD, and St Francis, born in Assisi in 1181.

Life in Umbria has always had strong religious and Papal associations. During the 13th century both Orvieto and Perúgia sheltered exiled Popes. Perúgia has been the scene of five Papal conclaves; four Popes have died there. Small wonder that Umbria is a region of splendid religious buildings, Romanesque and Gothic, and of painters such as Perugino and Pinturicchio, who have excelled in religious art.

The Middle Ages seem still alive today as one walks around the narrow, tortuous streets of Perúgia, Bevagna, Todi, Nórc — in fact, in almost any town of the reion. In Gúbbio medievalism seems blend with other-worldliness, making different from all other Umbrian citi Here is a little city where many houses the older part have 'doors of the dead' extra doors, close to the front door but a higher level, walled up, except wher corpse is taken out of the house for buri

Many of the cities are in themselv museums of art and architecture; great fountain in front of the cathedral Perúgia is the combined work of Nic and Giovanni Pisano; the huge basil of St Francis in Assisi has magnifice frescoes by Cimabue, Giotto, Simo Martini; the cathedral in Orvieto, w the external reliefs by Maitani, the fr coes by Signorelli inside, springs up the vision like an exotic flower in a c tage garden; Todi, Bevagna and ma other provincial centres have munici squares that are a miracle of perfecti Nature, too, has showered riches up Umbria; from the bastions of its h towns one looks out upon scenes of h and valley of unforgettable beauty; not from Spoleto is another example Nature at its loveliest, in the Fonti Clitunno (Springs of Clitumnus), su by poets from Virgil to Byron and C ducci.

Festivals The festivals of Umbria many and picturesque: Assisi – *Cal dimaggio*, 1 May, the celebration of Return of Spring; the main square is scene of the choosing of the *Madon Primavera* from among the prettiest gi of the city, all in fancy dress. Gúbbio Festival of the *Ceri* (Candles), 15 M which are not candles, but huge pillars decorated wood on which are mount the three patron saints of the city, bor through the street in procession and lat borne up the hill at a running pace by t

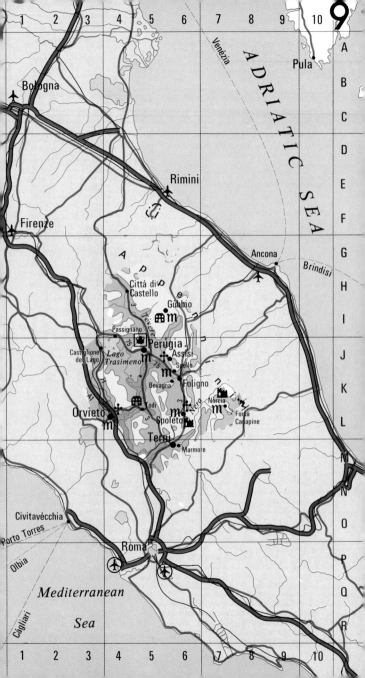

strongest youths of the district. Spello —
Corpus Domini, streets are carpeted in
flowers arranged in picturesque designs.
Orvieto — Corpus Domini, a caged dove
is flown on a wire over the heads of the
spectators in the main square before the
cathedral; the cage is surrounded by
fireworks which are ignited before the
flight begins. Foligno — The *Quintana*,
September (2nd Sunday), a parade in costume followed by a tournament of riders
whose aim it is to take a ring from the
outstretched hand of the figure of a Moor.

Assisi   J6

(pop. 25,372) The city of St Francis
seems impregnated with the spirit of that
gentle saint who died at the age of 44 in
1226. True, Assisi has other memories;
beneath the Temple of Minerva, now
transformed into the church of Santa
Maria sopra Minerva, are the remains of a
Roman forum, but the ever-present
thought in the minds of visitors is of the
beloved San Francesco.

The first great monument to visit is the
Basilica di San Francesco, begun in
1228. In the lower church are frescoes by
Simone Martini in the chapel of St Martin; there are also charming stained glass
windows, possibly to the design of the
same artist. In the upper church are frescoes by Cimabue, the master of Giotto,
and the splendid series, the *Story of St
Francis* by Giotto and his school. The
body of the saint, not discovered until the
beginning of the last century, is in the
simple crypt beneath the lower church.
Not one, but many visits are necessary to
savour to the full the beauty of this huge
basilica.

Another interesting church is that of
Santa Chiara, the founder of the Order of
the *Clarisse* (Poor Clares). This is a
Gothic building of the second half of the
13th century, with impressive arched
supports on the exterior, a huge rose window, the crucifix which according to the
legend spoke to St Francis, and a painting
on wood of Santa Chiara (1283). The
church of San Rufino, where St Francis
was confirmed, is a splendid example of
Umbrian Romanesque architecture; the
façade contains three rose windows, a
beautifully decorated central door and
two side doors. Unfortunately, the
interior was rebuilt in a manneristic style
that did not blend well with the exterior;
however, changes are now being made.

Leaving the town by the Porta Nuova
(east), and descending sharply for a mile
or so, one comes to the first convent of the
Poor Clares, San Damiano, where St
Francis was converted. The tiny church
is unspoiled and tranquil, and more than
any other place in Assisi speaks of the

spirit of the Saint. Some 2-3km/2mi we
of the town lies the great **Basilica di San
Maria degli Angeli** (16th-century) whic
houses the humble little church, the Po
ziuncola, St Francis' first church, and th
spot where he died, *'nudo sulla terra nud*
('naked on the naked earth').

The **Carceri**, the site of the solita
hermitage where he used to pray,
8km/5mi from Assisi. Another walk
short drive is to **Rivotorto** where a san
tuary rises over two huts, once lived in b
the saint. *Perúgia 24km/15mi.*

Gúbbio   I

(pop. 34,606) This is one of Umbria
many interesting cities, particularly
mid-May when the *Festa dei Ceri* is hel
an ancient pageant in which the youn
men of the city, dressed in costume, rac
through the narrow streets in three team
each team bearing an enormous woode
platform on which is mounted the figu
of a saint. After a banquet in the Palazz
dei Consoli, they race up the steep hill
the sanctuary of Sant' Ubaldo, where th
figures are deposited, to be fetched dow
again the following year. The view fro
the sanctuary is fine, and it can also b
reached by cable railway. In the Palazz
dei Consoli is a fine collection of works
art, and the famous Tavole Eugubin
seven bronze tablets covered with lette
ing and dating back well over 2000 year
The Palazzo Ducale, the Municipio an
the Palazzo del Bargello are all worth vi
iting, as is the cathedral. One wall of th
church of San Francesco was the wall of
house in which the saint once foun
refuge. In the church of Santa Mari
Nuova are some charming frescoes by th
Umbrian artist Nelli. The city also has
Roman theatre in which open air perfo
mances of Shakespeare and othe
dramatists are given during summe
evenings. *Assisi 57km/35mi, Perúg*
40km/25mi.

Nórcia   K

(pop. 7629) This is a good winter spor
centre. On the road from Spoleto, th
scenery becomes grander and grande
hills become mountains, and the litt
stream that runs beside the road turn
into a mountain torrent. It is an ancie
city, home at one time of the mother of th
Roman emperor Vespasian; in mo
recent days the birthplace of Sa
Benedetto (480—546 AD) and his twi
sister, Santa Scolastica. It was Sa
Benedetto who founded the religiou
Order of the *Benedettini*, and in the pri
cipal square of the little town is a statue
the saint. The small fortress was built
1554 for Pope Julius III; in the san
square is the church of San Benedett
7th-century with a 13th-century façad

he crypt once formed part of a Roman ouse, allegedly the house in which the aint and his sister were born. The hurch of Sant'Agostino is one of the ost interesting in this area, with altars a local baroque – unpainted – and with ome delightful, well-preserved frescoes f the Umbrian school. In a niche behind e altar is a precious statue in wood of an Sebastian, a favourite in country hurches for his power against the ague.

Forca Canapine (13km/8mi) is a plendid winter sports centre, and the otel of the same name is excellent, as is s restaurant. *Spoleto 50km/31mi.*

Orvieto L4

op. 25,090) This is one of the most picuresque cities of Umbria; built on a nound of tufa rock, it is breathtaking, hether one approaches it by rail or by ad. Several times Orvieto has been the fuge of Popes, and it has always been osely linked with Papal affairs. The nagnificent cathedral bursts upon one's sion as one makes one's way through e medieval streets. The building was egun in 1260. The splendid Gothic çade is superimposed upon a typical asilica; the architect is thought to have een Fra Bevignate, but some authorities e inclined to regard it as the work of rnolfo di Cambio. In 1309 a Sienese chitect, Lorenzo Maitano, took over the ork and changed the concept of the ructure. His façade is a splendid exame of Pisan Gothic, terminating in pin-

e Duomo, Orvieto

nacles clearly inspired by the French. The four pilasters decorated with bas-reliefs are superb. The mosaics are mostly 17th-century; the only remaining 14th-century ones are in the Victoria and Albert Museum, London. The interior is rich in works of art. In the Cappella di San Patrizio is a splendid series of frescoes, the work of Signorelli 1499-1504; the chapel on the other side of the cathedral houses the Miraculous Host, which prompted the building of the cathedral when it oozed blood in the hands of a doubting priest.

Another interesting church is that of San Domenico, probably the first church dedicated to the founder of the Order of Dominicans, of which, thanks to a building project of the early part of this century, only the transept remains. However, the lovely funeral monument to Cardinal de Bray, the work of Arnolfo di Cambio, is still there. The oldest church in the city is that of San Giovenale (1004). *Arezzo 119km/74mi, Roma 126km/78mi.*

Perúgia J5

(pop. 116,710) Perúgia is well situated, and is an excellent centre from which to visit other cities of this agreeably green heart of Italy. Almost 500m/1640ft above sea level, surrounded by the foothills of the Apennines, it rarely becomes uncomfortably hot in the summer months. Perúgia was originally an Etruscan city, and in its museum is a fine collection of relics of that time; the Arco Etrusco is a magnificent portal at the foot of Via Rocchi and Via Bartolo, the two steep streets running downwards from behind the cathedral. This archway is also known as the Arco d'Augusto, for it is a composite construction, with not only a Roman arch superimposed upon the original Etruscan, but also a Renaissance *loggetta* which was added during the 16th century.

The principal street, Corso Vannucci, runs from the Piazza IV Novembre down to the delightful gardens, Giardino Carducci, overlooking the fertile valley and the low surrounding hills. The cathedral is Gothic of the late 14th and 15th century, with some excellent stained glass; in its museum are some fine works of art by Umbrian and Tuscan artists, but the focal point in this square is the magnificent Fontana Maggiore, constructed in the late 13th century to celebrate the completion of an aqueduct bringing water to Perúgia from Montepulciano, and decorated with bas-reliefs of striking beauty by Nicola and Giovanni Pisano. The enormous Palazzo dei Priori occupies the other side of the square and was built over a period of more than three centuries; the oldest part is that facing the square, the newest is in Corso Vannucci, and the whole is a harmonious blending of the various styles. The palace also houses the Galleria Nazionale dell'Umbria – a splendid collection by Perugino, Pinturicchio, Duccio and others. Farther down the Corso is the Collegio di Cambio.

A pleasant walk from the square is down the steep Via dei Priori, a typical medieval street, which sweeps round into an open piazza in which are situated the delightful Oratorio di San Bernardino, with a façade decorated in bas-reliefs by Agostino di Duccio, and the huge ruined church of San Francesco al Prato. To the right is Via A. Pascoli, tree-lined and pleasant, which leads to Palazzo Gallenga, now the seat of the University for Foreigners, where students from all the nations come to study the language, art, literature and music of Italy. From Piazza Fortebraccio in front of the university, a walk up the steep Corso Garibaldi brings one to the charming little church of Sant'Angelo, worth visiting also for the views beyond. Another church that demands a visit is San Pietro, reached through the Porta San Pietro (another example of the work of Agostino di Duccio). The church is a museum in itself; note particularly the 16th-century courtyard, the unusual bell-tower, the magnificent choir stalls – with a superb view from the centre of the choir – and the paintings.

These are merely the chief points of interest in a city that has much more to offer to those who have time to wander lazily through its streets. An absorbing half-day excursion is to Ipogeo dei Volumni, an Etruscan tomb in the suburb of San Giovanni.

Spoleto   L6

(pop. 36,769) Spoleto is high above sea level and is dominated by a 14th-century fortress, with a spectacular viaduct nearby. Its civilization has developed from Umbrian, Etruscan and Roman origins and a Roman theatre, Roman walls, gates and a Roman house, allegedly once lived in by the mother of the emperor Vespasian, remain as witnesses of its early splendour. When the Longobards invaded Italy in the 6th century, the city became one of their dukedoms, and eventually it formed part of the Church state. Many of its streets still have a medieval aspect. The splendid cathedral of Santa Maria Assunta, a Romanesque building of the 13th century, has a marvellous mosaic high up on the west front, and an attractive portico of more recent date. The interior is baroque, with a bronze above the main portal by Bernini. There

is a fine pavement, and behind the ma[in] altar a famous fresco by Filippo Lipp[i] begun in 1467. In the Sacristy is a famou[s] crucifix painted on the parchme[nt] stretched on wood, the work of Alber[to] Sozio (1187). In the first chapel on th[e] right as one enters are frescoes by Pi[n]turicchio. The cathedral stands at o[ne] end of a sloping piazza in which, durin[g] the annual Festival of the Two Worl[d] (July), open air performances of suc[h] works as Verdi's *Requiem* are given.

Another lovely Lombard-Romanesqu[e] church is that of Sant'Eufemia nearb[y] with a charming ladies' gallery and a va[l]uable and anonymous triptych behind th[e] altar.

One has to obtain keys and permissio[n] to visit the Roman house and the littl[e] disused church of Santi Giovanni [e] Paolo, but both are worth the troubl[e] particularly the latter as among its man[y] frescoes is an extraordinary one depictin[g] the murder of Thomas à Becket. Farth[er] from the centre of the city are two oth[er] extremely interesting churches, San Pietro with its wonderful Romanes[que] que façade, and the church of San Salv[a]tore, constructed at the end of the 4th [or] the beginning of the 5th century (th[e] church is just beyond the cemetery). Th[e] 13th-century Palazzo Pubblico is now t[he] home of the art gallery, and another fi[ne] 14th-century palace, the Palazzo de[l] Signoria, houses the Museo Civico.

A pleasant excursion is to **Fonti d[el] Clitunno** (springs), 12km/7mi along t[he] main road to Foligno. These springs ha[ve] been sung by poets through the centuri[es] and half an hour is well spent wanderin[g] in the shade of the poplars and weepin[g] willows; a pair of swans glide over th[e] waters, and all around is peace. A litt[le] farther along the road is a tiny 5th-centu[ry] church. *Perúgia 57km/35mi, Rom[e] 133km/83mi.*

Todi   L[6]

(pop. 20,659) Todi stands on a heigh[t] like many Umbrian towns; it is encircle[d] by three sets of walls – Etruscan, Roma[n] and medieval. The main square is a[n] almost perfect example of mediev[al] architecture, with a Romanesqu[e] cathedral and three palaces: the Palazz[o] del Popolo and the Palazzo del Capita[no] del Popolo, both 13th century, and th[e] Palazzo dei Priori (14th century). It h[as] other interesting churches: San Fo[r]tunato, Gothic with delightful cho[ir] stalls, and at the foot of the entrance ste[ps] a statue of Jacopone da Todi, the 13[th] century writer; and a charming litt[le] church, built to a design by Cola di Ca[p]rarola, the Tempio di Santa Maria de[lla] Consolazione. *Perúgia 47km/29mi.*

LÁZIO

Lázio received its name from its earliest inhabitants, the Latini, at a time when it consisted of the Tyrrhenian coast south of the Tévere (Tiber), embraced by the Lazial and Tiburtine Hills, a territory that merited its name, which apparently indicated 'plainland'.

With the passing of time the area dominated by Roma increased and in the Middle Ages the name was abandoned, while the various additions took on different designations. In 1870, however, papal power ceased and the united province around Roma was established under its ancient name of Lázio, which nowadays extends north and east as far as the Apennines, south to the northern bank of the River Garigliano, with the Tyrrhenian forming its western boundary.

Mountains, hills, plain, one-time marshes (now mostly reclaimed) and a lengthy coastline – Lázio has a little of everything. South of the Tévere, the once volcanic nature of many of the hills has rendered the soil rich enough to encourage intensive cultivation. Progressing north and east towards the Apennines, one encounters first of all low, calcareous hills, rising to great heights along the northeastern boundary of the region.

Lakes are mostly of volcanic origin. Lago di Bolsena, Lago di Bracciano and the small Lago di Vico all come into this category, as do the little lakes, Albano and Nemi in the Colli Albani (Alban Hills).

Lying between the two Papal strongholds of Orvieto and Viterbo is Lago di Bolsena, in the heart of Etruscan territory, near such centres as Tarquínia where there is a fine Etruscan museum, and nearby some splendid painted tombs, Vetralla where there are unexplored rock tombs and Tuscánia with its lovely Romanesque churches.

The town Bolsena, too, has its history, for here is the church where, in the year 1243, in defiance of the doubtings of a sceptical celebrant, the Host dropped blood on the corporal and even down to the pavement before the altar. The corporal that featured is kept in a special reliquary in the cathedral of Orvieto.

Coming to less weighty matters, near the southeasterly corner of this lake is the little town of Montefiascone, long famous for its wine, the very wine that features in a sad little tale of the German Bishop Fugger of olden times, a gentleman who appreciated good wine so much

that he was wont to send his servant ahead of him on journeys to test the wine, and, if he found it good, to mark the place with the word *Est*. When he arrived at Montefiascone, the servant found the wine so superior to all the others that he wrote *Est, est, est*. When the bishop arrived, he called for the wine, sampled it, and was so entirely in agreement with his servant's verdict that he drank far too much of it, and did not live to tell the tale. Travellers have been warned – the wine IS good, but if tempted to over-indulge, remember the fate of poor Bishop Fugger.

Another pleasant lake is Bracciano, about 35km/22mi northwest of Roma. The eighth Italian lake in size, its waters abound in fish and in the town above is the splendid 6-towered Orsini castle of the 15th century.

After a busy but exhausting time in Roma, a visit to Lakes Albano and Nemi in the nearby Alban Hills, is agreeable. The former, elliptical in shape, is near the little town of the same name, which alas, is not best equipped to welcome visitors. It is well to proceed to Nemi nearby. This is a smaller lake, almost completely circular, lying far down within a surround of wooded slopes. There is a strawberry festival here in June, but it is usually possible to find exquisite strawberries as late as September. Both these lakes are of volcanic origin.

Down on the shore stands a museum in which are housed two Roman ships. Be warned. It is a good 2km/1mi down the slope, and on the return journey the 2km seem to have grown considerably. You will have asked in the town where to find the museum, and you will have been told 'Down there'; you have neglected to ask 'Is it open?', and consequently no-one has mentioned that probably it is NOT. The walk back is pleasant, but very long.

If one is driving and has a day to spare

ile in the vicinity of Roma, there are
any interesting places within reach.
Travelling from Roma along the Via
silina and branching off to the left after
out 37km/23mi, one comes first of all to
lestrina, a picturesque city of about
,000 inhabitants, 515m/1690ft above
a level and presiding over a wide valley,
pical of the scenery of this not very
ell-known part of Italy. Here in 1525
s born the famous composer who took
s name from that of the city. There is an
teresting museum and the immense
mple of Fortuna Primigenia (8th cen-
ry BC) and among the treasures in the
useum is a wonderful mosaic depicting
gypt at a moment when the River Nile
s in flood.

From Palestrina, retracing one's tracks
e can branch off again from Via Casili-
, this time to the right, to take a look at
gni, interesting for its surrounding
lls. Back once again to Via Casilina
e should travel on to Anagni (pop.
,500) a medieval city with a fine
manesque cathedral that has a splen-
d mosaic floor and lovely Byzantine-
e frescoes of the 13th century. It was in
s cathedral that Pope Alexander III
nounced the excommunication of
rbarossa. It was once the favourite
elling place of Pope Boniface VIII,
ose palace, now converted to other
es, still stands, and it was here in the
ar 1303 that William of Nogaret dared
slap the face of the aged prelate, a blow
m which he never recovered.

From Anagni, a winding road to the left
ngs one to the thermal town of Fiuggi,
ere those who wish may pause awhile
'take the waters'. Leaving Fiuggi and
ing Road No. 155 – which is fairly
ading – when one arrives at the turn-
g for Collepardo, it is as well to proceed
yond this point and uphill until arriv-
g at the Certosa (Charterhouse) of
isulti, which comes surprisingly into
w in the midst of a small forest of oak
es; a huge concentration of religious
ildings around the ancient church of
n Bartolomeo. There is much to visit
re, the great and small cloisters, the
apter house and an enchanting 17th-
ntury chemist's shop. One can also buy
excellent liqueur distilled from the
cally-grown herbs.

From Trisulti and down the winding
ad again, one goes on to Alatri, of about
,000 inhabitants, a city more than
0m/1640ft above sea level and famous
r its massive cyclopic walls which date
ck to the 4th century BC. The central
rt of the town has preserved a medieval
pect.

Driving back to Roma, you will probably feel that your day's excursion has
been rewarding.

The climate in Lázio varies from typically maritime along the coast, to temp-
erate with colder winters in the river valleys, then, as one nears the mountains, it
becomes continental with severe winters and, along the slopes of the Apennines, the possibility of heavy rain.
Roma has rain on an average of 80 days
per annum, and an average annual rain-
fall of 760mm/30in, the wet periods
reaching their peak usually from
October to December, with the
minimum in July.

Festivals Good Friday in Sezze, about
15km/9mi from Latina, has a procession
in costume representing, among other
things, the re-awakening of the dead – on
the men's costumes are painted
extremely realistic skeletons. Corpus
Domini is celebrated in many provincial
towns, Genzano di Roma for one, by 'pav-
ing' the streets with pictures composed
entirely of tiny flowers. In Viterbo 3 September sees the Procession of Santa
Rosa, in memory of a young girl who in
1243 saved the people of her town from
the tyranny of Frederick II; on the eve of
the festival a huge papier-mâché edifice
in the form of a bell-tower, with a niche
containing the image of the saint, is borne
through the streets by 80 men in white.

Cittá del Vaticano (Vatican City)   J4

Cittá del Vaticano, the seat of the Pope
and his court of ecclesiastical and civic
dignitaries, is an independent State, an
enclave with its own coinage and stamps
and its own radio transmitting station.
Constituted on 11 February, 1929 under
the Lateran Treaty between Italy and the
Holy See, it comprises the Basilica di San
Pietro in Vaticano, the Vatican Palace
and precincts, while the three basilicas of
Santa Maria Maggiore, San Giovanni
Laterano, San Paolo fuori le Mura are
included in its extra-territorial rights.

Roma (Rome)   J5

(pop. 2,364,727) Roma, true heart of Italy,
is not only capital of the Republic but, in
the Cittá del Vaticano, capital of the
entire Catholic world. Throughout Italy
one sees representations of a she-wolf
suckling twins, and on the left-hand side
of the slope rising to the Campidoglio
(Capitol – 1), in a cage let into the rock, is
another she-wolf, a reminder of the
mythical founding of the city. Ancient
Roma was famous for its power, its
architecture, its statuary, its culture and
its cruelty. The Colosseo (2) was scene of

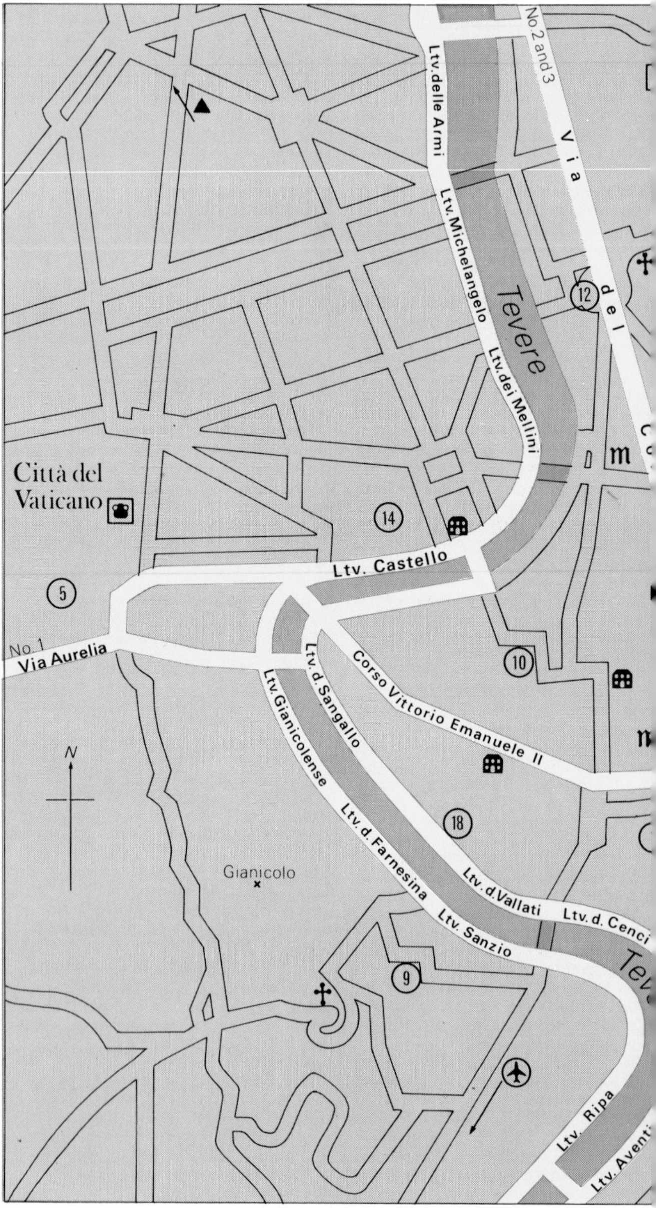

Città del
Vaticano

No 2 and 3

Ltv. delle Armi

Ltv. Michelangelo

Tevere

Ltv. dei Mellini

V i a   d e l

⑫

(5)

⑭

Ltv. Castello

No.1
Via Aurelia

⑩

Ltv. Gianicolense

Ltv. d Sangallo

Corso Vittorio Emanuele II

N

⑱

Gianicolo
×

Ltv. d. Farnesina

Ltv. d'Vallati

Ltv.d. Cenci

Ltv. Sanzio

Tev

⑨

Ltv. Ripa

Ltv. Aventi

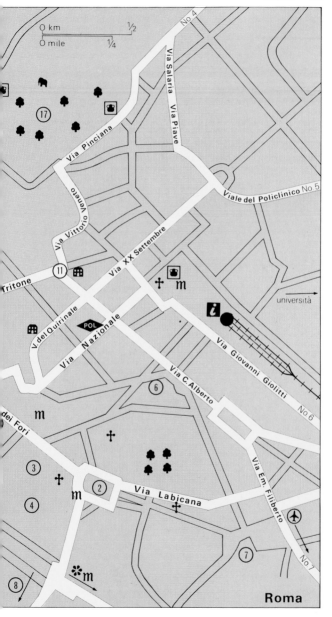

Roma

gladiatorial fights; the catacombs of San Callisto, Sant'Agnese and others are a tragic reminder of the privations suffered by Christians until the Edict of Milan (313 AD) allowed them freedom to worship openly. Sacked twice during the 5th century AD, Roma was reduced to a travesty of its former glory; Pope Gregory, writing nearly 50 years after the second disaster, speaks of a Roma with more empty spaces than houses, more sheep in its streets than human beings. But as the power of the Empire declined, that of the Church state grew, and the city flourished. For about 70 years following the year 1305, the Papacy established itself in Avignon, with a corresponding reduction of the population and standard of living in Roma; the Papacy returned, and once again Roma rose triumphant. In 1527 it was sacked by the combined forces of Spain and the Austrian Empire – it has survived to become a city which one can barely hope to know in a lifetime.

Imperial Roma. Relics of the ancient city are to be seen primarily in the region of the Foro Romano (3) and Colosseo where one may walk for a considerable time (preferably in the early morning or evening) tracing the outlines of the imperial city, the arches of Titus, Constantine and Janus, the Ara Pacis (Altar of Peace), the columns of Trajan and Marcus Aurelius, the Terme di Caracalla. From the Palatine Hill (4) with remains of Roman palaces one can wander down the Via Appia with its umbrella pines and tombs of famous Romans.

Christian Roma The present Basilica di San Pietro (5) was designed by Bramante (16th century) and built on the site of the previous basilica erected by Constantine on his conversion. The dome was the creation of Michelangelo, as is the lovely *Pietà* in the interior. The canopy over the altar and the circular colonnade in the Piazza are by Bernini, who also designed the Royal Staircase in the Vaticano. The baroque façade was designed by Maderno. The Vaticano is full of treasures: the frescoes of Michelangelo in the Sistine and Pauline chapels, the sculptured group of Laocoon (50 BC) in the Museo Pio-Clementino, the suite of rooms decorated by Raphael, the Pinacoteca, the Borgia Apartments. All these museums are open only 09.00 to 14.00.

The church of Santa Maria Maggiore (6) is 4th century, restored in the 16th century, with some fine mosaics of the 5th and 13th century. The main façade was designed by Fuga in the 18th century. San Giovanni in Laterano (7) has lovely cloisters, and nearby is the chapel containing Scala Santo, the stairs down

which Christ supposedly walked at Passion. They were brought to Rom Elena, the mother of Constantine. Basilica di San Paolo fuori le Mura rebuilt 1823, has a beautifully sculp Easter candle by Fuga, a confessio altar by Arnolfo di Cambio, and lo Romanesque cloisters. Santa Maria Trastevere (9) is a Romanesque build with fine medieval mosaics in the ap

Squares Roma is a city of lovely squa The Campidoglio was designed Michelangelo; the bronze equestr statue of Marcus Aurelius dates from AD. In Piazza Navona (10) is the Fo tain of the Rivers, designed by Berr who also designed the Fontana Tritone in Piazza Barberini (11). Pia del Popolo (12), with the churches Santa Maria dei Miracoli and Sa Maria di Montesanto, was planned a the sack of Roma in 1527, but the 1 century architect Valadier is larg responsible for its classical appearan One of the most picturesque comb tions of square and architecture is great staircase designed 1725–26 by Sanctis, and leading from Piazza Spagna (13) to the church of La Tri dei Monti. In a house to the right of th stairs Keats died in 1821.

Other Sights The bulk of Castel S Angelo (14) was a Roman sepulchre was transformed into a fortress in the 1 century. Popes have fled to it for saf Benvenuto Cellini was one of the prisoners who managed to escape from The huge white monument to Vitto Emanuele II stands near the Piazza V ezia (15) and contains the Tomb of Unknown Soldier. One of the lovel parks is the Pincio (16) which forms, w the Zoo, part of the great expanse of gr surrounding Villa Borghese (17). Thi now a museum which includes Titia *Sacred and Profane Love,* Canov statue of Pauline, Napoleon's sister, Raphael's *Deposition.* The Palazzo F nese (18) and the Museo Capitolino (should also be visited.

Excursions In addition to the magr cent fountains of the Villa d'Este, **Tiv** there are fabulous natural cascades in Via Gregoriana and in the cathedra splendid 13th-century *Deposition* wood, consisting of five figures. Not from Tivoli is **Hadrian's Villa** (2nd c tury BC) where there are the remains various buildings copied from those Emperor had seen or heard about. **Ca Gandolfo,** in a delightful position ab Lake Albano, is the summer residence the Pope. **Nemi** (4km/2½mi) is mirro in its lake, and is famous for its delici strawberries and wines. **Frascati** is a to

uperb villas, parks and fountains. Its
⁀e dates back to the time when it was
⁀nsignificant village and the roofs of its
⁀ses were covered with *frasche* (small
⁀ghs). **Óstia Antica** can be reached by
⁀ropolitan railway. Excavations have
⁀overed a city of the 4th century BC
⁀ a theatre, forum, flour mills, a
⁀ghtful fountain of Amore and Psyche
⁀some mosaic pavements, relics of a
⁀t port with a population of some
⁀,000. Not far away is the modern
⁀rt of Óstia.

rmation Roma is so vast that it is
⁀ntial to take one or more of the tours
⁀nised by CIT, Piazza Esedra. Other
⁀ul addresses are: Ente Provinciale per
⁀urismo, 11 Via Parigi; Comune di
⁀a, Assessorato per il Turismo, 68
⁀Milano; Rome Automobile Club,
Via Cristoforo Colombo.

rquínia   **H2**
⁀. 12,000) Visitors following the
⁀es of Etruscan civilization may well
⁀themselves travelling to Tarquínia.
⁀nd more than 5km/3mi from the
⁀rennian Sea, this small town gives
⁀the idea of being remote, not just
⁀the sea, but from the entire world.
⁀riginally Etruscan, it became impor-
⁀in Roman times, but when Roma fell,
⁀Tarquinians retired to the upper part
⁀heir hilly city and reinforced their
⁀ty with walls and a stronghold. In the
⁀dle Ages many of the houses erected
⁀towers of the type generally
⁀ciated with the Tuscan city of San
⁀ignano, many of which remain to
⁀day. There are three interesting
⁀anesque churches, Santa Maria di
⁀ello, where there is a charming cos-
⁀sque pulpit, San Pancrazio and San
⁀cesco, but the chief attraction is
⁀quínia is the Museo Nazionale,
⁀h is housed in the 15th-century Vit-
⁀chi palace. Here are to be seen Etrus-
⁀remains of extreme interest; the col-
⁀on of vases is splendid.
⁀ear the city are Etruscan tombs in the
⁀opolis which date from the 7th to the
⁀century BC. Among the finest of these
⁀ted tombs is that of the Auguri (end
⁀h century BC), the Tomb of the Baron
⁀l of the 6th century BC) and the Tomb
⁀e Leopards (end of 5th century BC).
⁀here are many interesting walks and
Lido di Tarquínia, about 5km/3mi
⁀y, has a fine stretch of sand.
⁀here is good accommodation to be
⁀, but this is limited, so book early.

voli   **I6**
⁀. 33,200) If staying in Roma, a visit to
⁀oli makes a welcome break from the
⁀le of the city.

Of ancient origin, Tivoli was much
liked by the Romans as a holiday centre.
The Temple of Vesta goes back to the last
years of the Republic, as does the Temple
of the Sybil.

The poet Horace loved Tivoli and had
a house in or near the city.

The Emperor Hadrian (2nd century
AD) had a villa built there, in the grounds
of which were erected replicas of the
monumental delights he had enjoyed
seeing during his many travels to distant
places.

The Villa Gregoriana is one of the
great attractions of the city, not least
because of the celebrated waterfalls
within its grounds, and the Villa d'Este, a
16th-century transformation of an
ancient convent, with splendid gardens
and fantastic fountains,is another of the
sights not to be missed.

The cathedral has works in the Sacristy
attributed to Bernini and the Romanesque church of San Silvestro merits a
visit.

Viterbo   **G3**
(pop. 48,120) This city, of Etruscan
origin and later a Roman colony,
developed greatly during the 10th century. It was a seat of the Popes during the
period of dissidence between the Popes
and Roma, and was the seat of the first
Papal conclave. After a period of contesta-
tion between Popes and emperors, in
1375 it came finally under the domination of the Papal state.

Traces of Pelasgic walls still remain,
and there are many evidences still
remaining of the one-time medieval
splendour; the whole district of San Pel-
legrino, for instance. The Palazzo Papale
(13th century) is a fine example of Gothic
Viterbese architecture, and has an
exquisite loggia.

The cathedral of San Lorenzo, originally built in 1192, but later restored in
1681, has a fine 14th-century bell-tower, a
baptismal font of the 15th century and the
tomb of Letizia Bonaparte.

In the church of San Sisto (11th to 12th
century) is a baptismal font of Roman
days.

The fountains of the city are famous,
particularly the Fontana Grande (1279)
and those in Piazza della Morte and
Piazza Pianoscarano.

There are thermal curative establishments, and around the city are delightful
walks to such interesting places as the
ruins of Ferentum, or the Villa Lante, a
fine Renaissance building by Vignola
with statuary by Giambologna at Bag-
naia, and the Cistercian abbey of San
Martino al Cimino.

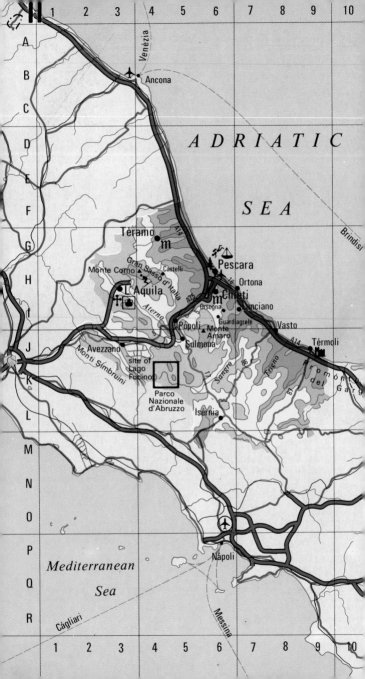

ABRUZZI AND MOLISE

Here are two more regions which are associated, with a coastline that runs from the mouth of the River Tronto northwards to just above the Gargano peninsula; on the west and south it is bordered by Lázio, Campania and the northern boundary of Púglia.

Historically the two regions are distinct; there is the Abruzzi proper, which includes the provinces of Chieti, Téramo, Pescara and l'Aquila, and Molise, which occupies the territory of Campobasso.

The highest peaks of peninsular Italy rise in the heart of the Abruzzi. There is the Gran Sasso which in Monte Corno arrives at 2914m/9560ft above sea level, and La Maiella where Monte Amaro is 2795m/9170ft. These chains of mountains, together with the Simbruini and della Meta mountains, make up a vast region of high peaks, with occasional large valleys.

Molise extends south of La Maiella; its physical aspect is not unlike that of the Abruzzi, and as one draws nearer to Campania the mountains become less lofty.

The rivers run perpendicularly to the coastline. Some, such as the Aterno, near Pescara, cut deep gorges down the mountain sides.

In spite of the high percentage of mountainous country, there is a good amount of forest and agricultural land. Among the major crops comes first of all potatoes, followed closely by wheat and maize; along the coast vegetables grow well. There is a certain amount of vine growing and olive groves; sugarbeet is also grown. Oddly enough the Abruzzi stand high in apiculture; saffron, which one time grew in considerable quantity round l'Aquila, is now declining.

Among the rich forests stands out the Parco Nazionale d'Abruzzi (National Park of the Abruzzi), instituted with the idea of protecting the region's wildlife.

Sheep-grazing has always thrived, the mountains providing summer pastures, the plains a milder winter climate; some fishing is carried out along the coast.

In spite of its resources of water, which have led to the installation of a considerable number of electric networks, there is a lack of great industries, except for sugar-refining in the region of the one-time lake Fucino and some chemical industries. There are, however, a fair number of smaller industries: pottery-making, particularly at Castelli in the province of Téramo, distilleries – the liqueur Aurum is a local product – and the making of 'confetti' (sugared almonds).

Tourism is well provided for all along the coast, and in the interior there are excellent opportunities for winter sports.

Both regions were inhabited in ancient times by fierce war-like tribes, but in the time of Augustus became part of the 4th Region.

There are relics of ancient Roma to be found all around; Chieti possesses a theatre, baths, temples, Téramo a theatre and an amphitheatre, and these are but two of numerous sites.

It was from the Longobards in the 6th to 7th centuries AD that first inklings of the present name appeared: to them the part around Téramo was known as Apruzzo.

At this time Molise was added to the Duchy of Benevento, and what is now Abruzzi fell to the lot of the Duchy of Spoleto, a condition that continued under the Franks, though in 843 AD an autonomous region, Marsia, developed in the interior.

In the 12th century the Pope ceded the region to the Normans, but this domination was sensed only in Molise until Frederick II came to the throne, when Abruzzi sided with him against the Church, at which time the city of L'Aquila came into being. Later, under the Angevin and Aragonese, the region followed the lead of Nápoli.

During the Middle Ages architecture rose to great heights in the region in numerous cathedrals and abbeys. At this time L'Aquila began to enrich itself with churches which, while they followed the examples of Lombardia and Púglia, maintained a certain individuality of style, mainly seen in a square façade with rectilinear balustrade, as in the church of Santa Maria di Collemaggio.

Following about 200 years of Spanish domination, and a short intervention by Austria, the region passed under the Bourbons of Nápoli; in 1860 it became part of the new Kingdom of Italy.

Molise largely follows the pattern set by Abruzzi, but mention must be made of a series of 9th century frescoes in the crypt of the church of San Lorenzo in San Vincenzo al Volturno, apparently unique in the world of art.

Festivals First Thursday in May at Cocullo in the province of L'Aquila a festival that might repel many, that of the *Serpari* (snake-catchers). The origins of this festival go back a long way; even Pliny makes mention of it. It has to do with the cult of the pagan goddess Angizia nowadays substituted by San Domenico, whose statue on the day of the festival is adorned by living snakes and then carried in procession through the streets of the little hill town (870m/2854ft above sea level) accompanied, one is happy to add, by the most able of the local snake-catchers.

Easter morning in Sulmona sees a statue of the Madonna borne aloft on the shoulders of youths in costume and borne through the streets.

On the Tuesday after Easter Orsogna in the province of Chieti holds the Festival of the *Talami*, when local children enact Biblical scenes.

L'Aquila   H3
(pop. 58,420) This is a delightful medieval city situated on a wide plateau surrounded by a circle of the Apennines. It is a fine centre for walks through breathtaking scenery, and is within easy reach of the lovely pinewoods of Róio and the skiing resort of **Campo Imperatore** on the Gran Sasso (excursions), the highest part of this section of the Apennines. The church of Santa Maria di Collemaggio, a 13th-century Romanesque-Gothic edifice with a charming façade in pink and white marble with three elaborate rose windows – the façade was added later – lies just outside the southeast walls of the town. The entrance doors are elaborate, and inside is the tomb of Pope Celestino V, a Renaissance work by Gerolamo da Vicenza. This huge church has also one of the few *porta Santa* (holy doors) used only in the years of a Papal jubilee. Returning along the Viale Francesco Crispi one comes to the Corso Vittorio Emanuele, lined with *portici* (arches), under which it is pleasant to sit and take a cup of coffee or an apéritif and watch the world go by. Behind this street is the lovely Basilica di San Bernardino.

In the Public Library are two volumes printed in 1482 by Adamo di Rotwil, dis-

ciple of Gütenberg, and a fine collecti of plain-song manuscripts. At the nort ern end of Corso Vittorio Emanuele is large park in one corner of which stan the striking castle built by the Spanish the 16th century, nowadays the home the Abruzzi National Museum. T cathedral has been largely rebuilt since was first constructed in the 14th centur and architecturally the nearby Chiesa d Suffragio (18th century), which has delightful cupola by Valadier, is far mo interesting. These two churches stand the Piazza del Duomo, the scene of a bu market on most mornings. One sight n to be missed is the Fountain of 99 Cha nels, close by the station.

While in L'Aquila an excursion not be missed is to the **Gran Sasso**. One c take a bus in the square, which pass through a series of charming little v lages until it reaches the terminus of t cable railway which conducts one in tv stages to the summit, from which t views are spectacular. *Ascoli Pice 109km/68mi, Pescara 104/65.*

Pescara   H
(pop. 94,000) In addition to being the ca ital of its province and a very busy indu trial city, Pescara is also one of the impc tant seaside centres of the mid-Adria coast. It has excellent hotels and resta rants and extremely good road and r communications.

Standing on the site of the ancient c of Alternum, Pescara was conquered the Romans in 214 AD and later destroy by the Longobards during the course the Barbaric invasions. Nowadays it p sents the appearance of a well-planne completely modern city.

The Italian poet Gabriele d'Annunz was born in Pescara.

There are many small beaches in t vicinity, and a lovely pinewood; excu sions to the **Gran Sasso,** the gre National Park of Italy, are not difficult arrange.

Térmoli   J
(pop. 11,000) This is an active little p near the peninsula of the Gargano, th spur-like promontory at the north Púglia on the Adriatic coast.

A busy little town, one of its interes for tourists is that it is one of the points embarkation to the fascinating **Trém** islands. It has a good beach, and thoug hotels are not numerous, it has go camping facilities.

It boasts a 13th-century castle, built Frederick II, and a very interesting 12 century cathedral.

Fishing is good at Térmoli, and there plenty of hunting inland during t autumn.

CAMPANIA

This region, to many foreign visitors, is the 'real' Italy, the region of the Tarantella, of sunshine, frivolous gaiety, of a sense of 'living for the day'; certainly, it has much of natural beauty to offer, and its inhabitants display an engaging desire to please.

Bounded on the west by the Mare Tirreno (Tyrrhenian Sea), its coastline offers a chain of delightful seaside resorts, vying one with another in natural beauty and in excellent tourist facilities. Coastal plains yield soon to the slopes of the Apennines, with here and there deep valleys. At times, for example around the Sorrento peninsula, the rocks rise sheer after a mere strip of blackish volcanic sand. The region is not lacking in volcanic manifestations: one has only to remember the not infrequent eruptions of Vesúvio, the bubbling witches' cauldron of the Solfatra near Nápoli and the buried cities of Pompei and Ercolano. Because of its volcanic nature the soil is fertile, yielding annually three or four crops, even though the terrace cultivation of hilly regions demands much hard work and tenacity of purpose.

The area was once so racked with malaria that the Greeks abandoned the plain on which stand the magnificent ruins of Paestum; fortunately that same fear kept away many who might have raided the temples and used their stone for other buildings. Malaria has now been conquered; the menace today, where Paestum is concerned, is that of the speculating builders who, contrary to the law, run up concrete excrescences nearer and nearer to the glory that was Greece.

Beauty, history and climate combine to render Campania congenial and attractive, and one should not content oneself with visits to the 'obvious' tourist spots. For instance, from Vico Equense it is possible to go by bus or car to the summit of Monte Faito, to ramble among the woods and to eat in one of several good restaurants; similarly, from Amalfi, it is almost a 'must' to travel up the hill – preferably by slow-motion *carozza* to visit Ravello, with frequent pauses on the way to rest the horse and admire the view, and once arrived to admire the beauties of the cathedral with the pulpit by Nicolò da Foggia, the other lovely church of San Giovanni del Toro, the Palazzo Rufolo and Villa Cimbrone; from the belvedere of the latter one has a marvellous view.

Visiting Vanvitelli's Royal Palace at Caserta, it is well to allow time to drive up to Vecchia Caserta, 7km/4mi away, a little almost forgotten town of Longobard origin with a Norman Romanesque cathedral of the 12th century seemingly untouched by time.

From Nápoli itself there are numerous 'extras'; apart from the obvious Pompei and Ercolano, there are the Campi Flegrei (Phlegrean Fields) and the Lake of Avernus, to mention but two.

Ninety per cent of Campania is given over to agriculture: vines, tomatoes, citrus fruits. Olives are grown on the calcareous slopes, vines on the volcanic soil, and the wine from these grapes is extremely good. Fishing and the preservation of fish is a big source of income, and the corals from the region are worked in many establishments. Probably the best pasta (macaroni, spaghetti *etc*) comes from Campania, said to be the true home of pasta. Around Sorrento it is possible to find excellent inlaid woodwork, and the working of cameos is another trade at which the craftsmen of the region are expert.

The islands off the coast, Capri, Íschia and Prócida, attract great numbers of tourists for their great beauty of scenery and their pleasing climate.

Capri So much has been written about this island that many people feel themselves familiar with it even before going there. If one is spending a holiday in the area of Nápoli, a visit to this island should be included.

Boats ply daily from Nápoli, Sorrento and Amalfi. Once arrived, a lift takes one speedily up the cliff into the town. The main street winds pleasantly uphill, lined with restaurants, bars and tourist shops. As one glances upwards one notices the hillside dotted with houses.

Capri was probably originally settled by the Phoenicians, but it first achieved notoriety under the Romans. The

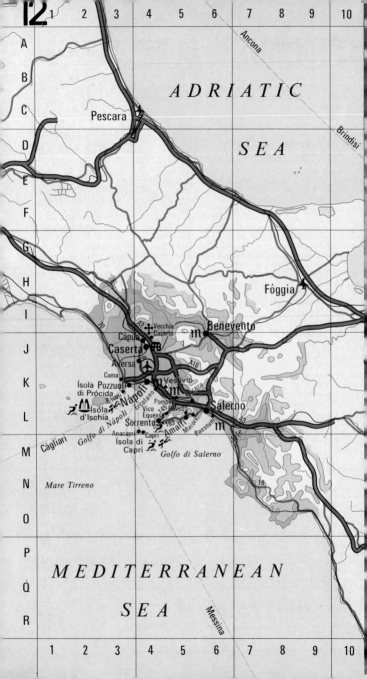

perors Augustus and Tiberius both
ew it. The latter had a 'stately pleasure
use' on Capri, and tales of his orgies
m a part of the folklore of the island.
he is shown the precipitous rock from
ich he is said to have cast discarded
ourites.

It is thought that Norman Douglas
ed the background of Capri for his
vel, *South Wind*. Dr Axel Munthe has
ndered it familiar to all who have read
s appealing *Story of San Michele,* and
e can still visit the house the building
which is described in the story.

One should visit the villa where
unthe lived, the 17th-century church of
nto Stéfano, the heights of Anacapri, or
lk to the cliff where once stood the villa
Tiberius. Then, down again on the
ore, it is possible to take a boat to fairy-
nd, alias the Blue Grotto. Once arrived,
u will change into an even smaller
at, and will probably be bidden to lie
t while this little cockleshell makes its
trance into the grotto, but once inside,
e reward is great. Water, walls, every-
ing one sees is of a deep pellucid blue;
e puts one's hand into the water and it
pears to be covered with silver.

It is possible to spend an entire holiday
Capri, but because of its great popular-
, very early booking is necessary.

hia is larger than Capri, and while it is
less beautiful, its beauty is of a less
phisticated order.

There are numerous boat services to
Íschia, and in addition to natural beauty,
the island offers a wide variety of water
sports, hunting and fishing.

Not only a holiday resort, it is also a
spa, with curative springs at Fornello and
Fontana, which produce strongly
radioactive water at a temperature of
65°C/148°F.

The late Renaissance baptistery of the
church of dell'Assunta is interesting, as is
the 15th-century Aragonese castle and
the botanical garden.

There are numerous excellent hotels
and restaurants and visitors are well provided for.

Prócida lies between Nápoli and Íschia
and is a pleasant little island, reminiscent
of an oriental village with its white
houses. It provides for tourists in that
there are lovely walks to be taken, with
many picturesque viewpoints on the way.

There are only two hotels, but it is
within easy reach of both Nápoli and
Íschia by boat.

In the abbey of San Michele there is a
fine ceiling painting by Luca Giordano.

Near Nápoli is a trio of lakes that
has come down in mythology. Homer and
Virgil both sang the fame of Avernus,
Lucrinus and Fusaro, and Roman
emperors and the aristocracy of their day
revelled in the splendours nature offers
there. Avernus presents a somewhat
alarming aspect; here one stands amid
the ruins of the villas, thermal establishments, temples and tombs of the day

pri

when Roma was at its greatest. This lake, once thought to be the entrance to the Nether Regions, has become even more awe-inspiring, for something seems to have gone wrong with part of the drainage system, and effluent that ought by rights to go far out to sea, has been known to arrive there.

Lucrinus still attracts holiday-makers to the narrow stretch of sandy shore dividing it from the sea; Fusaro, almost entirely circular, is separated from the sea by pinewood; it is famous for the production of oysters. Nearby stands the Royal Casino built in 1782 by Vanvitelli for the Bourbon King Ferdinand II.

These are among the best-known lakes; there are many more, but of less importance.

The 8th century BC saw the Greeks established along the coast, at Paestum, Nápoli and Cuma. These were menaced in the 6th century by the Etruscan founders of Cápua, then in the year 330 BC we see that city united with Roma against the Sannites who advanced from the interior, from which time the Romanization of Campania proceeded until under Augustus it formed, with Lázio, part of the 7th Region. Then, under Domitian, it became a province in its own right. This territorial unity held good under the Ostrogoths and the Byzantines, but fell apart when the Longobards arrived and established first of all a principality at Cápua and then in 900 AD extended this to Benevento, which became a Longobard duchy, while the Byzantines still maintained power in the Duchy of Naples. In the 9th and 10th centuries AD Amalfi broke free and, establishing its autonomy, became a great naval power, the rival of Pisa and Génova – the Amalfitani Naval Code was of infinite importance during the Middle Ages.

The fact that the region was divided into many sections made it an easy prey to the Normans who, stemming from the region of Aversa in 1030, gradually spread until, by 1077, they not only held Cápua but annexed Salerno and in 1139 Nápoli. Campania became identified with the Kingdoms first of Sicília then of Nápoli and later what was known as the Kingdom of the Two Sicilies. In the 12th and 13th centuries it formed a part of the Norman-Swabian dynasty then, at the beginning of the 16th century, under the Angevins and the Aragonese it became important, with Nápoli as the capital city. For over 230 years it suffered Spanish domination, and a viceroyalty was established. It received its autonomy under the Bourbons and this lasted with small interruptions under Napoleon until 1860,

when Garibaldi sealed its unity with t[ ] Kingdom of Italy.

Campania is a region richer than ma[ ] in relics of antiquity. Paestum is pu[ ] Greek, Cuma, Pompei, Ercolano Roma[ ] Pozzuoli is rich in remains of Imperi[ ] Roma; some part of the one-time Temp[ ] of Serapis is now under water, and for th[ ] reason more fascinating to behol[ ] Benevento has a Roman triumphal arc[ ] Bácoli huge cisterns, while Cápua boas[ ] several villas, and almost everywhere it[ ] possible to find bridges and sepulch[ ] which speak of Roma. Paleochristian a[ ] too, can be seen; Nápoli has the baptiste[ ] of San Giovanni in Forli and t[ ] catacombs of San Gennaro extra Mœn[ ] The Longobard period is remembered[ ] monuments at Cápua and Beneven[ ] and the churches that rose between t[ ] 11th and 13th centuries are splend[ ] combinations of Classical, Byzantin[ ] Arabo-Norman and Lombard style. The[ ] came a period during which were co[ ] structed the splendid pulpits and bron[ ] portals to be seen in many churches, [ ] example the bronze doors of the cath[ ] drals of Amalfi and Atrani, broug[ ] from Constantinople. In the Palaz[ ] Rufolo at Ravello are examples of char[ ] ing Arabo-Sicilian stonework. Under t[ ] Angevins and the Aragonese one sees t[ ] Gothic and Spanish influence in citi[ ] such as Cápua. During the Renaissan[ ] and baroque periods the region as a who[ ] echoed what was seen in and arou[ ] Nápoli, for example Vanvitelli's Roy[ ] Palace at Caserta of the 18th century.

In the 17th century a great school[ ] painting centred upon Nápoli with su[ ] representatives as Salvatore Rosa, Ruc[ ] polo and others.

Festivals Hardly a 'festival' but a serio[ ] affair at Nápoli and Pozzuoli is the co[ ] memoration ceremony of San Genna[ ] when the blood of the saint liquefies –[ ] does not – in the church of San Genna[ ] in Nápoli before a wildly excited crowd[ ] the faithful. The more solemn of the tv[ ] annual occurrences is on 19 Septemb[ ] the anniversary of the saint's martyrdo[ ] the other takes place on the eve of the fi[ ] Sunday in May. Because of the inten[ ] crowds, it is not easy to witness either[ ] On 29 June of every year in the little v[ ] lage of Cetara not far from Amalfi t[ ] statue of San Pietro is borne through t[ ] streets, followed by a procession.

The most festive of the festivals of Náp[ ] – which has several – is that of *Pied[ ] rotta* on 8 September of every year, wh[ ] a gaily caparisoned procession leaves t[ ] church of Piedigrotta and parad[ ] through the streets of Nápoli to t[ ] accompaniments of fireworks, music a[ ] neral revelry. The following morning, the vicinity of the Aquarium is held nat might be termed a children's *edigrotta*, a parade of young children, nose fancy dress must be made only of èpe paper – a little festival well worth a sit.

malfi L5

op. 6803) This is one of many fine sea-le resorts along the coast between ápoli and Salerno. In the Middle Ages was an important Marine Republic, nking with Venezia in volume of trade ith Constantinople and the Orient. The arine Laws of Amalfi were the codex of arine commerce until as late as 1570, d the original Tavole Amalfitane can ll be seen in the Municipio.

The splendid cathedral, standing at the ɔ of a long flight of steps, its eye-tching façade crowned by a mosaic of ırist enthroned, recalls its medieval ɔry. It dates back to the 9th century, but was rebuilt in 1103, when the lovely ıradise Cloisters were added. In 1066 e splendid bronze doors were brought ɔm Constantinople. The cathedral is dicated to Sant'Andrea, whose remains e buried beneath the altar. There is an teresting fountain in the square, and it amusing to walk in and around the ıare and the narrow streets to enjoy the ısy life of the town and the open air arket. Also worth visiting are the stored Arsenal, where at one time boats ere built, and a former Capuchin con-nt.

One of Amalfi's attractions is a boat trip the Grotta di Smeraldo, where the light ves the water an almost unbelievably ıutiful colour, In the cathedral of **rani** with its magnificent bronze doors, e former dukes of Amalfi were pro-aimed. If you are spending some days in nalfi, a pleasant leisurely excursion – eferably by horse-drawn carriage – is the steep, winding hill to **Ravello**.

There are numerous hotels, two of ıich were originally convents, which ve been beautifully converted and offer cellent – but not cheap – hospitality. ıe can breakfast in what were once ɔisters. One of these convents is across e road from a one-time watch-tower, a ıic of the days of Saracen invasions, and ıs has been converted into a most reeable bar and tearoom, with stairs ding down to the hotel's excellent ıvate beach.

From Amalfi, another pleasant walk ɔng the cliffs is to the small coastal vns of **Minori** and **Maiori**, once too significant to merit a mention other an as fishing villages, but now rapidly veloping into good tourist centres.

Nápoli (Naples) K4

(pop. 1,150,390) It would be hard to find a city more beautifully situated, a huge bay, houses rising up in terraces to the hills behind, with Vesuvius, ever watchful, ever menacing in the background. Climatically, Nápoli is fortunate, mostly sunny, often extremely hot, but with a freshness from the sea that prevents it from becoming unbearably sultry. A rich, florid city with an almost oriental splendour in its buildings, it is over-populated, vociferous and kindly. Apart from the more obvious sights, the tourist should also walk down some of the crowded side streets, the *Bassi*, where a whole family lives in one large room in the basement of a tall Palazzo, where much of the day's work is done in the street. Modern Nápoli has wide streets and up-to-date houses, but the real Nápoli is the city of the *Bassi,* the palaces that remind one of bygone glory.

The waterfront is extremely beautiful. The huge Castel Nuovo, built in the time of Charles I of Anjou (1280) and recon-structed during the 15th century, has an interesting triumphal arch and the rooms of the Bourbon kings, one of which leads to the Tower of the Beveretto, looking out to the sea. There is a fine museum in the castle. Follow the waterfront to the Palazzo Reale in Piazza Plebiscito; on the other side of the square is the 19th-century church of San Francesco di Pao-la, designed by Pietro Bianchi. Again on the front are two of Nápoli's famous restaurants, Zi' Teresa and Bersagliera. Continue along the bay to the fishing sec-tion at Mergellina, passing through the green, shaded Villa Comunale, pausing to visit the Aquarium. Close by is the church of Santa Maria di Piedigrotta, a 14th-century building, which is illumi-nated during the *Festa di Piedigrotta*.

Back in the city centre, at the junction of Via E. Pessina and Via Foria, the Museo Nazionale has a splendid collec-tion of archaeological treasures, mosaics, sculpture and paintings. Walk north along the Corso Amedeo di Savoia to the Parco di Capodimonte where Charles of Bourbon used to hunt game. The palace is now a museum with a fine collection of paintings by Bellini, Titian, Parmigiano, Correggio. By the Sanità bridge are the church and catacombs of San Gennaro; the catacombs (2nd century AD) are on two levels, and contain wall paintings. The lighting is not good.

Another walk starts from the church of Santa Chiara (east of Via Monte Oliveto). Although badly damaged in 1943, the church has been restored, and the clois-ters with majolica columns are in a

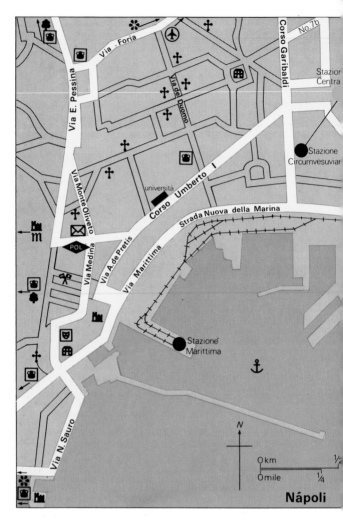

Nápoli

charming setting. Farther along is the church of San Domenico. St Thomas Aquinas taught in the adjoining convent. Along Via Duomo is the church of the Gerolomini, the centre of Father Borelli's work to help the poor of the city, and across the road lies the 13th-century cathedral. Here is celebrated the Miracle of the Liquefaction of the Blood of the Patron Saint (7 May). Upon the degree

and speed of liquefaction depend the fortunes of Nápoli for the following year. To the north of the nave, one may descend to the church of Santa Restituta, the first Christian basilica of Nápoli. The low screens (*plutei*) dividing the presbytery of this church from the nave have some absorbing bas-reliefs.

Excursions are many. Coaches go to **Vesúvio,** or one can take the Circu-

suvian Railway to **Pugliano** from
hich buses connect with the chairlift.
his particular trip could be combined
ith a visit to **Ercolano** which was sub-
erged under a wave of molten lava. Dur-
g the reign of the Bourbons, the district
as a resort for wealthy families, and
ere are still some delightful villas, parks
d gardens. It was at this time that exca-
tions began to reveal much of the old
oman city which now offers a fascinat-
g insight into Roman life.

There are also daily coach tours to
mpei, which was buried under a blan-
t of dust at the same time as Ercolano
9 AD). Here, the services of a guide are
sential, if one is to appreciate the amaz-
g temples, forums and private houses.
he museum contains many works of art
om this city, once a pleasure resort of
althy Roman citizens. **Caserta**
7km/17mi) is a busy provincial town
here Vanvitelli built the 'Versailles of
aly' for the Bourbon king. This elegant
lace, surrounded by delightful gardens,
ntains a private theatre, a series of
onderfully furnished rooms, and a fine
rtrait gallery. There is an excellent
staurant in the park.

It is also well worthwhile travelling a
rther 7km/4mi uphill to the old city,
ecchia Caserta, of Longobard origin,
here one finds a scattering of ancient
ouses that give one the feeling of having
epped back into the Middle Ages. There
also a splendid Norman-Romanesque
thedral, built in black and the local yel-
w tufa rock, and boasting a fine pulpit
d some early mosaics.

The building of the Royal Palace of
aserta, and the consequent demand for
cal labour, led to the almost complete
sertion of the old city for the new.

avello
L5

op. 2530) Ravello, on the spur of a
ountain dividing two valleys, has a
od climate, several hotels and some
lendid panoramic views. The cathedral
s two magnificent pulpits, one of 1272,
d an earlier one of 1130. The latter is
corated with a head and two profiles,
e work of Nicolò da Foggia, and the
lumns of the pulpit rest on 'peram-
lating' lions. The Palazzo Rufolo, in
e gardens of which are splendid exam-
es of Moorish architecture, and the
lla Cimbrone, also with lovely gardens
d with a breathtaking panoramic view
om the belvedere, are two lovely villas.
here are charming Romanesque clois-
s in the church of Sant'Antonio. Two
easant walks are to **Scala** (1km/½mi), or
wn the long hill to **Minori** where there
a Roman villa. *Amalfi 4km/2½mi.*

Salerno
L6

(pop. 110,995). The Roman city became
part of the Longobard Duchy of
Benevento in the 6th century; then, in the
9th century, an independent principality,
falling eventually into Norman hands in
1076. The famous Salerno School of
Medicine, founded in the 9th century,
flourished until the beginning of the last
century. The old town rises up towards
the hills behind the bay; along the shore
is the modern part, with gardens and a
promenade. The city offers all kinds of
seaside amusements, and there are pleasant walks to be taken in the district. In the
old part is the cathedral of San Matteo, an
11th-century building with an attractive
courtyard and covered forecourt. The
interior is richly decorated and houses
many treasures including a splendid pulpit and, in the crypt, two bronze statues of
the patron saint whose bones are buried
there. The Museo del Duomo also has
many precious exhibits including a famous 12th-century *Exultet*. In the church
of San Giorgio are frescoes by Solimena;
the Chiesa dell' Annunciata was
designed by Vanvitelli. Salerno also has
another interesting museum, the Museo
Provinciale.

The ancient Greek city of **Paestum**
(40km/25mi) is reached easily by rail or
road. Here are the temples of Neptune
and of Ceres, and a fine basilica dating
from the 4th century BC. There is also a
fascinating museum, and city walls that
cover over 4km/2½mi with four city
gates. In the vicinity are medieval coastal
towers erected as a means of defence
against Saracen raiders.

Sorrento
L4

(pop.11,768) This is one of the loveliest
seaside resorts in the vicinity of Nápoli.
At Easter the streets are gay with orange
trees and flowering almonds, and there is
an interesting and very solemn procession on Good Friday when the statue of
Christ reclining is borne through the
streets by black-robed, cowled figures, to
the accompaniment of funeral music.
The main square has a monument to the
poet Torquato Tasso who was born in
Sorrento in 1544. In this square, too, are
carrozzas (little carriages) with plumed
horses, and numerous shops selling the
lace, embroidery, and inlaid woodwork
for which the town is famous. In the tree-
lined Via Correale is the Museo Correale
with a fine collection, and with a splendid
view from the belvedere. The bathing
beach is small, and the sands, being volcanic, are blackish, but bathing is good.
There are boat trips to **Capri** and
Amalfi, and interesting walks.

PÚGLIA AND BASILICATA

Two more regions usually associated, occupying the southeastern extremity of the peninsula from a little north of the spur-like peninsula, Gargano, down to the 'heel' of Italy, cut off from Calábria by the spine of the Apennines.

Taking first of all **Basilicata**, known also since 1932 as Lucania, this western section is largely mountainous; its few rivers are unpredictable, floods and landslides are not infrequent and, except in the north where grapes are cultivated, agriculture is difficult. Lack of good roads and hydroelectric power combine to render the region backward as regards heavy industry, though native craftsmanship reaches a high level. Since the end of World War II State intervention has provided schools, hospitals and aqueducts, roads are being improved, conditions are better, but the old traditions die hard. A region once notorious for brigandage, this is now one of the least turbulent regions of the South.

Potenza, the main city, 822m (2697ft) above sea level, is the highest capital in peninsular Italy; the air is good, but windy. Melfi merits a visit for its fine cathedral, and another important city is Matera, built mainly on the edge of an abyss in the rocky plain.

When in the 8th and 7th centuries BC the Greeks founded colonies along the Ionic coast at Metapontum, Siri and Eraclea, this region enjoyed the fruits of a high civilization, dispersed in the 6th century BC when the Lucanians from the interior advanced and gradually established themselves.

Under Roma, Basilicata was included in the 3rd Region, but was not regarded as being very important.

The museums of Matera, Potenza and Metapontum have much to show by way of prehistoric remains, but there is little evidence left of the Greek period except for the splendid Tavole Palatine (Doric columns) at Metapontum. Of Roman days remains an amphitheatre at Venosa.

Under the Barbaric invasions, aided by increasing epidemics of malaria, the population was considerably reduced. A part of Basilicata was added to the duchy of Benevento, then in 847 AD it became part of the principality of Salerno. Next came the Byzantines and by the middle of the 11th century the beginning of Norman domination. Not until the 12th cen-

tury the name Basilicata was used.

The Middle Ages saw a great flowering of architecture, modelled on that of Púglia, Sicília, Campania and even France. The last is manifest in the great cathedral of Acerenza and the abbey of the Sacred Trinity at Venosa. While the cathedral of Matera is purely Pugliese, that of Melfi is redolent of Sicília, especially as regards the bell-tower.

The Normans, and later the Angevins, liked Basilicata and under them it enjoyed a period of prosperity, but from the 14th century onwards Nápoli became the centre of power and Basilicata fell into a decline, living in political isolation troubled by quarrels between the various dynasties and feudatories. Faraway events had little effect on the torpor into which the region had sunk.

From 1815 onwards the ferments of the *Risorgimento* began to circulate, but it was not until 1860 that Basilicata became recognized as a part of the Kingdom of Italy.

The influence of Venezia is seen in that such painters as Vivarini and Cima da Conegliano are represented in the churches of Matera and Migliónico.

Festivals *Corpus Domini* is celebrated at Potenza by a procession during which flowers of ginestra (broom) are thrown to the crowds. In Accettura near Matera 2 May sees a great procession in honour of the patron saint Giuliano. Matera on 2 July holds the *Festival of the Madonna della Bruna*. A statue of the Madonna is taken through the streets accompanied by a parade in costume. In the evening the papier-maché cart is pulled to pieces and the spectators take pieces home for good luck.

Púglia has few high mountains, Monte Calvo in the Gargano rises 1056m (3464ft) above sea level, Montecornacchia, in the eastern Apennines just over 1100m (3609ft); otherwise, e region is flat. A wide stretch of plain-nd, the Tavoliere Capitanata, follows e coastline from north to south, backed the so-called Terra di Bari, which pet-s out south of the town of Francavilla, ving way to the slightly higher Murge arantine, Murge Salentine and Terra di ranto, which constitute the Salentine ninsula.

There are few rivers, so most of the cessary water comes from an aqueduct, by the River Sele in Campania, but en this is insufficient. Forests, except the magnificent Foresta Umbra on the argano, are practically non-existent. arcity of water has enforced specializa-n in crops demanding little: vines, ich produce grapes equally good for le use and for wine-making, olive es, which grow to a fantastic size and ld excellent oil, almond trees, the nuts m which are world-famous. Thyme, ge and rosemary flourish, and on the lentine peninsula, peas, beans and matoes, and there is a modest cultiva-n of citrus fruits − otherwise, agricul-e is limited to cereals and forage.

Fishing supplies local needs, and is ried on not only along the coast, but in two lakes, Lésina and Varano, north the Gargano. The bay of Táranto has g been famous for large, succulent sters and mussels.

As regards industry, the only bauxite nes in Italy are situated in the Gar-no; the salt marshes of Margherita di voia, to the north of Barletta, are the st important in Europe. Along the ast are several large refineries.

Bari and Bríndisi have long been portant for communications with the t; Táranto is one of Italy's two naval es, La Spezia in Liguria being the her.

From the 8th century BC a flourish- Greek colony had Táranto as its ital; then followed a period of prosper- under the Romans until the Fall of me, after which came attacks by the zantines, the Longobards and the nks, and also by Saracen raiders along coast.

In the 9th century AD the Byzantines ablished command. From the 11th tury marine trade with Amalfi and the lmatian and Levantine ports was car- on.

Next came Norman domination of the ion. The Crusades and trade with the t brought prosperity. When the Swa-ns took over from the Normans, glia was not only rich, but had a period splendour in the fields of art and litera-e.

Later, under the Angevins and the Aragonese, decline set in. Venezia assumed much of the marine commerce. Turkish raids, particularly around Ótranto, made the condition of coastal cities desperate. The decadence was aggravated by famines, malaria and the plague that raged over Europe. The Spanish period (1503−1707) served only to aggravate the sad case.

Under the Bourbons things improved. For one thing, they were horse-lovers and during their domination the Tavoliere around Fóggia was used for pasturage, until the city and its surroundings seemed like an Italian Wild West. (This pasturage was abolished by law in 1860). The decade 1805−15 saw Púglia once again prosperous. In 1860 it was added to the newly-formed Kingdom of Italy.

The region is rich in prehistoric dol-men and menhirs. Greek vases found in various necropolises can be seen in the museums of Táranto, Bari, Lecce and Ruvo. There are two great archaeological complexes at Canne della Battaglia and Egnázia. Roman remains are plentiful, among them the two pillars not far from the port of Bríndisi, which mark the end of the Via Appia, and amphitheatres in Lecce and Lucera.

From the 11th to the 14th century came the erection of splendid cathedrals and churches in which the native Roman-esque is embellished with oriental ele-ments. In Táranto and Ótranto the cathedrals adhere to the Roman basilical form, and the latter has a fine mosaic floor. Many such buildings contain sculptural elements of great beauty, epis-copal thrones, pulpits, bronze doors, por-tals and windows displaying Byzantine and oriental motifs. France and the Holy Land were mainly responsible for the Gothic influence noticeable from the 12th century onwards. During the 13th and 14th centuries numerous castles were built, among them Castel del Monte near Andria, the hunting lodge of Fre-derick II.

There is little Renaissance architec-ture, and in art can be seen the influence of Venezia.

In the 17th century a particular type of baroque appeared in Lecce, peculiarly suitable to the easily-worked local stone which assumes a warm, golden hue with the passage of time. During this period, too, a local school of painters developed, strongly influenced by Nápoli, but with a certain individuality; in the 19th century the painters Altamura and Toma were much admired.

There is an odd little architectural enclave not far from the world-famous caves of Castellana, the region of the *trulli*. The small centres of Fasano and Alberobello possess groups of small houses, circular in form, white-walled, with conical stone roofs. The origin of the form is lost in the mists of antiquity, but the houses to be seen today date back to 1555 when the peasants of Conversano asked the local feudator, Count Acquaviva, if they might establish themselves in the territory. Permission was granted, but only on condition that any buildings should be built entirely of stone, without the aid of mortar or plaster. The most spectacular group of *trulli* is at Alberobello, where there are over a thousand.

Festivals Bari, 17 May, the *Festival of San Nicola* whose relics were brought from the monastery of Mira in 1097. The statue of the Saint is borne out to sea in a fishing boat to receive the homage of the faithful who go out in boats to visit him. Ostuni, last Sunday in August, a parade of 'well-dressed' horses with a prize for the best. The trappings are most elegant, with ribbons and flowers; final touc[h] are administered not in the stables bu[t] the houses of the owners. Hardly a 'fe[sti]val', but the Trade Fair of the Leva[nt] held every September in Bari is of gr[eat] importance in relations with the Ori[ent]. On September 26 the patron saints [of] Bitonto, Cosma and Damian, are borne [in] procession; pilgrims arrive from near a[nd] far, and the most devout carry ligh[ted] candles on their shoulders.

The Trémiti (Tremites)

These isles are off the coast of the G[ar]gano, that spur-like promontory that j[uts] out from the coast at the northern extre[m]ity of Púglia. To reach them, one can ta[ke] a steamer from the little port of Rodi [on] the Gargano, or from Térmoli at [the] southern end of the Abruzzi, or travel [by] the swifter hydrofoil.

In order of size the group compris[es] San Domino, San Nicola, Capraia a[nd] Pianosa. There is a small hotel on S[an] Domino and there are camping sites [on] San Nicola.

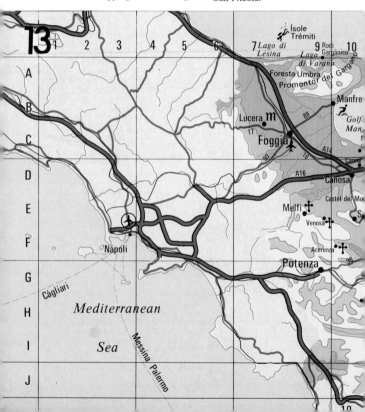

Bari D13

(pop. 323,060) Bari is one of the busiest commercial cities of the province, trading with the East and Middle East. In the middle two weeks of September is the international trade fair, the *Fiera del Levante,* one of the most important in Europe; in May there is an International Festival of Military Bands. On May 7, a solemn procession recalls the transference to Bari of the bones of its patron saint, San Nicola. The next day a procession of pilgrims and sailors carries an effigy of the saint shoulder-high to the Piazza Mercantile; after a mass in the open air, the effigy is mounted on a sloop and taken out to sea, where it is visited by pilgrims and brought back to land in the evening.

The city is divided into two parts, the modern commercial centre, and the old city. Here, the church of San Nicola, a Romanesque building of the 11th and 12th centuries, has a delightful façade, one of the richest in this region. In the cathedral is preserved a valuable *Exultet* (the prayer recited on Easter Sunday during the blessing of the Easter candle).

Not far from Bari are the famous caves of **Castellana** (40km/25mi), and it is within handy reach of the little town of **Alberobello** (67km/42mi) with its outlandish *trulli,* small white stone houses with conical roofs. A pleasant bathing resort which complements the facilities of Bari is **Torre a Mare.** Seafood in this area is excellent.

Barletta C11

(pop. 69,000) This is a city of pre-Roman origin, first known as Canusium, later as Barulum and finally Barletta. It lent its name to one of the famous events in Italian history, *La Disfida di Barletta,* when Ettore Fieramosca, a soldier of fortune, issued a challenge to one of the attacking French – the room in which the challenge was uttered is still to be seen in Barletta.

The cathedral (1267) is splendid inside and out, appearing smaller than it is in

actual fact, because of the surrounding buildings. Another treasure of the city is the Colossus, an Imperial bronze statue, 5m/16ft high, dating back to the 4th or 5th century and brought back from the Orient in the 13th century.

Having looked carefully at these and other architectural beauties Barletta has to offer, come back along the coastal road and make your next stop at **Trani,** 14km/8mi away; a small but flourishing maritime and commercial centre up to the 15th century when it passed into the hands of Venezia. Trani is famous among other things for bell-founding.

It is a quiet little place nowadays but has a cathedral that is beautiful, and a bell-tower beside it for which the adjective beautiful is hardly adequate. Standing as it does, right on the shore, one can look through the portal and passageway at its base and see one of the most charming seascapes imaginable.

The next stop should be at **Biscéglie,** after another 8km/5mi, and here is another marine centre with yet another interesting 11th century church, that of Sant'Adoneo, erected by the Normans and dedicated to the saint of Rouen. There is a splendid font here.

After another 8km/5mi you come to lovely **Molfetta,** where at Easter-time is held one of those solemn religious processions so dear to the people of southern Italy.

The interesting part of Molfetta is the medieval section, down towards the sea, where stands the old cathedral (not to be confused with the nearby new cathedral, a 17th-century edifice). This older, Romanesque building is fortunate in having remained both inside and out as it was originally. It is recognizable from the outside by its three imposing cupolas, rather the shape of open Japanese parasols.

The little harbour of Molfetta is enchanting, and after such a tour as has been suggested, one returns to Bari with the feeling of having spent one's time well. *Bari 55km/34mi.*

Bitonto   D12

(pop. 38,500) Bitonto is an extremely interesting city of Apulia for those who admire Romanesque architecture, of which its cathedral is one of the outstanding examples. The entire façade, and particularly the right-hand side, might well be called a poem in stone. Inside there is a splendid pulpit (1240) the work of Master Bonifacio, and the crypt with its thirty columns, no two of which are alike.

The church of San Francesco has a fine 13th-century Gothic portal and the

very old abbey of San Leo has interesti 15th-century cloisters. Another archit tural jewel is to be found in the Loggia Sylos Calò, and it is rewarding to w through the 15th-century Gothic porta the Sylos Labina mansion to see lovely Loggia in the courtyard.

Bitonto is within easy road and rail d tance from Bari and is worth a visit.

Bríndisi   G

(pop. 73,000) This has been a major p throughout its history which goes back pre-Roman days. Virgil, born n Mántova, died at Bríndisi in 19 BC. T old — and interesting — part of the to contains several monuments. Not from the port are the two columns ma ing the end of the ancient Via App Nearby is the 12th-century church of S Giovanni al Sepolcro, now a museu The cathedral was rebuilt during the 1 century, and little remains of the earl edifice. About half a mile from the city the imposing Castello Svevo, begun 1227 by Frederick II, later enlarged Ferdinand of Aragon and at present seat of the Comando Militare Marittim

There is a splendid beach at the th mal resort of **Torre Canne.** Grapes, dr figs and melons are especially good Bríndisi, and there are numerous rest rants where one may enjoy marine fo

Lecce   H

(pop. 76,305) This is an agricultural a industrial centre, a good tourist cen about 41km/25mi from Brínd 14km/8mi from the pleasant seas resort of **San Cataldo,** and one of finest Italian baroque cities, cent round the Piazza del Duomo. T cathedral is 12th-century, and was alte in the 17th century by the architect Zi balo, who added a fine bell-tower fr which there is a lovely view of the c The Vescovado (Bishop's Palace) and Seminario Vescovile complete the co position. The church of Santi Nicol Cataldo, to the north of the city, ha stupendous baroque façade; anot highly decorative church by Zimbalo that of Santa Croce. The lo yellowish-brown stone lends itself be tifully to the intricacies of this particu style of architecture. The town also p sesses a Roman theatre and amp theatre, and 16th-century castle.

Matera   G

(pop. 40,000) This town is well wort visit. It is a busy commercial centre also has lovely buildings, such as fine Apulian Romanesque cathec (1268—70), and the churches of S Domenico and San Francesco.

Possibly the greatest attraction, however, lies in the houses and churches xcavated in the rock on which the upper ty stands, particularly the little church Santa Maria de Idris which has a walk ading to another hypogeum (under-ound church) with Byzantine frescoes the 12th century.

tranto I19

op. 4070) This busy agricultural and mmercial centre of Roman origin was important city during the Middle ges. It has a fine Romanesque cathe-al, restored in 1481, but possessing a lendid mosaic floor, featuring among her characters King Arthur of Round able fame (1166). There is also a charm-g Byzantine church, San Pietro, with a lindrical dome and three semi-circular ses.

Added to which, fish in Ótranto is ccellent, so that a visit to this little part of tiglia is by no means a waste of time.

otenza G9

op. 44,490) This city, 823m/2700ft ove sea level, is the highest city in ninsular Italy. The air is good, but it is windy city. Parts are old and shabby, but ere is also an elegant section and it has a ne cathedral and two Romanesque urches (San Michele Archangele and n Francesco). Note the wooden portal the 12th-century convent of the latter. the Town Hall is the Roman sar-phagus of Rapolla, said to have spired Jacopo della Quercia when he signed the much admired tomb of aria del Carretto in the cathedral in ucca.

uvo D12

op. 23,500) 260m/853ft above sea level. nis is a city scorched now and again by a fling *scirocco* that seems to take away wish or power of movement; neverthe-ss, it is one of the 'musts' of Apulia.

Within easy reach of Bari by train, it asts yet another of the lovely Apulian omanesque cathedrals, with a charming se window and a bell-tower that started e as a cylindrical defence tower in orman days.

In the period when Apulia was Magna recia, it was famous for the making of ottery vases, which were exported to the other country, Greece. During excava-ons, a vast number of these vases were ought to light in Ruvo, objects of great eauty, decorated with heroic and ythological scenes, coloured and azed, and in almost perfect condition. eedless to say, many of these found eir way into various museums all over

the world, but the little Museo Jatta in Ruvo still has over 1800 pieces, things of a rare beauty that should be seen by any-one visiting the city.

Apulia is dotted with castles built by the Norman kings, and from Ruvo one can go by car or taxi to visit the most famous – **Castel del Monte.** Enquire in advance about opening times, as it may be necessary to get special permission to visit the interior of the castle. Not only is this castle one of the showpieces of Nor-man architecture, it is one of the architec-tural masterpieces of the whole world. Needless to say, the king who had it erected was Frederick II, who used it as a hunting lodge. The architect was one Nicola da Foggia, whom many believe to have been that Nicola who, when Fre-derick II died and his court was dispersed, travelled through Italy until he came to Pisa and became known as Nicola Pisano.

Táranto H15

(pop. 193,000) This city, tucked away under what one might call the 'instep' of Italy is a busy industrial centre, but also a very interesting town to visit.

Originally it was one of the most flourishing cities of Magna Grecia, in the days when the southeast coast of Italy was heavily settled by Greeks.

It consists of the old city and the new and, not surprisingly, the most interest-ing architecture is to be found in the former. There is the 12th-century cathedral of San Cataldo which rose on the site of an earlier 4th-century edifice; there is a castle which was largely rebuilt in the late 15th century by Ferdinando of Aragon, and a fine 19th-century Municipio (Town Hall).

At one time Táranto was famous for wool and for the dyeing of wool with a purple dye made from a certain kind of mollusc peculiar to the district. It is also said that the inhabitants of Táranto were responsible for the introduction of cats into Europe.

Nowadays one of the chief industries of Táranto is the cultivation of oysters, said to be the finest in Italy. The writer Nor-man Douglas was of the opinion that the inhabitants of Táranto were of a sluggish nature, thanks to their overeating of mus-sels, which are also found in considerable quantities.

Táranto has two ports, a military one and a civil, and its two cities, old and new, are united by a drawbridge.

The Museo Nazionale is one of the finest in Europe for its collection of pre-cious prehistoric relics.

CALÁBRIA

Calábria occupies what we might call the 'toe' of Italy, bordered by Campania on the north, by the Mare Tirreno (Tyrrhenian Sea) on the west, the Ionian on the east, and on the map looks as though it had just kicked Sicília into the Mediterranean.

Largely mountainous, on the west the mountains drop precipitously down into the sea and coastal strips are narrow; on the east, the plateaux of the Sila intervene before wider coastal strips are reached, especially in the north and central parts of the region. In the far south rise the wooded heights of Aspromonte, Montalto, the highest point, 1956m/6417ft above sea level.

There are numerous bays around the coasts and the fine sands – some of a pinkish hue because of the presence of coral – are an attraction to tourists, as the chestnut woods of the Sila, for about one-fourth of Calábria is under forest, in spite of de-forestation in former days by the poorer members of the population who regarded trees as 'thieves of the soil'. Many people see in the mountains of Calábria a strong resemblance to those of the north rather than to the typical southern landscape.

There are three great plains, that of Sant' Eufémia on the bay of the same name, the Plain of Rosarno behind Gióia Táuro, and finally the area around Réggio, all on the Tyrrhenian side, while on the Ionian there is the Plain of Sibari in the north, and the March of Crotone.

Rivers are few and liable to flooding, swift-running, which gives rise to shortage of the water essential to agriculture. One river, the Busento, which divides the older part of Cosenza from the newer, is said to be the river whose stream was diverted around 410 AD so that the treasure of King Alaric of the Visigoths might be buried safely in its bed. Many have hunted this fabled treasure, but so far it has not come to light.

Calábria has many natural beauties. The rock Scilla, which, with the whirlpool Charybdis, was sung of by Homer and Dante, lies 15km/9mi north of Réggio. Between Catanzaro and Crotone the landscape seems more lunar than terrestrial; the Ionic coast is splendid in its great desolation; this is the coast deserted by the Greeks who fled, and by the local population who took to the hills to escape the scourge of malaria, a danger now eliminated but which served to drive away even the raiding Corsairs.

There are numerous lovely bays along the Tyrrhenian coast from which can be seen the Ísole Eólie and at times Monte Etna in Sicília.

At least two famous men were born in Calábria; in 1508 the philosopher Telesio was born in Cosenza; in 1613 the painter Mattia Prete was born in Mancuso in the Sila, now a holiday centre. In another town of the Sila, San Giovanni in Fiore, there is the tomb of the mystic Gioacchino di Fiore mentioned in the third book of Dante's *Divine Comedy*.

Here and there are apparently untouched medieval towns such as Corigliano Calabro, 219m/718ft above sea level.

In the 16th century a group of Albanians fled their own country and settled in a few Calabrian towns, among them Spezzano, where even today their native language, customs and songs persist.

The Tyrrhenian coast is lined with huge olive groves, plantations of citrus fruit, bergamot in particular, the foundation of many essences. Figs grow well and are a source of income.

Tuna and sword fish are caught in large numbers along this coast.

Calábria is still a poor region, and lack of suitable employment has led to much emigration. Things are improving, however, and efforts are being made to attract tourists; good hotels are springing up in the larger centres and there are a fair number of camping sites.

Under the colonizing Greeks in the 7th to 6th centuries BC Calábria enjoyed a period of great splendour, especially in Réggio, Crotone and Sibari. Hostile to Roma in the wars against Pyrrhus and Hannibal, the region became subject to her after the second Punic War and, in the 2nd century BC, colonies were founded and the road from Cápua to Réggio traced out. When the Empire fell, Calábria lapsed into a state of misery. Some help was given by Theodoric in the period 494 to 526 AD then, with the incursions of the Longobards, the territory was divided and the area of Cosenza was assigned first to the duchy of Benevento, later to the principality of Salerno.

Saracen raids imposed a heavy tax on the inhabitants, but the Normans brought peace and security (11th to 12th century AD).

In later years Calábria shared the destiny of the south, and Angevins and Aragonese impoverished the region.

In 1848 there was a peasant rising against the Bourbons, suppressed by Garibaldi, and in 1860 Calábria became a part of the United Kingdom of Italy.

There are many relics of ancient civilization in the museums of Réggio, Catanzaro, Cosenza and Crotone. Excavations at Locri still reveal evidences of the past. On Capo Colonna near Crotone one column remains of the one-time Temple of Giunone. Near Vibo Valentia and along the coastal esplanade at Réggio are remains of imposing Greek walls. The Roman period left baths in Réggio, a theatre at Gioiosa Iónica.

Byzantine art and architecture were widely diffused up to the Middle Ages: Rossano preserves a splendid Greek Gospel, its red pages written on in letters of silver; in the Episcopal Palace in Cosenza is a Byzantine cross of exquisite workmanship. The architecture of the baptistery at San Severino, the church of the Cattolica in Stilo, the church of San Marco at Rossano is pure Byzantine, and the cathedrals of Tropea and Gerace, the Roccelletta near Squillace are examples of this allied with Romanesque. The Gothic did not begin to penetrate until the early 13th century. The influence of the Renaissance is stronger in painting than in architecture. Réggio possesses a fine example of the work of Antonello da Messina, Morano Calabro boasts a Vivarini. Sculpture by Laurana and Gagini is fairly widely dispersed. During the 17th and 18th centuries came a period of fervid building to replace earthquake damage.

One may wonder at the 'newness' of Réggio di Calábria, bearing in mind that it was founded in the 8th century BC. Much of the original city perished in the earthquake of 1908.

Festivals At Easter-time in Réggio, Karacolo, Mammola, Tiriolo and Vibo Valentia comes the rite of the *Affruntata*, a procession during which there is an encounter between the statue of the Madonna and that of the risen Christ. In the early days of May in Tropea comes the *Festival of the Camel*; in the evening fol-

lowing a day of jollifications, a young man places on his shoulders the image of a camel constructed of fire-crackers which are then ignited as he course through the streets accompanied by a band of drums and tambourines.

Palmi on the last Sunday in July celebrates the festival of the Madonna with a long procession of decorated boats.

Also in Palmi on 16 August, a procession of the faithful who, for grace received, cover themselves with prickly branches.

Belvedere Marittima   G4

(pop. 10,500) For those wanting a really quiet yet delightful holiday along the coast of Calábria, Belvedere would be ideal. There is but one hotel, quite moderately comfortable, but the owner also has a series of fairly well-equipped seaside bungalows which he rents during the season.

The small town is tranquil; its main interest is the daily departure and return of the fishing fleet. Swordfish are found here and make an appetizing dish, as do the local sole.

On a hill above the town is the frowning bulk of an Angevin/Aragonese castle and a couple of churches. Little narrow streets wind in and out of this upper part and add to the charm of this upper town.

A pleasant walk takes one along the shore to the nearby town of **Diamante**, even smaller, but again with possibilities for sea bathing and with some lovely panoramic views.

Both these places have a long way to go before they qualify as regular tourist resorts, but they are well worth exploring

Belvedere Marittima is on the main railway line to Réggio di Calábria, and the station is busy. Communications to other coastal cities farther south, such as **Páola, Amantea, Tropea** and so on, are facilitated by this railway line, and it is even possible to go as far as **Cosenza** though this last is less easy, because after turning inland to approach the hilly city one travels on a rack type of railway and progress is decidedly slow and jerky.

Páola   I.

(pop. 15,000) This is an agricultural centre, the main products of which are oil and wine, but it has a good stretch of sandy beach, and with the growing importance of Calábria as a resort province, is rapidly taking on the aspect of a holiday resort.

An interesting excursion by bus or car from Páola is to the **Santuario di San Francesco,** which is set in an extremely picturesque position at the mouth of the River Isca.

Scilla

The sanctuary buildings themselves are extremely interesting and the journey there and back is panoramic and agreeable.

Réggio di Calábria   O3

(pop. 152,350) This is the capital of the province and is a busy tourist centre, important for its export of citrus fruits and various essences manufactured from these, particularly that of bergamot.

Its climate is excellent, it has an excellent coast and is a good centre for excursions either on the mainland or over the Stretto di Messina and into Sicília.

In the days when Greece had established southern Italy as Magna Grecia, Réggio was of great importance, which did not cease when the region fell under Roman rule. During the Middle Ages it was repeatedly sacked, but enjoyed a further flowering under the Normans. It has suffered the ravages of several serious earthquakes, the most recent in 1908 when it was almost completely devastated and many relics of the past destroyed.

Part of the ancient castle remains, and is now the seat of the geophysical observatory.

There are interesting walks, and from the slopes of Aspromonte can be enjoyed a fine panorama. Réggio is in the midst of the so-called 'violet' coast embracing the centres of **Scilla, Bagnara, Palmi** and **Monte Sant'Ella.** The site of the ancient city of **Locri** is within easy distance.

Siderno   N6

(pop. 15,500) This is a charming seaside resort on the eastern coast of southern Calábria. It has its own port and is a fairly busy industrial centre set in an agricultural and olive-growing district.

Hunting and fishing are good and bathing is excellent and well provided for.

There is a long, wide stretch of sand separated from the main part of the town by attractive gardens.

9km/6mi away is an excellent camping site.

Siderno is on the Ionian sea coast, and the inhabitants take pride in the fact that the Ionian is not among the seas that has suffered pollution from modern industry.

Tropea   L4

(pop. 7000) This town, which lies at the southern end of the Golfo di Sant'Eufémia in Calábria, is a very picturesque tourist centre with its own port.

During the 9th century AD it was captured by the Saracens, but later came under the rule of the Angevins and later again of the Aragons.

It has many interesting buildings, including the 9th-century cathedral which, in addition to some fine 16th-century bas-reliefs, has a lovely marble ciborium among its treasures. The 12th-century church of San Francesco and its chapel of a century later are interesting to visit, and in the church of the Annunciation there is a charming 16th-century group of marble statues.

Tropea has an excellent beach, and fishing and other nautical sports are well provided for. Photographers will doubtless wish to 'snap' the picturesque church of Santa Maria dell'Isola which stands out against the sky from its position atop a high cliff.

Tourism, which is fairly new to Calábria, is fast developing and hotels are springing up at the various beauty spots along the coast.

SICÍLIA

Sicília is the largest island in the Mediterranean, lying between the southern extremity of the peninsula and the African coast. It has a special statute and enjoys particular forms of autonomy, which are shared with the Ísole Eólie, the Egadi, the Pelage, Ustica and Pantelleria.

Mostly mountainous, its heights culminate in the great volcanic complex of Monte Etna. There is a large fertile plain inland from Catánia and others in the southwestern corner of the island, and around the Bay of Gela, while behind Palermo lies the fertile and beautiful area known as the Conca d'Oro (Golden Valley).

The climate is typically Mediterranean. Summers are very hot and dry and the rainy season of the winter months is so short that finding sufficient water for crop irrigation is an ever-present problem. The rivers alternate between dry, stony beds in the summer and raging torrents in winter.

In spite of this difficulty, Sicília is an agricultural region. Once the granary of Italy, in spite of reckless deforestation it still produces large quantities of wheat and oats, and its production of citrus fruits represents almost four-fifths of the national yield. Vines give good-quality wines of high alcoholic content; Malvasia is the special wine of the Ísole Eólie, Marsala comes from the district of the same name, and the wines of Pantelleria are well known. Among other products are almonds, olives, walnuts, figs, carob beans and pistachio nuts; tomatoes and artichokes are also grown in large quantities and Sicília grows most of the cotton produced in Italy. Sheep, cattle and goats are raised, and fishing prospers, especially for tuna, which supplies a sizeable canning industry.

Sulphur and rock salt are mined, and oil drilling has proved successful near Ragusa and Gela, which supply the refineries at Augusta on the east coast.

Much of the attraction of Sicília comes from its checkered history and the many monuments that signalize the various dominations. This, plus perfect coastal scenery and climatic conditions coupled with excellent hotels, brings visitors in their thousands.

It is not difficult to reach Sicília; steamers from Nápoli travel to Palermo and Messina; there are air services to Palermo, Trápani and Catánia, and a ferry from Réggio di Calábria.

Siracusa (Syracuse) was great and powerful under the first Dionysius, who died in 388 BC. In his day was built the Castle of Eurialus, still extant and regarded as one of the finest examples of military architecture. When the Romans attacked Siracusa in the 2nd century BC their defeat was due to the ingenuity of the famous mathematician Archimedes who designed the large cranes that overturned many vessels, and destroyed others by means of 'burning glasses' which set them on fire.

Although small groups of Spanish and Italian colonists arrived, not to mention the Phoenicians who founded the city of Palermo, they were outnumbered by the Greeks who occupied first the eastern shores and then gradually forged their way along the southern coast, where they founded the city of Agrigento.

Relics of Greek civilization still stand in the Valley of Temples near that city, in the theatres in Siracusa and Taormina and in the now deserted sites of Segesta and Selinunte.

Following the defeat of Carthage, the Romans tried again, this time successfully; first Siracusa and later the entire island fell under their power. It was they who discovered and exploited the rich deposits of sulphur and other natural resources.

In memory of their stay there is a Roman theatre at Siracusa, and near the city of Piazza Armerina, 50km/31m southeast of Enna, stands the 5th-century Villa di Casale with attractive and well preserved floor mosaics.

Following the Barbaric invasions of the mainland, Sicília came under the domination of Byzantium, and from about 535 AD Greek was once again the official language and the church adopted the Greek ritual.

By the 8th century AD Mohammedanism was endeavouring to eradicate Christianity, and Sicília was one of its points of attack. In 827 the Moslem Arabs invaded; in 831 they captured Palermo, in 878 Siracusa was destroyed. Under their rule commerce prospered, taxes were lowered, religious toleration of a sort existed. They installed an excellent irrigation system; citrus fruits, cotton, mulberry trees and their attendant silkworms were introduced. Arab weights and measures are still in use today, and many Arab words have remained in the language, for example *maggazzino* (warehouse).

In the 1030s a Byzantine force landed in Messina, among them Harold Hardrada, later one of the invaders of England. In 1060 came Roger d'Hauteville, first of the Norman kings who were the rulers of the island for over 200 years.

Under the Normans, particularly Roger II and Frederick II, Sicília rose to an unprecedented peak of splendour. These two kings were outstanding in every way. Roger, though a Christian, was crowned in a mosque in Palermo, and in the church of the Martorana in that city there is a mosaic depicting him wearing the cloak and stole of an apostolic legate, with a Greek crown being placed on his head by Christ himself; yet he was reputed to maintain a harem. He it was who initiated the building of the great cathedral at Cefalù. When, for lack of male heirs to William II, the crown went to the Hohenstaufen dynasty, Frederick II of Swabia proved to be one of the greatest emperors of all time. Even today, looking at the tomb of this great ruler in the cathedral of Palermo, one feels one is in the presence of royalty. His court at Palermo attracted men of culture: poets, artists, musicians, scientists. He lived in regal luxury, more Oriental than European, and it is rumoured that he, too, maintained a *seraglio*.

With the passing of the Normans, the picturesque history of Sicília ends with the possible exception of the incident known as the *Sicilian Vespers* of 1282 when the allegedly too-friendly relations between a French soldier and a Sicilian woman sparked off a war which ended with the defeat of the invading French.

From this time on the history of the island was one of foreign domination on the part of Italy, France and Spain. In 1347 it was swept by the Black Death, a plague said to have caused the death of a good third of the population.

Internal revolts from time to time led to banditry and Sicília received the not entirely undeserved reputation of being a turbulent island, for which its past history might well furnish an excuse, and yet at the same time explain the enchantment that lingers over the one-time *Trinacria* of Virgil.

Sicília has something of everything to offer. Vestiges of the past remain, not only in art and architecture, but in the very features and characteristics of the people. The gay painted carts that are such a feature of rural Sicília depict legends that go back into mythology; the puppets one enjoys at street-corner 'theatres' are by no means of recent growth.

Among its lesser joys are the out-of-this-world pastries of Palermo, and that delicious ice-cream cake known as *Cassata Siciliana*.

The little terracotta statuettes are the product of local craftsmen who have inherited their skill from past generations. The embroidered blouse you admire, and which is not your size, can be copied within twenty-four hours in exquisite handwork.

Festivals Holy Week is celebrated in every city of Sicília with processions in costume. *Palio dei Normanni* (Horse race in costume) 13 August, at Piazza Armerina. In Messina 15 August sees the *Procession of the Vara*, a great float surmounted by a pyramid of angels with the statue of the Virgin at its peak.

Ísole Eólie o Lipari (The Aeolian or Lipari Isles) A14

This group of islands lies between Nápoli and Sicília and is passed by steamers travelling between Nápoli and Messina.

In the *Aeneid*, Virgil refers to them as *Aeolia*, the kingdom of the god of storms and winds, Aeolus, but in spite of this reputation, the climate of the islands is so mild and agreeable as to recommend them for winter holidays. This refers particularly to Lípari, the ancient Meligunis and the largest island of the group which comprises seven in all: Lípari, Filicudi, Alicudi, Salina, Vulcano, Panarea and the fearsome Strómboli which, despite its ever-active volcano, boasts three hotels.

Approach is easy by steamer and the speedier hydrofoils from Nápoli, Palermo, Catánia, Taormina and Milazzo near Messina.

All seven have good hotels and good camping possibilities.

There is no end to the attractions for visitors; walkers find countless beauty spots to be explored; all the islands have wide, sandy beaches, stupendously tall, rugged cliffs, grottoes and floating islands, and there are possibilities for excursions of all types, from yachting and motorboating to a trip on one of the large fishing vessels, while underwater fishing is popular. One of the most popular attractions is a night visit to the crater of Strómboli. Fishing is carried on in a big way, and it is pleasant at nightfall to watch the local fleet going out to sea with the *lampare* alight. (These are lights facing down into the water to attract passing shoals of fish).

Pantelleria　　　　　　　　　J2

Pantelleria is an extremely interesting little island, lying off the shores of Trápani on the western coast of Sicília. It is not the easiest place to visit, since boats call only twice weekly, nor for accommodation, as there are only two hotels and those of fourth category.

Nevertheless, for the hardy traveller Pantelleria presents many attractions. Extremely mountainous, rising in the centre to more than 800m/2625ft above sea level, it is of volcanic origin, and the many eruptions have tortured its cliffs

into fantastic shapes. It is also of grea archaeological interest, being the ancien Cossyra. Among the treasures to be exp lored are the *Sesi* (prehistoric tombs), neolithic village and the Phoenicia acropolis.

Hunting and underwater fishing can b enjoyed, and the wines, particularly th local *passito* (not unlike Moscato) a extremely good.

Agrigento　　　　　　　　　G

(pop. 47,000) This city, on the souther shores of Sicília, is built on two hills from which one can see the Mediterra nean. **Porto Empédocle,** the coasta town, and a centre for deep-sea fishing, only about 5km/3mi away.

Agrigento had its beginnings almos 600 years before the birth of Christ, whe it was a Greek colony. Its original nam Girgenti, by which it was known unti 1927, is reminiscent of the Arab domina tion of the island.

It is a fascinating city to visit, and sinc it possesses remains of no fewer than 2

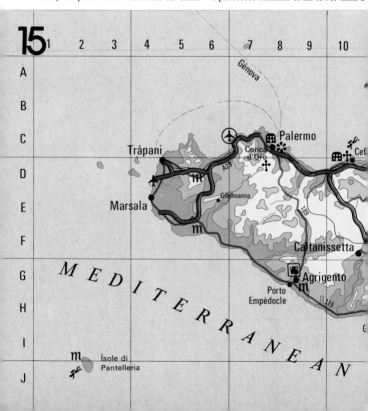

Greek temples, most of them situated in the lovely Valley of the Temples which lies between the two hills, it is a mecca for archaeologists. The most famous of the temples is that of Hercules, recognizable by the tapering of its remaining eight columns; twenty-five columns still stand of the Temple of Giunone Lacinia (5th century BC), and it presents a most evocative vision of what the Valley must have looked like in its early days. The remains of the great Temple of Olympic Jove and that of Castor and Pollux are also impressive, while the almost perfect Temple of Concord is one of the loveliest to be found in that part of Italy and Sicília known as Magna Grecia. These are but the highlights of the stupendous collection to be found in the Valley, which in the month of February becomes even more beautiful, the flowering almond trees decking the temples with a shower of blossom. February is an ideal month in which to visit Agrigento and to take part in the Festival of the Almond Trees.

Coming nearer, but not very near, to the present day, Agrigento also boasts a fine Romanesque-Gothic church, that of San Nicola, and the 14th-century cathedral has a sepulchre, that of De-Martinis, that is a treasure of art.

Not surprisingly, the Civic Museum of History offers a fine collection of treasures of archaeological interest, while, in the museum of the cathedral is the sarcophagus of Phedra, dating back to the 2nd century AD.

Hotels are various, a few excellent, others mediocre; there is a camping ground nearby, and several restaurants and trattorias where the food is good.

The modern bathing beach of **San Leone Bagni,** near Porto Empédocle, is well equipped.

Catánia   F14

(pop. 363,000) This city, standing in the middle of the east coast of Sicília, occupies an extremely picturesque position below the towering height of Monte Etna.

Conquered by the Romans in 263 BC, it enjoyed alternating periods of great prosperity and equally great depression, but under the Emperor Augustus it was regarded as the most flourishing city in Italy, and under the Saracens and Normans it continued to prosper until it suffered considerable damage in the earthquake of 1169. It soon recovered itself and began again to flourish under the Aragon rulers until another earthquake in 1693, from which time many of the buildings we admire today were constructed.

The central part has agreeable 18th-century architecture, but as a town it is not well-kept, and during the past 20 years it has grown rapidly and without any definite town planning.

It is criss-crossed by streets all of which seem to be climbing up towards Etna; one of the most famous streets is Via Etnea, which runs in a perfectly straight line for a length of 3km/2mi.

The cathedral, originally of the 12th century, was rebuilt after the earthquake of 1693. (The painter Vincenzo Bellini is buried in the chapel of Sant'Agata). In Piazza Duomo, the square in which the cathedral stands, is a famous Elephant statue; the elephant is the symbol of Catánia and it is said that in paleolithic days elephants roamed the island of Sicília.

The Ursino Castle, now the seat of the Civic Museum, was one of the many erected by Frederick II half-way through the 13th century.

For those who like baroque architecture, Catánia offers many examples, such as the Biscari Palace.

It lies in a rich agricultural district and its main sources of wealth are agriculture and oranges; forests of chestnut trees line the slopes of Etna and add to its picturesque aspect. The best month to see Etna in its glory is February, when almond trees are abloom, snow still covers the slopes and the sea is of an almost unbelievable blue.

Going from Catánia to Taormina along the coastal road one passes many interesting little places; **Acicastello**, where there is a black castle which once belonged to (yes, you are right!) Frederick II; then a few miles further along the same road you come to **Acitrezza**, the setting for Verga's famous novel *I Malavoglia*. Out in the sea stand the Cyclops, huge rocks which according to legend were those thrown by the giant Polyphemus in an effort to hit Ulysses.

Proceeding even further one reaches one of the most interesting towns in this part of Sicília, **Acireale**, an almost entirely baroque city, the jewel of which

is the church of San Sebastian. This is said to be a very 'close' town, a place where folks keep themselves to themselves, and are extremely jealous of the traditions of this little place.

Cefalù   D1

(pop. 13,000) One can go to Cefalù for a seaside holiday, and a most enjoyable one, for it is a well-equipped place, but to visit the city without paying homage to the 12th-century cathedral is to miss one of the great churches of the Middle Ages.

This massive building stands on a height in the rear of the town. It is approached by a flight of steps and presents an austere façade flanked by two square towers. Internally there is a fine presbytery, and the bowl of the apse is dominated by a huge mosaic representing Christ, the Pancreator.

Behind the cathedral are the remains of a megalithic temple to Diana, and nearby is the very interesting Mandralisca Mansion, with a fine collection of paintings.

A short, steep bus or car ride from Cefalù takes one to the sanctuary hill town **Gibilmanna**, 800m/2625ft above sea level, where even today you can see the village women fetching water from the well, bearing the vessels on their heads.

Lying midway between Palermo and Messina, Cefalù is easily reached from either by road or rail.

Not far away is a well-run tourist village.

Palermo   C8

(pop. 585,000) Spectacular is the adjective for this very busy and very beautiful city, whose checkered history has endowed it with a wealth of varied architecture.

Palermo was originally founded by the Phoenicians, but became Roman about 250 years BC. After the rout of the Byzantines by the Saracens in the year 831 AD it knew a period of great prosperity, which continued even after the arrival of the Normans, who made it the capital of the island. King Roger II and King Frederick II were the monarchs who brought Palermo to the height of its splendour.

Under the French rule imposed upon it after the fall of the Norman kings, it first of all rebelled, in the incident that has come down in history as The Sicilian Vespers in the year 1280, and then, until 1860, passed successively into the hands of the Angevins, the Aragons and the Bourbons.

It is still a busy port and has an excellent and much-frequented tourist section. A city of great natural beauty, it has also some of the finest public parks in Italy.

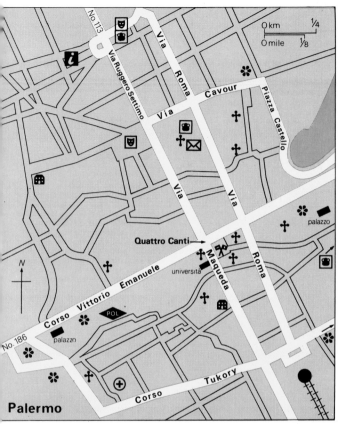

Palermo

The things and places one ought to visit are numerous. The most famous and spectacular square is that of the Quattro Canti (Four Corners), which is a good point of location when wandering around the city. The 12th-century cathedral (north of Corso Emanuele) is breathtaking; in it are the tombs of the Norman kings. The 11th-century church of San Giovanni degli Eremiti has interesting Arab cupolas; in the church of the Martorana (Santa Maria dell'Ammiraglio) are wonderful mosaics. In the Oratorio della Compagnia del Rosario di San Domenico is a painting by Van Dyck; the Oratory of the Company of San Lorenzo has a precious Caravaggio.

The erstwhile palace of the Norman kings was restored in the 18th century and of the original 12th-century fabric remains only the Pisana Tower and the Palatine Chapel, which latter must be added to the sightseer's list for its wonderful musive decoration and its marvellous wooden ceiling. The castle known as La Zisa is a fine example of 12th-century Muslim architecture.

Palermo has a fine National Museum, an astronomical observatory and an interesting Botanical Garden.

Having seen all these, a visitor can spend literally days before exhausting the many other interesting churches and buildings around Palermo, such as the nearby Convent of the Cappuccini, the not-to-be-missed cathedral of Monreale – note particularly the lovely cloisters and the mosaics that line the interior walls of this cathedral. Yet another interesting church is that of San Giovanni dei Lebbrosi (11th century).

From 13 to 15 July of every year there is the colourful Festival of Santa Rosalia, patron saint of the city.

Hotel accommodation is good and plentiful and there are many excellent restaurants.

Siracusa (Syracuse)   H15

(pop. 83,000) This city, not surprisingly, when one thinks of its checkered history, has much to offer visitors.

Its excellent port is built partly on the mainland, partly on the island of Ortigia, the site of the original town, now joined to the mainland by a bridge.

Founded by the Greeks almost 800 years before the birth of Christ, Siracusa had a long reign of glory, having become, by 485 BC, the principal Greek city in Sicília. Its outstanding rulers were Dionysius the Tyrant, and his not much less tyrannical son, Dionysius the Younger.

Roman occupation led to the decline of its power, and Siracusa never again rose to its one-time heights of prosperity, but it possesses today relics of that past splendour that give us an insight into what it must once have been.

A little outside the city itself, looking towards Africa, which it is said can be seen on a very clear day, is the great military fortification of the older Dionysius, the Castle of Eurialus. Siracusa has also a fine semi-circular Greek theatre of the 4th to 3rd century BC, and even earlier is the pagan altar nearby, dedicated to Gerone. Still in the same area is a Roman amphitheatre of the time of the emperor Augustus. All these are to be found not far from the one-time huge lime-quarries, now transformed into public gardens, Here, too, is the so-called Ear of Dionysius, a cave the formation of which resembles that of the human ear.

There is also the Spring of Arethusa around which is woven the charming legend of the nymph of that name who, pursued by the river God Alpheus, implored the aid of the goddess Diana, who responded by changing her into a spring.

King Frederick II left his mark in Siracusa by way of remodelling the 11th-century Maniace Castle.

The National Archaeological Museum is interesting; among its many exhibits is what must surely be the coyest statue of Venus extant.

Archimedes, the great mathematician, was a native of Siracusa, a fact commemorated by a handsome fountain in the square of the same name.

In the convent attached to the churc of San Giovanni are interestin catacombs, and the cathedral, in spite its 18th-century façade is, internally, th 5th-century reconstruction of what wa formerly the Temple of Athena.

A few years ago work was begun o what was intended to become a moder cathedral, dedicated to the miracle working Madonna delle Lacrime, a hol image whose eyes at certain times wer seen to be filled with tears. A lot of poo property was demolished in order t accommodate this new building, which i being built out of the offerings of th many poor parts of the city.

Siracusa is well equipped with hotel and from it there are many interestin excursions to be made.

Taormina   D1

(pop. 8000) 206m/676ft above sea level. I a country where many lovely place abound, it is pointless to indicate any on in particular as the most beautiful, bu certainly Taormina ranks very high o the list. Lying on the eastern shores o Sicília, midway between Catánia an Messina, the coastal road to either o these offers panoramic views.

The French writer Roger Peyrefitt wrote of this lovely city that 'Taormina to Sicily what Sicily is to the world'; th poet Horace felt that it was a place 'wher one would wish to live, forgotten an forgetting'.

Taormina seems to offer something everything, panoramic beauty and a wor derful climate first of all, semitropica vegetation, clumps of prickly pear her and there, lining the little lanes leadin down the ravines to the soft, sand beaches and the deep, blue sea; a wealt of hotels and restaurants to suit all pock ets, camping grounds, too, and, walkin through the town one passes medieva mansions, several Romanesque-Gothi churches, and the austere 16th-centur cathedral, the old convent of Sa Domenico (now a luxury hotel), with i lovely old cloisters. In Taormina are th remains of a large Graeco-Roman theatr with Monte Etna forming a spectacula and permanent backdrop. There is th arena which was once the scene of moc sea-fights, and these are but a few of th many interesting sights to be seen.

The tourist in search of souvenirs wil find an abundance in the littl craftsmen's shops along the narro streets. Glance at the women sitting i cottage doorways, embroidering exquis ite silk blouses, and you will see tha hardly one is wearing glasses.

Taormina is a definite 'must' for any one visiting Sicília.

SARDEGNA

ardegna is the second largest of the islands of the Mediterranean. Its geological foundations go back to the paleozoic age. Prevalently mountainous, its highest peak is in the Gennargentu range, and here are plains and tablelands to vary the landscape, while the coastline is an invitation to all who love the sea.

A mere 180km/112mi from the mainland, it is fairly accessible by boat and plane; in fact, there are more than 100 flights daily, and modern ferries capable of transporting not only people, but caravans and boats, and once arrived, there is an excellent network of roads. Nevertheless, because of the popularity of the island, there are sometimes tiresome hours of waiting for available transport.

Sardegna is divided into four provinces, Cágliari, Sássari, Núoro and Orisno, each furnished with reliable tourist information offices (see Useful Addresses, p 19).

The climate is mild and around the past there is little possibility of rain. Tourism is developing rapidly, especially in the north, along the far-famed Costa Smeralda (Emerald Coast), paradise of the 'jet set', the Golfo dell'Asinara (Bay of Asinara), the archipelago of La Maddalena and Santa Teresa di Gallura. In all of these one has the choice of a host of well-run hotels, but very early booking is essential.

The south, east and west are somewhat less well-geared for tourists, but even here a fair choice of modern and reliable accommodation exists.

There are camping sites around the coast and inland, youth hostels at **Alghero, Arzachena, Bari Sardo, Calasetta** and **La Maddalena,** to mention but a few. The exotic and expensive Club Mediterrane has a tourist village on La Maddalena.

Everyone has heard praises of its coastal joys, but Sardegna offers inland treats as well, which throw some light on its strange, almost mysterious history. Though the origin of the population is uncertain, it is known that during the neolithic age navigators used to land in Sardegna, followed onwards from the 7th century BC by Phoenicians, Greeks, Etruscans, Carthaginians, Romans, Vandals and Byzantines, all of whom have left their mark.

From the 7th century onward, the Byzantine empire having gone into a decline, a form of self-government arose in the form of four *Giudicati* centred on Cágliari Porto Tórres, Arborea and Gallura. Later, during the 11th century, began the conquest of the island by the maritime republics of Pisa and Génova. Then during the 13th and 14th centuries we see Sardegna under Spanish domination until about 1700 when there was a short period of Austrian rule. Following this it was given to the House of Savoy, and thus came into being the Sardinian/Piemontese Kingdom, from which in 1861 King Victor Emmanuel II was called to be first king of United Italy. Now, although within the limits of the Italian Republic, Sardegna is more or less self-governing.

Going around the island one notices a particular characteristic of its most ancient civilization, the *nuraghi,* cone-shaped megalithic structures, the stones piled one atop the other without the aid of mortar or cement. The purpose of these has puzzled archaeologists through the ages; some imagine them to have been fortresses, others see them as places of worship; others again regard them as dwellings. There are about seven thousand on the island, and one is unlikely to pass one's holiday without encountering a few. They date back at least as far as 1500 BC.

Then, too, the island has the reputation of being inhabited by the 'little people', the fairies, who are said to have had their habitations in the *domus de Janas,* grottoes cut into the rock and consisting of small windowless chambers, though many believe these to be tombs.

Coming to more recent antiquities, there are the Roman towns of **Nora, Antas, Tharros; Cágliari** has a fine Roman amphitheatre, and there are numerous Romanesque churches, Spanish castles and towers.

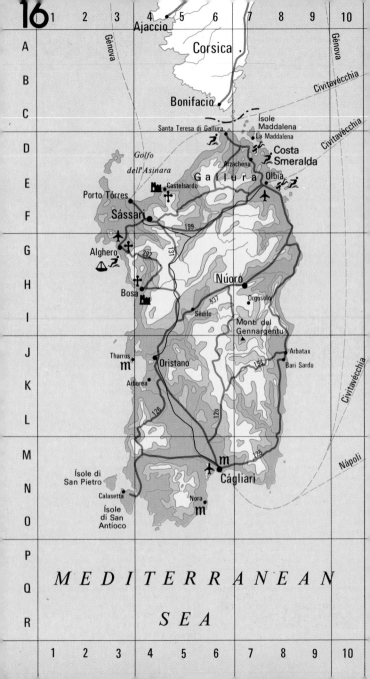

All of Sardegna is interesting; Alghero, addition to its fine beach, grottoes and a cropolis, has a fine Aragonese-Gothic thedral, and nearby are *nuraghi*. Here u can see the working of coral, for hich the island is famous, and there are pendous views for camera enthusiasts; osa has the remains of the Malaspina stle and a fine Romanesque church; in astelsardo, in addition to the Doria Case e and the 16th-century cathedral, you n see the local basket-makers at work.

To add to your knowledge of where to and what to see, the Assessorato al urismo della Regione Sarda, Viale rento 69, Cágliari, publishes an excel nt little handbook, *Sardegna Guida,* in alian, French, German and English.

Thinking of souvenirs to buy, Sardi an handwork has its origins in the tradi ns of the past; there are carpets woven hand looms, and this craft has been tended to include wall hangings and holstery fabrics, the designs of which e traditional and unusual. Because cer in regions are rich in china clay, there is nsiderable production of ceramics, par cularly in Cágliari and Sássari. Hand orked embroideries on scarves or usehold linen are exquisite, but fficult to find.

Silverware, articles in gold and corals e obtainable in a variety of types, as are sket-work, carved wood and articles ade of the local cork.

Where eating is concerned, the ham of e wild boar is exquisite as are the eggs mullet and tuna fish, preserved as only e Sards know how. Sucking pig is other speciality, and sweets are particu rly good — try *sebada,* a fritter stuffed th cheese and seasoned with bitter ney.

Vernaccia, a dry wine, is the favourite ne; if you prefer a sweet wine, try Mal sia or Moscato.

Some excellent little ports provide pecially for tourists travelling in their n boat, **La Maddalena, Porto Tórres** d **Arbatax** among them.

estivals Orgósolo — 16 January nt'Antonio — bonfire and procession. ast Sunday in May, Sássari — *Sardinian wvalcade.* Sédilo — 6-7 July, *palio* in stume around the medieval walls. íssari — 14 August, Large, heavy votive ndelabra carried in procession by Sards m all over the world who have man ed to come home for the festival.

KEY WORDS

academy — accademia
airport — aeroport
arch — arco
armoury — armeria
baker's shop — panetteria
baths (spa) — terme
beach — lido, spiaggia
bell-tower — campanile
bridge — ponte
butcher's shop — macelleria
camp site — campeggio, camping
castle — castello
cathedral — duomo
chapel — cappella
chemist's shop (pharmacy) — farmacia
convent — convento
dairy — latteria
exchange — cambio
ferry — traghetto
fortress — fortezza
forum — foro
fountain — fontana, fonte
gallery — galleria
gardens — giardini
greengrocer (fruit and vegetable market) — erbivendolo
hospital — ospedale
hotel — albergho
house — casa
information office — ufficio informazioni
inn — locanda
library — biblioteca
market — mercato
monastery — monastero, certosa (Carth-usian)
motel — autostello, motel
museum — museo
palace — palazzo
park — parco
parking — parcheggio, posteggio
parking meter — contatore per parcheg-gio, parchimetro
picture gallery — pinacoteca
police — polizia
policeman — poliziotto
police station — commissariato, ufficio di polizia
railway station — ferrovia, stazione fer-rovia
restaurant — ristorante, trattoria
shore — spiaggia
sports stadium — stadio
square — piazza
station — stazione
supermarket — supermercato
swimming pool — piscina
telephone — telefono
theatre — teatro
tobacconist's — tabaccheria
town hall — municipio
tunnel, gallery — galleria
zoo — zoo, giardino zoologico

INDEX

All main entries are printed in heavy type. Map references are also printed in heavy type. The map number precedes the grid reference.

Abano Terme   38–9 **49, 40**
Abetone   **70 E4,** 72
Abruzzi and Molise   **96,** 97–8
  festivals   98
Accettura (festival)   106
Accommodation   12–13
Acicastello   120
Acireale   120
Acitrezza   120
Addresses, useful   19
  camping information   13
Aeolian Isles
          117–18, **118–19 A14**
Agrigento
          118–19, **118–19 G9**
Alássio   **52 J3,** 53
Alatri   91
Alba   **24 K6,** 25–6
Albenga   **52 I3,** 53–4
Alberghi diurni   13
Alberobello   107–8, 109
Alghero   125
Amalfi   **100 L5,** 103
Anagni   91
Ancona   **81 G7,** 82
Aosta   **24 F3,** 26
Aosta valley
  see Tremonte and Valle d'Aosta
Aquiléia   **38–9 F14,** 40
Arbatax   125
Architecture   6–10
  Tuscan-Romanesque   71
Arezzo   **70 I9,** 72
Arquá Petrarca   40
Art   6–10
Ascoli Piceno   **81 K8,** 82
Asinara, bay of   123
Assisi   **85 J6,** 86
Asti   **24 J6,** 26
Atrani   103

Bagni di Lucca   75
Barbana (island)   42
Bari   **108–9 D13,** 109
Barletta
          108–9 C11, 109–110
Basilica di Santa Maria degli
  Angeli   86
Basilica di Sant' Apollinare in
  Classe   67
Basilicata *see Púglia and
  Basilicata*
Bassano del Grappa
          38–9 F9, 40
Behaviour, general   18
Bellágio   21
Belvedere Marittima
          112 G4, 114
Bergamo   **28 H5,** 30
Biscéglie   110
Bitonto   **108–9 D12,** 110

Blue Grotto (Capri)   101
Boarding houses (*pensions*)   13
Bologna   **60–1 D11,** 62–3
  town plan   62
Bolsena (lake and town)   89
Bolzano   **38–9 C7,** 40–1
Bordighera   **52 K1,** 54
Borromean islands   20, 26
Bosa   125
Bracciano (lake and town)   89
Bréscia   **28 I7,** 30
Bressanone   **38–9 A8,** 41
Bríndisi   **108–9 G17,** 110
Burano   36–7
Busseto   65

Calábria   112, 113–15
Camogli   **52 H7,** 54
Campania   99–105, **100**
Camping   13–14
Campo Imperatore   98
Campo nell'Elba   71
Canne della Battaglia   107
Cáorle   **38–9 G13,** 41
Capri   99–101
Carrara   76
Cascata delle Marmore   84
Caserta   105
Castel del Monte   111
Castel Gandolfo   94
Castelfidardo   82
Castellana   109
Castell'Arquato   **60–1 B6,** 63
Castelsardo   125
Castiglione del Lago   84
Catánia   **118–19 F14,** 119–20
Cattólica   **60–1 F16,** 63
Cefalú   **118–19 D10,** 120
Cernóbbio   21
Cérvia   **60–1 D15,** 63
Cesena   **60–1 E14,** 63–4
Cesenatico   **60–1 E15,** 63
Cetara (festival)   102
Chianciano Terme **70 K8,** 73
Chiavari   **52 H7,** 54–5
Chieti   97
Chioggia   47
Chiusi   73
Cigarettes and cigars   17
Cinque Terre, Le   57–8
Città del Vaticano   **90 J4,** 91
City States *see Comunes*
Cividale   **38–9 E14,** 41
Clothing   18
Clothing sizes   19
Coculla (festival)   98
Cogorno   57
Collegio Alberoni   57
Comácchio   **60–1 B14,** 64
Como   **28 G3,** 30
Comunes   6

Corigliano Calabro
Corniglia
Cortina d'Ampezzo
          38–9 B10, 4
Cortona   **70 J9**
Cost of meals
Cremona   **28 K6, 3**
Cùrrency
Customs

Desenzano
Diamante
Drinks *see Food and Drink*
Duty-free allowances

Egnázia
Elba   **70 L3,**
Electricity
Emerald Coast (Sardegna)
Emerald Grotto
  Grotta di Smeraldo)
Emília-Romagna   60–8, **6**
Ercolano
Exchange rates
Exchange offices

Faenza   **60–1 D13,**
Falconara
Fano (festival)
Fasano   107
Ferrara   **60–1 B12, 64**
Festivals   (see   also   regio
  introductions)
  Music
Fiascherine
Fidenza   **60–1 B7,**
Fiésole
Firenze (Florence)
          70 G6, 73
  town plan
Fiuggi
Fluid measures
Foligno (festival)
Fontana   1
Fonti del Clitunno
Food and Drink   14–
Forca Canapine
Forli   **60–1 E14,**
Fornello   1
Forte dei Marmi   **70 F3,**
Frascati   94
Friuli and Venezia Giulia   37–

Gallinara (island)
General information   16–
Génova (Genoa) **52 H6,** 55
  town plan
Genzano di Roma (festival)
Gibilmanna   1
Grado   **38–9 G14,**
Gran Sasso

ttammare | 82
bio | 84, **85 I5,** 86

drian's Villa | 94
tory | 6
els in Italy | 12–13

péria | 52 J3, 56
ormation, general | 16–18
s (*Locande*) | 13
ia | 101
a del Giglio | 78

acolo (festival) | 114
y Words | 125

Maddalena (islands) | 123
Maddalena (port) | 125
Spezia | 52 I9, 56
kes (northern) | 20–3, 22–3
mo | 21
arda | 21–3
o | 21
vico | 20
aggiore | 20
isurina | 20
ta | 20
sia | 20
arese | 20–1
es (other):
bano | 89
vernus | 101–2
saro | 102
crinus | 102
mi | 89
asimeno | 84
aquila | **96 H3,** 98
agna | **52 H8,** 56–7
io | 89–95, **90**
Cinque Terre | **52 I8,** 57–8
ce | 108–9 **H18,** 110
co | 21
horn *see Livorno*
ici | 52 I9, 58
o degli Estensi | 64
o degli Scacchi | 64
o delle Nazioni | 64
o di Jésolo | 38–9 **H12,** 42
o di Pomposa | 64
o di Spina | 64
o di Tarquínia | 95
o di Volano | 64
nano Pineta | 42
nano Riviera | 42
nano Sabbiadoro | 38–9 **G13,** 42
uria | 51–9, **52**
ari Isles *see Aeolian Isles*
orno (Leghorn) | **70 H3,** 75
nbardia (Lombardy) | 28, 29–33
reto | **81 H8,** 83
cania *see Púglia and Basilicata*
cca | **70 G4,** 75–6
ni | 59

Macerata | 82
Magistri Comacine | 29
Maiori | 103
Mammola (festival) | 114
Manarola | 57
Mántova (Mantua) | **28 K9,** 31
Marche (The Marches) | 80–3, **81**
Marciana | 71
Marina di Carrara | **70 F2,** 76
Marina di Massa | **70 F2,** 76
Maróstica (festivals) | 37
Matera | 106, **108–9 G12,** 110–111
Mazzorbo | 36
Meals, cost of | 15
Medical insurance (US visitors) | 18
Medical treatment | 18
Melfi | 106
Merano | **38–9 B7,** 42–3
Messina (festival) | 117
Metapontum | 106
Metric conversion tables | 19
Milano (Milan) | **28 I3,** 31
town plan | 32–3
Minori | 103
Miramare (castle) | 46
Modena | **60–1 C10,** 65
Molfetta | 110
Molise *see Abruzzi and Molise*
Montallegro, Sanctuary of | 59
Monte Argentario | 78–9
Monte Bignone | 59
Monte Faito | 99
Monte Righi | 56
Montefiascone | 89
Montegrotto Terme | 40
Monterchi | 73
Monterosso | 57
Mortola | 59
Motoring | 12
Mottarone | 26
Murano | 36
Music festivals (*see also regional introductions*) | 16

Nápoli (Naples) | **100 K4,** 103–5
town plan | 104
National Park (Abruzzi) | 97
Nemi (town) | 94
Newspapers | 17
Nórcia | **85 K7,** 86–7
Novacella, convent of | 41
Numana | 82

Oneglia | 56
Opera (*see also regional introductions*) | 16
Orgósolo (festival) | 125
Orsogna (festival) | 98
Orvieto | **85 L4,** 87
Osimo | 82

Óstia | 95
Óstia Antica | 95
Ostuni (festival) | 108
Ótranto | **108–9 I19,** 111

Padova (Padua) | **38–9 H9,** 43–4
town plan | **43**
Paestum | 99, 105
Palermo | **118–19 C8,** 120–2
town plan | **121**
Palestrina | 91
Palmária | 58
Palmi (festivals) | 114
Palombina | 82
Pantelleria | 118, **118–19 J2**
Páola | **112 I5,** 114–15
Papal Audience | 18
Parma | **60–1 B8,** 65–6
Passariano (Villa Manin) | 46
Passetto | 82
Passports | 16–17
Pavia | **28 K3,** 31
Pensions | 13
Perúgia | **85 J5,** 87–8
Pésaro | **81 F5,** 83
Pescara | **96 H6,** 98
Peschiera | 23
Piacenza | **60–1 A5,** 66
Piazza Armerina (festival) | 117
Piemonte and Valle d'Aosta (Piedmont and Aosta Valley) | 24, 25–7
Pienza | **70 K8,** 76
Pisa | **70 H3,** 76–7
town plan | 77
Pistóia | **70 F5,** 77–8
Poggio thermal centre | 71
Pompeii | 105
Pomposa, abbey of | 65
Porto Azzurro | 71
Porto Empédocle | 118
Porto Garibaldi | 64
Porto San Giórgio | 82
Porto Santo Stéfano | **70 N6,** 78–9
Porto Tórres | 125
Portoferraio | 71
Portofino | **52 H7,** 58
Portofino Vetta | 58
Portonovo | 82
Portovénere | **52 I9,** 58
Postage | 17
Potenza | 106, **108–9 G9,** 111
Pozzuoli | 102
Praglia, abbey of | 44
Prato | **70 G6,** 79
Prócida | 101
Public conveniences (*see also Alberghi diurni*) | 18
Public holidays | 18
Púglia and Basilicata | 106–11, **108–9**

Punta del Faro 58
Rapallo 52 H7, 58–9
Ravello 99, 100 L5, 105
Ravenna 60–1 D14, 66–7
Recanati 82
Réggio di Calábria
112 O3, 115
Réggio Nell'Emília
60–1 C9, 67
Riccione 60–1 F16, 67–8
Rímini 60–1 F16, 68
Riomaggiore 57
Rivotorto 86
Roma (Rome) 90 J5, 91–5
town plan 92–3
founding of 6
Roman Empire 6
Ruvo 108–9 D12, 111

Sacile (festival) 40
St Francis of Assisi 36, 84, 86
Carceri 86
Salerno 100 I.6, 105
Salsomaggiore Terme
60–1 B6, 68
San Benedetto 84, 86–7
San Benedetto del Tronto 82
San Borgonovo Val Tidone 66
San Cataldo 110
San Damiano (convent) 86
San Fruttuosa 58
San Gimignano 70 I7, 79
San Giovanni 71
San Lazzaro degli Armeni (island)
35–6
San Leo 81 F3, 83
San Leone Bagni 119
San Marino 60–1 F15, 68
San Maurizio 56
San Michele (island) 36
San Michele di Pagana 59
San Remo 52 J2, 59
Sansepolcro 72–3
Santa Maria degli Angeli, basilica
86
Santa Scolastica 84, 86–7
Santa Teresa di Gallura 123
Sant'Apollinare in Classe,
basilica 67
Santuario di San Francesco
114–15
Sardegna (Sardinia)
123–5, 124
Sarzana 52 I10, 59
Sássari (festivals) 125

Savona (festival) 51
Sculpture, Renaissance 8
Sédilo (festival) 125
Segri 91
Senigállia 81 G6, 83
Sezze (festival) 91
Shops, opening hours 18
Sicília (Sicily) 116–22, 118–19
Siderno 112 N6, 115
Siena 70 I7, 79
town plan 78
Siracusa (Syracuse)
118–19 H15, 122
Sirmione 22
Sluderno 20
Sorrento 100 L4, 105
Spello (festival) 86
Spina, necropolis of 64
Spoleto 85 L6, 88
Sport 15–16
spectator sports 15–16
winter sports 16
Springs of Clitumnus 88
Staglieno 56
Stamps 17
Stra 47
Stresa 20, 24 E7, 26
Sulmona (festival) 98

Tabiano Terme 60–1 B7, 68
Taormina 118–19 D15, 122
Táranto 108–9 H15, 111
Tarcento (festival) 40
Tarquínia 90 H2, 95
Telephones 17
Tellaro 58
Téramo 97
Térmoli 96 J9, 98
Theatrical events (see also
introductions) 16
Tinetto 58
Tino 58
Tipping 18
Tiriolo (festival) 114
Tivoli 90 I6, 95
Tobacconists 17
Todi 85 L5, 88
Toilets (see also Alberghi diurni)
18
Torcello 37
Torino (Turin) 24 I4, 26
town plan 27
Torre a Mare 109
Torre Canne 110
Torrette 82
Toscana (Tuscany) 69–79, 70

Tourist villages
Trani
Travel 10–
Trémiti (islands)
108, 108–9
Trentino/Alto Adige
Trento 38–9 E7,
Treviso 38–9 G10, 44
Trieste 38–9 G16, 45
town plan
Trisulti, charterhouse of
Tropea 112 L4, 1
Turin see Torino
Tuscany see Toscana

Údine 38–9 E14,
Umbria 84–8
Urbino 81 G4,
Useful addresses see Addresses

Valle d'Aosta see Piemonte a
Valle d'Aosta
Vallecrosia
Vatican City see Città
Vaticano
Vecchia Caseta 99, 1
Vegliasco
Veneto 34–50, 38
Veneto proper 34
Venezia (Venice)
38–9 H11, 46
town plan 48
islands of the lagoon 35
Venezia Giulia see Friúli a
Venezia Giulia
Venice see Venezia
Ventimiglia 52 K1,
Vernazza
Verona 38–9 H6, 47–
town plan
Vesúvio 104
Viaréggio 70 G3,
Vibo Valentia (festival)
Vicenza 38–9 G8,
Vignola 60–1 D10,
Villa di Marlia
Villa Manin
Villa Mansi
Visas 16–
Viterbo 90 G3,
Volterra 70 I5,

Weights
Winter sports

Youth hostels